Tolkien's Art

Tolkien's Art

A Mythology for England

Revised Edition

JANE CHANCE

THE UNIVERSITY PRESS OF KENTUCKY

Publication of this volume was made possible in part
by a grant from the National Endowment for the Humanities.

Scholarly publisher for the Commonwealth,
serving Bellarmine University, Berea College, Centre College of
Kentucky, Eastern Kentucky University, The Filson Club Historical
Society, Georgetown College, Kentucky Historical Society, Kentucky
State University, Morehead State University, Murray State University,
Northern Kentucky University, Transylvania University, University of
Kentucky, University of Louisville, and Western Kentucky University.

Editorial and Sales Offices: The University Press of Kentucky
663 South Limestone Street, Lexington, Kentucky 40508–4008

05 04 03 02 01   5 4 3 2 1

Library of Congress Cataloging-in-Publication Data

Chance, Jane, 1945-
   Tolkien's art : a mythology for England / Jane Chance. — Rev. ed.
   p. cm.
   Includes bibliographical references and index.
   ISBN 0-8131-9020-7 (pbk. : acid-free paper)
   1. Tolkien, J. R. R. (John Ronald Reuel), 1892-1973—Criticism
and interpretation. 2. Tolkien, J. R. R. (John Ronald Reuel), 1892-
1973—Knowledge—England. 3. Fantasy literature, English—History
and criticism. 4. Epic literature, English—History and criticism. 5.
Medievalism—England—History—20th century. 6. Mythology,
Germanic, in literature. 7. Middle Earth (Imaginary place). 8.
England—In literature. 9. Mythology in literature. I. Title.
PR6039.O32 Z698 2001
828'.91209—dc21   2001002584

Manufactured in the United States of America

CONTENTS

PREFACE AND ACKNOWLEDGMENTS

The pleasure of revising a book originally written and published over twenty years prior stems from the opportunity to correct mistakes and delete outmoded interpretations, but also to measure the contribution it has made, if any, to the field. In the case of Tolkien, such an opportunity allows for the crucial addition of insights gleaned from the publication of his *Letters, Unfinished Tales,* the twelve volumes of *The History of Middle-earth,* several other editions and translations of Old English works, and two children's stories, *Mr. Bliss* and *Roverandom,* as well as the critical and scholarly books that have appeared since 1979.

The first point made by *Tolkien's Art*—that Tolkien wished to construct an overarching mythology that was embedded in all his published fiction except for the fairy-stories and his medieval parodies—has been legitimized by Tolkien's letter 131, to Milton Waldman at Collins. That Tolkien wished to create this mythology *for England,* a nation he believed lacked any coherent mythology comparable to the Germanic or Finnish mythologies, is also attested in that important letter. Thus the title of this monograph—*Tolkien's Art: A Mythology for England*—can be seen in its first edition to have anticipated the publication of letter 131 and, with it, Tolkien's own analysis of how his corpus of creative writing fits into a discernible schema.

The second point made in this study—that Tolkien did not compartmentalize the writing of his scholarly or

vii

philological essays and notes and the writing of his fiction (that is, his professional contribution to medieval studies from his personal and private creating, or vice versa)—is also clear throughout Tolkien's *Letters* and the plethora of critical essays and books that have been published by other scholars since 1979. In this regard, the more philological study of Tom Shippey's *The Road to Middle-earth,* first published in 1982, several years after my own study, follows a course similar to my own. When Shippey's book was revised in 1992, a subtitle was added to the cover of the paperback edition, *How J.R.R. Tolkien Created a New Mythology.* The argument that Tolkien created a mythology *for England* out of the literatures in Old and Middle English and also Old High and Middle German, Old Norse, Finnish, and Welsh, has now become clearly articulated on philological and literary grounds. A fuller annotated bibliography of items up to 1990 appears in Jane Chance and David Day's "Medievalism in Tolkien: Two Decades of Criticism in Review," published in an issue on *Medievalism: Inklings and Others* that I edited for *Studies in Medievalism* in 1991, pp. 375–88.

My argument in *Tolkien's Art* focuses only on the Old and Middle English literature Tolkien taught and wrote about and the ways in which his knowledge of and familiarity with those poems and treatises affected both his more minor works and the mythology that connected his three major works, *The Hobbit, The Lord of the Rings,* and *The Silmarillion*—truly a tribute to England. Other Tolkien scholars have subsequently attempted to define the phrase "mythology for England" in varying ways, not, I assume, in an attempt to correct my argument (they do not cite this book) so much as to interpret and extend Tolkien's obviously striking statement of intention in letter 131: among them, Jared Lobdell, *England and Always: Tolkien's World of the Rings* (1981); Carl F. Hostetter and Arden R.

Smith, "A Mythology for England," in *Proceedings of the J.R.R. Tolkien Centenary Conference, Keble College, Oxford, 1992,* edited by Patricia Reynolds and Glen H. Goodknight, *Mythlore* 80 and *Mallorn* 30, in one volume (Milton Keynes, England: Tolkien Society; Altadena, Calif.: Mythopoeic Press, 1995), pp. 281–91; and Anders Stenström, "A Mythology? For England?" in the same Reynolds and Goodknight, pp. 310–14.

And similarly, following (or at least paralleling) my idea of tracing much of Tolkien's own medievalization of his mythology by examining his scholarship on *Beowulf* and other Old and Middle English works, Tom Shippey, Andy Orchard, Bruce Mitchell, Jonathan Evans, George Clark, and others have extended our knowledge of the parameters of Tolkien's learning and how it informed his fiction: in Shippey's "Tolkien and the *Gawain*-poet," in Reynolds and Goodknight, pp. 213–20; Mitchell's "J.R.R. Tolkien and Old English Studies," in Reynolds and Goodknight, pp. 206–11; Orchard's "Tolkien, the Monsters, and the Critics: Back to *Beowulf*," in *Scholarship and Fantasy: Proceedings of the Tolkien Phenomenon, May 1992, Turku, Finland,* edited by K.J. Battarbee, Anglicana Turkuensia, no. 12 (Turku: University of Turku, 1992), pp. 73–84; Evans's "The Dragon-Lore of Middle-earth: Tolkien and Old English and Old Norse Tradition," in *J.R.R. Tolkien and His Literary Resonances: Views of Middle-earth,* edited by George Clark and Daniel Timmons (Westport, Conn., and London: Greenwood Press, 2000), pp. 21–38; and Clark's "J.R.R. Tolkien and the True Hero," in Clark and Timmons, pp. 39–52.

It is gratifying to have such company in the argument I make in this book, whatever flaws it may have had; it is reassuring to find that time has validated a critical approach that may have seemed too new or too glib (or too lonely) at the moment I first offered it. (The recent reprinting of the chapter on *The Lord of the Rings* in Harold Bloom's *Modern Critical Interpretations* volume on Tolkien is equally reassuring.) I have made a conscious attempt to acknowledge the views of other scholars throughout at appropriate moments as a means of thereby strengthening my own initial arguments or of rephrasing them where necessary.

Perhaps it is now impossible to discuss *The Lord of the Rings* or *The Silmarillion* in only one essay or chapter; certainly the importance of the latter as an original work of mythology has yet to be fully understood, especially given Christopher Tolkien's monumental edition of *The History of Middle-earth* (1983–96) and the new collection edited by Verlyn Flieger and Carl F. Hostetter, *Tolkien's Legendarium: Essays on "The History of Middle-earth,"* Contributions to the Study of Science Fiction and Fantasy, no. 86 (Westport, Conn., and London: Greenwood Press, 2000), which reveal how much remains to be analyzed about Tolkien's methods of composition and the scope of his mythology. The shape of my comments on both works, especially *The Silmarillion,* in two chapters is appropriate only within the limitation implied by the book's thesis, which relates back to the importance of Tolkien's *Beowulf* essay. Because in so many ways *The Silmarillion* is indebted to the Finnish mythology of the *Kalevala* and to epic concepts of vengeance more akin to Old Testament justice than to New Testament mercy, my treatment in this study is by necessity less than complete.

Whether Tolkien would have approved of or agreed with such critical analyses of his own works is at this point moot; we do know he detested putting forward himself or publicity about himself and his personal life. As Rayner Unwin notes, "Tolkien was a very private person. . . . [H]e was a reluctant publicist" (in "Publishing Tolkien," *Mallorn* 29 [1992)]: 42). And whether or not Tolkien's works will stand the test of time is not within our lot to know, so that the Tolkien enthusiast's need to defend Tolkien's title of "author of the century," as a result of the recent Waterstone's poll of 25,000 readers in Great Britain in 1997, may be unnecessary and even gratuitous. A work like *The Hobbit* that has been translated into more than thirty languages or one like *The Lord of the Rings*, into more than twenty, has already demonstrated the virtues of both accessibility and elasticity, if not endurance. An author who has sold fifty million copies of his works requires no justification of literary merit.

Chapter 1, "The Critic as Monster: Tolkien's Lectures, Prefaces, and Foreword," was delivered in a shortened form as a paper at the Twelfth Annual Medieval Conference, Western Michigan University, Kalamazoo, Michigan, on 7 May 1977. Portions of chapter 2 were delivered as a paper ("The Role of the Narrator in Tolkien's *Hobbit:* 'The King under the Mountain'") at Rice University's English Department Reader-Response Colloquium, 3 February 1979; a slightly altered version of the same chapter appeared in *North Dakota Quarterly* 47 (Winter 1979): 4–17. The conclusion originated in a review published in the *Zest* section of the *Houston Chronicle*, Sunday 11 September 1977, p. 13. Permission to reprint the above has been granted. Permission to quote from Tolkien's writings has been released by George Allen and Unwin (Publishers), Houghton Mifflin Co., and HarperCollins Publishers Ltd. (for extracts from Tolkien's books); by the *Observer* (for extracts from a letter to the editor, published on 20 February 1938); and by Mrs. C. Meleck (for extracts from "Beowulf: The Monsters and the Critics," first published in *Proceedings of the British Academy*, 1936). The Macmillan Press has granted permission to reprint the book (first published in Great Britain in 1979).

I am indebted to Rice University's Fondren Library and Interlibrary Loan for heroic efforts to obtain works by and about Tolkien. Rice University and the English department generously provided a summer research grant in 1976 that permitted me to complete the first three chapters; they also provided graduate and undergraduate assistance in the checking of transcriptions and documentation and funds for the final typing of the manuscript. Sue Davis produced a nearly error-free typescript from my rough copy. My colleagues the late Professor Will Dowden, Kathleen Murfin, and Candy MacMahon charitably volunteered to help me read page proofs, for which I am very grateful. The Macmillan Press, especially Mr. Tim Farmiloe, Ms. Julia Brittain, and Mrs. Jean Kennedy, helped in many ways, not least of which was obtaining permissions on my behalf and producing this book so efficiently and well in such good time.

Thanks are extended to my good friend Jackie Boyd and to former graduate student (now colleague) Thad Logan for their care in reading portions of this work and making tough but necessary criticisms, and to Randel Helms, who commented in detail upon the first chapter and generally encouraged my progress with the book. I am especially grateful to those students and friends, Jay Rudin in particular, who supplied the stimulus for this study in the Lovett College course on Tolkien that I taught at Rice in the spring of 1976, and who wholly convinced me, had I any doubts left, that Tolkien is a major writer.

For the revision, I am additionally grateful to English department secretary Jamie Cook for correcting the scanned copy of the previous edition and to English department editorial assistant Theresa Munisteri for her able correcting of style. Thanks to the leave granted me by the Office of the Dean of Humanities for the spring semester 2001, I have been able to complete revisions in a timely manner. To Interim Humanities Dean Gale Stokes I am indebted for the funds to pay an indexer. I would also like to thank Michael and Kathleen Hague for their generosity in allowing me to use a portion of an image published previously in Michael Hague's 1984 *Hobbit* for the cover art.

Note: Tolkien prefers certain spellings that are used where appropriate in this study—for example, Dwarves (not Dwarfs), Faërie, King of Faery (in "Smith of Wootton Major"), fairy-stories, sub-creation (not subcreation), and so forth; I have, however, capitalized the names of his species for consistency. *The Fellowship of the Ring* is abbreviated throughout as *FR*; *The Two Towers* as *TT*; *The Return of the King* as *RK*; *The Lord of the Rings* as *LR*. Citations from volumes are indicated in the text by means of parentheses and Arabic numbers for volume and page number(s).

INTRODUCTION

I was from early days grieved by the poverty of my own beloved country: it had no stories of its own (bound up with its tongue and soil), nor of the quality that I sought, and found (as an ingredient) in legends of other lands. There was Greek, and Celtic, and Romance, Germanic, Scandinavian, and Finnish (which greatly affected me); but nothing English, save impoverished chap-book stuff. . . .

Do not laugh! But once upon a time (my crest has long since fallen) I had a mind to make a body of more or less connected legend, ranging from the large and cosmogonic to the level of romantic fairy-story—the larger founded on the lesser in contact with the earth, the lesser drawing splendour from the vast backcloths—which I could dedicate simply: to England; to my country. It should possess the tone and quality that I desired, somewhat cool and clear, be redolent of our "air" (the clime and quality of the North West, meaning Britain and the hither parts of Europe; not Italy or the Aegean, still less the East), and, while possessing (if I could achieve it) the fair elusive beauty that some call Celtic (though it is rarely found in genuine ancient Celtic things), it should be "high," purged of the gross, and fit for the more adult mind of a land long steeped in poetry. . . .

—J.R.R. Tolkien
Letter 131, to Milton Waldman
of Collins (c. 1951)

1

Before the publication of Tolkien's biography and his letters, it was popularly believed that the Hobbit stories narrated to his children "conquered and remade Tolkien's imagination" to the point of "reshaping even his responses to the literature he studied as Rawlinson Professor of Anglo-Saxon at Oxford," as well as influencing his theories of mythological imagination implemented in his later creative works.[1] But with the publication of these and other works by and about Tolkien, it has become clearer that the relationship may have operated the other way around, that is, with his fictional stories and his own developing mythology of Middle-earth reshaping his responses to medieval literature.

Indeed, Tolkien regarded himself, according to Humphrey Carpenter in his biography, not as "an inventor of story" but as a "discoverer of legend."[2] The earliest expression of Tolkien's "discovery" in fact was a poem he had written in 1914 after a vacation in Cornwall, "The Voyage of Earendel the Evening Star," later to become chapter 24 of "Quenta Silmarillion," the long middle section of *The Silmarillion*. Such expressions were intended to provide a historical and poetic context for the private languages of Quenya (or High-Elven) and Sindarin (or Common Elvish) that Tolkien had begun constructing in 1912, languages that he modeled upon Finnish and Welsh, respectively, and that were themselves inspired by his exploration of the Northern mythologies of the *Elder* (poetic) and *Younger* (prose) *Eddas*.[3]

This poem itself, however, had been inspired by a line from Cynewulf's Old English *Crist*, "Eala Earendel engla beorhtost" (Behold Earendel [Evening Star], brightest of angels). "Earendel," the "evening star" (also called "morning star"; in actuality, the planet Venus) that heralds the coming of day and the sun akin to John the Baptist announcing the arrival of Christ, was used by Tolkien as a

2

model for Eärendil (Quenya for "sea-lover") the Mariner in the stories of *The Silmarillion*.[4] Neither the Old English language in which Cynewulf's poem was written nor its religious subject matter should come as a surprise to the Tolkien reader: Tolkien, a professor at Oxford and a "staunchly conservative Tridentine Roman Catholic" (in the words of Clyde Kilby),[5] taught and published research on Old and Middle English literature. It is appropriate that the seeds for Tolkien's "mythology for England" sprang from those medieval literary, religious, and cultural sources and the ideas in which his life was steeped.

Tolkien's publications on medieval English literature and language began as early as 1922, with his *Middle English Vocabulary* published for use with Kenneth Sisam's *Fourteenth Century Verse and Prose*, continued in 1925 with a joint edition of *Sir Gawain and the Green Knight*, with E.V. Gordon, and were followed by an essay in 1929 on the *Ancrene Wisse* and *Hali Meiðhad*. These publications preceded *The Hobbit* (1937), which was begun as early as 1928–29, with Tolkien's children having heard some episodes from it before 1930.[6] Indeed, when asked about the sources of *The Hobbit*, Tolkien replied, in a letter published in the *Observer* on 20 February 1938, that it derived from "epic, mythology, and fairy-story." Specifically, Tolkien acknowledges as his "most valued" source *Beowulf*, "though it was not consciously present to the mind in the process of writing, in which the episode of the theft arose naturally (almost inevitably) from the circumstances." He adds that his tale of *The Hobbit was* consciously based on a "history of the Elves," the unpublished *Silmarillion*. If Tolkien wished to develop a "mythology for England" akin to the Northern mythologies of the Eddas, what better way than to use those Old and Middle English works native to his country in fashioning his own works?

It is the general purpose of this study to show how

his creative works reflect his interest in medieval English literature, especially Old English, as expressed through his scholarship on and critical studies of such works. Because his relatively minor fictive works reveal this dependence more clearly in some ways than his greatest, *The Lord of the Rings*, a larger proportion of the analysis than their literary value warrants will be devoted to discussions of *The Hobbit*, the fairy-stories "Leaf by Niggle" and "Smith of Wootton Major," and medieval parodies like *Farmer Giles of Ham*. The minor works thus provide foils for the trilogy, in which medieval ideas metamorphose into art more successfully and subtly.

The Silmarillion, however, poses a critical problem in that it was begun in 1914, and although it might be viewed as an early and even minor work, it was not finished during Tolkien's lifetime, existed in multiple recensions, and was only edited and published posthumously by Tolkien's son Christopher in 1977, four years after the author's death. It will, therefore, be treated as a late and even an unfinished work, both influenced by and influencing other literary works published throughout his life, and certainly no longer expressing only the interests and ideas of his youth. Indeed, in the twelve volumes of *The History of Middle-earth* edited by Christopher Tolkien and published between 1983 and 1996, we can see how *The Lord of the Rings* and *The Silmarillion* were carved out of multiple recensions of almost every book and chapter and from other, unused materials relating to the mythology of Middle-earth. As Christopher Tolkien declares in his foreword to *The Silmarillion* (1977), these "old legends ('old' now not only in their derivation from the remote First Age, but also in terms of my father's life) became the vehicle and depository of his profoundest reflections. In his later writing mythology and poetry sank down before his theological and philosophical preoccupations: from which arose incompatibilities of tone."[7] Clearly source and influence become inextricably mixed in this particular work—and all Tolkien's work.

The most important scholarly study by Tolkien with parallels in the creative works is his 1936 Sir Israel Gollancz Lecture entitled "Beowulf: The Monsters and the Critics" (published in 1936 in an academic periodical and reprinted much later in several well-known *Beowulf*-studies anthologies).[8] Although required reading for any *Beowulf* student,[9] it has not yet appeared on the required reading list for *The Lord of the Rings*, a work that many literary critics believe to be equal in greatness to the Old English epic and one that is gradually, through the work of Anglo-Saxonists writing on Tolkien, being perceived as extremely important in its influence on Tolkien's mythology.[10] In the *Beowulf* lecture Tolkien attempted to resolve the long-standing critical debate over whether the poem was "pagan" or Christian by concluding that it was *both:* Germanic heroic values and Christianity coexist within the epic.[11] Tolkien's own works grapple with the same conflict: Is a good warrior also a good man? Does a warrior owe primary allegiance to his lord (*dryhten*) or to the Lord God (*Dryhten*)?

It is the social role and religious image of the lord and king through which Tolkien expresses his deepest philosophical and theological ideas. Significantly, Tolkien refers to the hero Beowulf and not to the poem *Beowulf* in the title of his seminal article, "Beowulf: The Monsters and the Critics."[12] Why should the king Beowulf occupy such a central position in the title when the poem's monsters chiefly demand Tolkien's attention in the article? A pattern emerges upon an examination of the titles of other Tolkienian works. Either the title centers on the hero ("Beowulf," *The Hobbit,* "Leaf by Niggle," "Smith of Wootton Major," *The Adventures of Tom Bombadil, Farmer Giles of Ham*) or, antithetically, on the hero's chief adversary ("The Homecoming of Beorhtnoth Beorhthelm's Son," *The Lord of the Rings, The Silmarillion*—the history of the Silmarils, symbol of the lowest human desire, that is, to appropriate things of value that belong to others).

The specific purpose of this study is to explore the reasons for this pattern of heroic conflict by tracing the development of the adversary (the dragon, the monster, the critic, the king) through Tolkien's early works, culminating in the trilogy and *The Silmarillion*. Irresponsible lordship—like that demonstrated by Beorhtnoth in the Old English poem "The Battle of Maldon" and criticized in Tolkien's verse drama, "The Homecoming"—most troubles Tolkien. The lord often commands his men to die for him, not out of a zeal to protect the tribe, but out of pride, to boost his own name. The subordinate, acting out of love and loyalty, obeys his lord but tragically so when such obedience results in unnecessary death. Responsible lordship, as exemplified in the sacrifice of one's own desires on behalf of others, especially the tribe, represents a healing and even redemptive act—symbolized by Aragorn's role in the House of Healing as he conveys the miraculous herb kingsfoil from wounded warrior to warrior and, of course, by God the Father's role in offering his only son for sacrifice in order to heal humankind, Christ himself becoming, as medieval poets often called him, the archetypal Physician.[13] The good lord, then, Tolkien usually casts in the role of healer or artist (healing and artistry both constructive acts, one physical and one spiritual)—but the evil lord he casts in the image of monster or dragon.[14]

The dragon in *Beowulf,* like Grendel, signifies the *feond mancynnes* (the enemy of mankind) and of God, so that the battle between Beowulf and the monsters on a higher level means that "the real battle is between the soul and its adversaries" (p. 73). The figure of the monster externalizes the evil within each soul. Hence in the article's

6

title, "Beowulf: The Monsters and the Critics," Tolkien focuses upon the hero Beowulf and his adversaries—the monsters and the critics—and not upon the poem *Beowulf.* More anagogically, such a battle between a hero and a *feond* also signifies the conflict between humankind and its ultimate enemy, death. Tolkien imagines the *Beowulf* poet surveying past heroes so that he "sees that all glory (or as we might say 'culture' or 'civilization') end in night" ("Beowulf," p. 73). As a result, in this world, as Germanic heroic values have it, "man, each man and all men, and all their works shall die" ("Beowulf," p. 73). So the *Beowulf* poet—who has composed a poem that we still read today, in translation and the original Anglo-Saxon, long after the poet has passed away—represents for Tolkien the hero of the title, an idea conveyed by the article's last line and final metaphor. Tolkien expresses his confidence in the permanence of *Beowulf,* given its similar language, geographical setting, and nationality of the author—"it must ever call with a profound appeal"—only, however, "until the dragon comes" (p. 88). Even art will eventually perish before the final adversary of all creation, the antithesis of its Author—total annihilation. The dragon thus concretely realizes those allegorical personifications of Sin and Death whom Milton portrayed as the offspring of Satan's mind in *Paradise Lost.*[15] The figure of the dragon recurs, in varying form, throughout Tolkien's works.

In Tolkien's prose nonfiction, especially the lectures and forewords, the "monster" is the critic-scholar who prefers history and philology to art for art's sake, reflecting by his choice a ratiocination sterile, stale, and dead, in contrast to the alive and joyful imagination of the artist-hero with whom Tolkien identifies. Although Tolkien was himself a philologist and learned and then taught various early languages that formed and inspired many of his own invented languages, he kept hidden from his colleagues at

Oxford for a very long time his own creative writing. Only late in his life was it revealed how prolific a writer he had been, not of scholarly and philological articles and books acceptable to the university at which he worked, but of the stories and epics for which he has attracted fifty million readers. This analogy between Tolkien and the *Beowulf* poet is explored in chapter 1 of this study, "The Critic as Monster: Tolkien's Lectures, Prefaces, and Foreword."

In chapter 2, "The King under the Mountain: Tolkien's Children's Story," the monster is the dragon Smaug in his role of King under the Mountain guarding Dwarf treasure in *The Hobbit*. But more sentient "monsters" populate this children's story—Thorin the Dwarf-king, the Master of Dale, and the Elvenking. Their heroic antagonist is the Hobbit artist Bilbo, who as the story progresses becomes increasingly skillful in his role as burglar. In addition, the pompous narrator (criticized as an aesthetic flaw in studies of the novel) also emerges as a human monster whose critical and patronizing comments subvert the impact of the very story he narrates. Thus, this children's story fictionalizes the ideas in Tolkien's lectures on *Beowulf* and the fairy-story.

In chapter 3, "The Christian King: Tolkien's Fairy-Stories," the adversary is depicted as a more abstract monster: the critical neighbor Parish in "Leaf by Niggle" and the unskilled but pretentious Master Cook in "Smith of Wootton Major." Interestingly enough, the artist as hero (Niggle and Smith) attempts to emulate the pattern of the archetypal artist, Christ as the Word, who is represented in the stories as the Second Voice in "Leaf" and Alf the King of Faery in "Smith." Sacrificing one's art in order to help one's neighbor or renew society resembles the greatest sacrifice—of Himself—offered by the Son of God. In these stories Tolkien fictionalizes ideas from his fairy-story lecture and the *Ancrene Wisse*.

In chapter 4, "The Germanic Lord: Tolkien's Medieval Parodies," Tolkien's excursions into mimesis in the parody of the Breton lay ("The Lay of Aotrou and Itroun"), Middle English romance and fabliau (*Farmer Giles of Ham*), Old English alliterative verse ("The Homecoming of Beorhtnoth Beorhthelm's Son"), and the *imram*, or "voyage" ("Imram"), define the king in chivalric terms as a lord motivated by excessive pride to the detriment of his tribe and himself. His subordinate, whether a *ceorl* (a man, that is, a free man) or a knight, represents a mock hero who symbolizes the lower class rebelling against the aristocratic nonsense of the chivalric code. The "monster" assumes a social as well as moral dimension. The parodies are modeled upon various kinds of medieval genres and specific works, Breton lays, *Sir Gawain and the Green Knight*, the *Canterbury Tales*, "The Battle of Maldon," and "The Voyage of Saint Brendan."

In chapter 5, "The Lord of the Rings: Tolkien's Epic," Sauron as archetypal and abstract Evil projects a monstrous adversary far more terrifying in his formlessness than the lesser adversaries described as leaders and kings—Saruman, Denethor, Boromir. (Sauron's fragmented self symbolizes the divisiveness of his evil; his Eye searches the countryside while his Lieutenant as his Mouth addresses the free peoples at the Gate to Mordor.) Monsters whose evil suggests a more physical viciousness like wrath, gluttony, or avarice reflect this in their form—Balrog, Shelob, Gollum. In contrast, the human and Elven kings who battle these monsters function more as servants than as masters—especially Aragorn, long disguised as the humble ranger Strider. The medieval conflict between the Germanic value of valor in battle to support one's lord, an expression of the virtue of obedience and love, and the Christian virtue of charity in sacrificial acts to support one's neighbor and God Tolkien reconciles finally through

the sacrificial (Christian) act of the free peoples, who heroically battle (in Germanic fashion) Sauron's Lieutenant
to divert attention from the real threat to Sauron, the
humble servant Sam who aids Frodo in his trek toward
Mount Doom. This sacrificial act in macrocosm counter-
points Gollum's sacrifice of himself in battle with Frodo
to save his master or lord—the Ring, to whom he has
sworn fealty. However, Gollum's battle with Frodo is motivated not by the loving desire of the subordinate to support his lord but instead by his selfish desire to become
his lord—an act of disobedience. In contrast, the battle
with the Lieutenant is motivated by the love of the masters and kings, specifically Gandalf and Aragorn, a love
directed toward those seemingly unimportant halflings
Sam and Frodo, who are themselves servants of the free
peoples. The trilogy thus unifies many of the themes and
concepts found in the minor works of Tolkien, which were
themselves influenced by various medieval English poems
and his own scholarship on them.

Finally, in the conclusion Tolkien's posthumous
Silmarillion will be examined as a "Book of Lost Tales," a
mythological collection whose emphasis on philology and
history and whose debt to the Northern mythologies mark
it as a work belonging to an early stage in the development
of Tolkien's art, but whose emphasis on the vexed role of
the creator of the Tengwar and Silmarils—Fëanor,
Noldorin prince and greatest of the children of Ilúvatar—
brings this early work into line with Tolkien's latest work.
Creation of art carries with it both joy in expression and
desire for its possession and keeping. Further, this work's
biblical (Old Testament) sense of justice thematically anticipates the contrasting and more specifically Christian
ethos found explicitly or implicitly in Tolkien's other
works. Nevertheless, it does exhibit the same religious
themes of pride and fall and the same images and sym-

bols of bad kingship analyzed in those previous works, especially in the figures of Melkor, Sauron, Fëanor, and Ar-Pharazôn, but without the buttressing of Germanic heroic and chivalric concepts. As its mythology inspired the writing of later works and as its publication ensures a complete history for the Middle-earth described in so many of Tolkien's greatest works, it constitutes an appropriate coda to Tolkien's life as a philologist and historian, philosopher and theologian—and artist and mythologist.

Chapter 1

THE CRITIC AS MONSTER

Tolkien's Lectures, Prefaces, and Foreword

> Nonetheless I think it was a mistake to intrude
> *Language* into our title in order to mark this
> difference [between "*Lit.*" and "*Lang.*" in English
> Departments], or to warn the ignorant. Not least
> because *Language* is thus given, as indeed I suspect
> was intended, an artificially limited and pseudo-
> technical sense which separates this technical thing
> from *Literature.* This separation is false, and this
> use of the word "language" is false.
>
> The right and natural sense of Language
> includes Literature, just as Literature includes the
> study of language of literary works.
>
> > —J.R.R. Tolkien, "Valedictory Address
> > to the University of Oxford, 5 June 1959"

When Tolkien delivered the Sir Israel Gollancz Memorial Lecture of 1936, he changed the course of *Beowulf* studies for the next sixty-five years and also permanently altered our understanding of the Old English poem. As a scholarly essay, "Beowulf: The Monsters and the Critics" sought to demonstrate the coexistence of Germanic and Christian elements in the poem, especially in the figures of its monsters, Grendel and the dragon, formerly viewed as peripheral to the work's main theme and structure. By so arguing, the essay provoked a controversy over its Germanic and Christian aspects that continues to be debated today, although in more subdued fashion. As a work of prose nonfiction by a great writer, however, the article has only recently begun to claim the attention of scholars interested in explaining the shape of Tolkien's mythology, although it has never been analyzed as a work of creative art in itself (a seeming non sequitur, given its prosaic and scholarly shape and form).[1]

This study seeks to illuminate the way in which the *Beowulf* poem and article so fully catalyzed Tolkien's imagination that few of his creative works escaped its explicit or implicit influence. Tolkien's article chiefly centers on three points. First, what he calls *"Beowulfiana"*—meaning the accretion of *Beowulf*-related studies—is "poor in criticism, criticism that is directed to the understanding of a poem as a poem."[2] Previously, according to Tolkien, scholars of Old English had investigated only *Beowulf*'s historical, folkloric, or philological importance and had not perceived the literary merits of the poem. This problem—which has been attributed by some Tolkien scholars to the curriculum battle between "Lang." and "Lit." factions within the British university—is not entirely appropriate here: that conflict positioned those who believe in the superiority of philology as a subject of the curriculum against those who advance literature as a priority, especially those who would relegate "Anglo-Saxon" to a status lower than other branches of study.[3] The myopic scholars in Tolkien's essay, who are mostly hypercritical or judgmental philologists and historians primarily interested in the past history of words and old stones and artifacts, but not in the powerful effect that works of art and words used for rhetorical effect can have on the reader's sensibility, will be termed "critics" in this study for the purpose of analyzing this Tolkien essay on *Beowulf.*

Second, the responsibility for this lapse in aesthetic judgment rests solely with the critic lacking that mythic imagination that the poem evokes and not with the poem itself. Third, when the critic does then examine the poem as a poem he wholly misunderstands it. To illustrate these points, Tolkien cites W.P. Ker (an Anglo-Saxon scholar cited in a passage by another Anglo-Saxon scholar, R.W. Chambers), who believes that *Beowulf's* weakness lies in placing "irrelevances" at the center and "serious things" on the outer edges (p. 59). By "irrelevances," Tolkien explains, Ker means the monsters and by "serious things," presumably the poem's historical and legendary background.

Such an adversarial relationship between the *Beowulf* poet, the *Beowulf* critic, and the *Beowulf* monsters so captures Tolkien's imagination that he entitles this article "Beowulf: The Monsters and the Critics," that is, with the name of the hero and his adversaries listed as subject and not the poem. If Beowulf as the hero battles with monsters (Grendel and the dragon) and with the critics who have misunderstood him (W.P. Ker and R.W. Chambers), then, Tolkien fantasizes, the critics must be adversaries, or monsters—just as Tolkien the fantasist and fiction writer, by defending Beowulf, must be the hero. This implicit fantasy is carefully developed through a series of metaphors in this article and becomes explicit in his Andrew Lang Lecture of 1938, on the subject of fantasy and fairy-stories.

The problem with this fantasy is that Tolkien himself as a critic remained interested in the history and philology of Anglo-Saxon and Middle English, as is evident from his prefaces to critical editions and translations of medieval works; he also used his knowledge of Anglo-Saxon and Germanic philology to construct his invented languages and his mythology of Middle-earth. Indeed, as

Tom Shippey has noted, Tolkien thought philology itself was a speculative, imaginary venture in its attempt to reconstruct Primitive Germanic and Prehistoric Old English by means of tracking sound changes.[4] How then can Tolkien identify with the hero opposing monstrous evil when, as philologist, he also occupies the role of the monster-critic?

That Tolkien was capable of embracing seemingly contradictory positions has been attested by Clyde Kilby by means of a trait that he describes as "contrasistency": "I felt that Tolkien was like an iceberg, something to be reckoned with above water in both its brilliance and mass and yet with much more below the surface. In his presence one was aware of a single totality but equally aware at various levels of a kind of consistent inconsistency that was both native—perhaps his genius—and developed, almost deliberate, even enjoyed. The word, if there were one, might be 'contrasistency.'"[5] For his biographer Humphrey Carpenter, this doubleness takes the form of a divided self. Tolkien provides an illustration of both concepts in the foreword to *The Lord of the Rings,* in which he establishes himself as a Frodo-like hero in his artistic role and, in his critical role pontificating upon the meaning of his own work, as a Saruman or Sauron-like monster. This divided self surfaces throughout Tolkien's fictive works and exists as a symbolic badge of fallen and imperfect human nature. Human nature is good—but also evil, as *Beowulf* is Germanic—but also Christian. We turn, first, to an examination of the stages in Tolkien's development of his fantasy—and Fantasy—in the lectures.

I. THE LECTURES: THE SCHOLARS W.P. KER AND ANDREW LANG AS MONSTERS

Tolkien in the *Beowulf* article defends the "irrelevances" of the poem—the monsters—responsible for that structural "disproportion" so disliked by Ker. Seeing instead a "balance" expressed as "an opposition of ends and beginnings . . . a contrasted description of two moments in a great life, rising and setting; an elaboration of the ancient and intensely moving contrast between youth and age, first achievement and final death" ("Beowulf," p. 81), Tolkien argues that the monsters reflect threats to Beowulf at two crucial moments in his life. As a young man the hero appropriately aids the Danish king Hrothgar by successfully battling with the monster Grendel in the first half, or the "rising moment," of the poem; and in the second half as an old king he aids his Geats, so he thinks, by battling with the dragon in the "setting moment" of the poem and of his life.

As an adversary the Old English monster possesses three significations for Tolkien. *In a Germanic sense,* the monster functions thematically as *feond mancynnes,* the enemy of humankind with whom such monsters ally in Nordic mythology—chaos, unreason, death, and annihilation. Because the monster battles only with "man on earth" it conveys the ancient theme "that man, each man and all men, and all their works shall die. . . . [The *Beowulf* poet] sees that all glory (or as one might say 'culture' or 'civilisation') ends in night" ("Beowulf," p. 73). *In a Christian sense,* the Germanic monster represents the enemy of God as well as of humankind, sin, and spiritual death. Although the poem should not be read as an allegory of the *miles Christi* who battles the Adversary with his breastplate of righteousness and shield of faith inherited from Ephesians 6, still, the battle assumes Christian proportions: Tolkien notes that "there appears a possibility of eternal victory (or eternal defeat), and the real battle is between the soul and its adversaries" ("Beowulf," p. 73). *In a modern sense,* finally, the monster signifies the adversary of the *Beowulf* poem: the critic who misunderstands it because of his predilection for history and philology instead of art, for dead ratiocination instead of live imagination. Allegorically the monster represents the final adversary of humankind, the dragon Death fought by the artist with the weapon of his art in the hope that its eternal life will defeat this dragon—as John Donne notes, in other words, "Death, *thou* shalt die."

Although Tolkien develops the first two significations through plain expository prose, this last signification he develops through a cumulative rhetorical sequence of five allegorical and metaphorical exempla interspersed throughout the article. The first exemplum portrays the poem *Beowulf* as a medieval hero on a journey-quest whose initiation is hampered by those allegorical guides supposedly helping him. Those guides of history, philology, mythology, archaeology, and laography (folklore) represent the interests of modern scholars that stifle communication between the poem and its readers:

> As it set out upon its adventures among the modern scholars, *Beowulf* was christened by Wanley Poesis—*Poeseos Anglo Saxonicae egregium exemplum.* But the fairy godmother later invited to superintend its fortunes was Historia. And she brought with her Philologia, Mythologia, Archaeologia, and Laographia. Excellent ladies. But where was the child's name-sake? Poesis was usually forgotten; occasionally admitted by a side-door; sometimes dismissed upon the door-step. "*The Beowulf,*" they said, "is hardly an affair of yours, and not in any case a protégé that you could be proud of. It is an historical document." ("Beowulf," pp. 52–53)

Poesis, or poetry-for-poetry's sake, as a humble and

male servant (rather than an arrogant female master or superior) is denied access to the hero because he seems a pedagogical churl: the ladies sneer that "Only as [a historical document] does [*Beowulf*] interest the *superior* culture of to-day" ("Beowulf," p. 53; my italics). In his lowly status Poesis (or the poem *Beowulf*) resembles other humble Tolkienian heroes or guides of heroes—Farmer Giles, Niggle, Smith, and the Hobbits from their agrarian background. In contrast, the ladies as effete scholars ally with such arrogant adversaries as King Augustus Bonifacius, Tompkins, Nokes, the Lord of the Rings, Sauron himself, and his former master Morgoth, or Melkor—and the superior culture of today.

In his next exemplum Tolkien switches focus from poem to poet and transforms the supposedly helpful godmother and guides into "friends" and "descendants" who misunderstand and abuse the poet (called merely "a Man"). The conflict centers now on a tower of old stones taken from a house of his father that the Man has built to "look out upon the sea"—that is, figuratively to see better or to gain perspective or wisdom. But the friends and descendants view the tower differently: not interested in farsightedness and perceptivity, they refuse even to climb the steps and instead gaze myopically at their old stones. Wishing "to look for hidden carvings" or to seek "a deposit of coal under the soil" ("Beowulf," p. 55), they seem as materialistic and shortsighted as the Dwarves of *The Hobbit* and *The Lord of the Rings*. Their myopia mirrors their lack of spirituality: they fulfill their destructive, selfish inclinations by pushing over the tower, digging under its soil, and generally disregarding the moral and legal rights of the tower builder. The parable intimates that modern students and readers ("friends," so-called) and even modern scholars ("descendants") prefer discovery of its sources and influences (the stone blocks' hidden carvings and coal deposits) to enjoyment and use of the whole poem (tower) in order to attain insight about life (to climb its steps and view the sea). Their "sensible" source-hunting overwhelms the tower builder's delight in the "nonsensical tower," as the friends term it. Unfortunately, the tower builder remains wholly alone, his friends more unkind than any enemies, his descendants more distant and alien than any strangers.

In the third exemplum the critic metamorphoses into the monster of the jabberwock, an unnatural creature that symbolizes the perversion of those students and critics—the "friends" and "descendants" in the first two exempla. This creature creates cacophony through a "conflicting babel" of opinion: "For it is of their nature that the jabberwocks of historical and antiquarian research burble in the tulgy wood of conjecture, flitting from one tum-tum tree to another" ("Beowulf," p. 56). They no longer constitute a physical danger to others because of their myopia, which resembles that of the "friends" and "descendants": "Noble animals, whose burbling is on occasion good to hear; but though their eyes of flame may sometimes prove searchlights, their range is short" ("Beowulf," p. 56). Such shortsightedness hints at a greater spiritual danger to the jabberwocks as well as to others, for the "conflicting babel" of their opinions reminds us of the confusion of tongues at the Tower of Babel as the epitome of the sin of pride (and of course in the previous exemplum the critics in *their* pride destroyed the tower of the artist). Pride and selfishness, myopia, a "conflicting babel" of opinion, destructiveness, chaos—all characterize the critic, truly a monster.

By the fourth exemplum—actually, a metaphor—Tolkien can finally identify the conflict he has portrayed abstractly thus far as a "battle" between hero and monster, in this case, a real critic, an Anglo-Saxon philologist:

"[Chambers] gives battle on dubious ground" ("Beowulf," p. 65). Chambers misunderstands the poem, or "battles" with it, because he argues that the story of Ingeld, for example, remains a real center of *Beowulf,* its monsters mere "irrelevances" ("Beowulf," p. 59). However, because Tolkien has depicted *Beowulf* and its poet as protagonists (knight, tower builder) and the critic as antagonist (false female guide, false friend and tower destroyer, jabberwock), it becomes clear that Chambers "gives battle on dubious ground" as a monster rather than as a hero, whose role is occupied here by the true and humble friend of the poem, Poesis itself, or (we might say) Tolkien, defender of myth. Ironically, Chambers as critic-monster specifically opposes the monsters of *Beowulf*—his adversary is as well Grendel and the dragon.

Further, the actual battle may not resemble a heroic contest between two opponents so much as the murder of an innocent animal in the scientific laboratory of the experimenting vivisectionist. The critic opposes the *Beowulf* monsters because as a rational being he misunderstands and dislikes what he would call "frivolity," meaning "flight of fancy." Yet for Tolkien, "A dragon is no idle fancy" but "a potent creation of men's imagination" ("Beowulf," p. 64). *Beowulf*'s dragon, in Tolkien's opinion, can be criticized only because it does not seem "dragon enough, plain pure fairy-story dragon" ("Beowulf," p. 65). As a personification of malice, greed, and destruction, or the evil side of heroic life, *Beowulf*'s dragon symbolizes *draconitas,* an abstract idea and generic type rather than a concretely depicted, individualized monster ("Beowulf," p. 65). For Tolkien, a "plain pure fairy-story dragon" should not be explained or it will die; so its defender, like the critic, "unless he is careful, and speaks in parables, . . . will kill what he is studying by vivisection, and he will be left with a formal or mechanical allegory, and, what is more, probably with one that will not work. For myth is alive at once and in all its parts, and dies before it can be dissected" ("Beowulf," pp. 63–64). The rational human or the critic seems not only a monster but a murderer, a homicide like Grendel.

As such, the critic exercising his rational faculty must still battle with the artist who delights in his imaginative faculty, for "[t]he significance of a myth is not easily to be pinned on paper by analytical reasoning. It is at its best when it is presented by a poet who feels rather than makes explicit what his theme portends; who presents it incarnate in the world of history and geography, as our poet has done" ("Beowulf," p. 63). Although the poet may die, his work, like the dragon a "potent creation of . . . imagination," will live on, mutely battling with misunderstanding critics and the ravages of time and death. In the last lines of the article, Tolkien claims of *Beowulf* that it will "ever call with profound appeal" to those who live in England and speak English because of its similar origin and language "until the dragon comes" ("Beowulf," p. 88). That final critic in Tolkien's fifth and final metaphor is the last dragon—complete chaos, complete annihilation and darkness.

In the contemporaneous Andrew Lang Lecture of 1938, "On Fairy-Stories," Tolkien develops more explicitly the earlier implicit fantasy concerning the adversarial relationship between the artist and the critic in the *Beowulf* article through a contrast between himself as lover of fairy-stories and the analyst and compiler of fairy-stories in the archetypal critic Andrew Lang. In the short preface to his Andrew Lang Lecture Tolkien sketches the "overbold" lover of fairy-stories as a medieval romance hero seeking "a rash adventure," a "wandering explorer" who grows inarticulate in trying to report the "richness and strangeness" of the land.[6] Such an adventurer need not have

21

"studied them professionally," for only a childlike wonder will result from these adventures in Faërie. To approach Faërie as a professional seeking not wonder but information, like any lost adult on a trip, is to "ask too many questions" so that the gates to Faërie will be shut and the keys lost ("On Fairy-Stories," p. 3).

Such a professional was Andrew Lang, who collected fairy-stories in twelve books of twelve different colors appearing in print as early as 1889. Because Lang's "collections are largely a by-product of his adult study of mythology and folk-lore" ("On Fairy-Stories," p. 36; my italics), he includes in his books selections inappropriate to the true fairy-story, such as travelers' tales, dream tales, and beast fables, all in some way connected with the primary (real or adult) world. Lang regards a fairy-story as a means to an end rather than an end in itself—interesting as an example of the monkey's heart topos, but not interesting as a story. Lang's interests are scientific (at least in intent): "[T]hey are the pursuit of folklorists or anthropologists: that is of people using the stories not as they were meant to be used, but as a quarry from which to dig evidence, or information, about matters in which they are interested" ("On Fairy-Stories," p. 18). In addition, Lang so misunderstands the nature and purpose of fairy-stories that he intends his collections only for literal children, to be used to satisfy both the "belief" in and "appetite" for marvels of the young ("On Fairy-Stories," p. 36).

But "belief" and "appetite" must be distinguished. As a child Tolkien experienced a desire for dragons ("On Fairy-Stories," p. 41) but not for belief: "[A]t no time can I remember that the enjoyment of a story was dependent on belief that such things could happen, or had happened, in 'real life'" ("On Fairy-Stories," p. 40). Further, Tolkien truly came to love fairy-stories *only as an adult.* "It is parents and guardians," he admits, who like Lang (the latter addresses his collections to these parents because they and not their children possess the money to purchase them) "have classified fairy-stories as *Juvenilia*" ("On Fairy-Stories," p. 44). Both the parent and the scientist assume only the child can experience a desire for marvels.

Although Tolkien warns that "[t]he process of growing older is not necessarily allied to growing wickeder[,] . . . the two do often happen together" ("On Fairy-Stories," p. 44). To combat this tendency, adults must not play at being children who have never grown up but instead regain an innocence or wonder similar to that of the child in Wordsworth's "Intimations of Immortality." This wonder allows the adult to escape from the weariness of living in the primary world, in the twentieth century with its burgeoning scientific and materialistic values, and to experience the sudden joyous "turn" of the eucatastrophic happy ending available in what Tolkien defines as the "sub-creation" of the secondary world—in "Literature" as the antithesis of "Drama." The latter is preferred by the critic because Drama reveals the dyscatastrophe inherent in tragedy and because, from the critic's point of view, it sheds the pretense that a secondary world exists beyond the primary one ("On Fairy-Stories," p. 51). In the secondary world of fantasy Tolkien can realize his own "happy ending"—the overthrow of the arrogant British critic—which he cannot realize in the real world.

At the time the Lang lecture on fairy-stories was written, Tolkien had completed and quotes a portion of a significant poem, "Mythopoeia," that emblematizes the artist as Philomythus, "Lover of Myth," and the critic, a scientist, as Misomythus, "Hater of Myth." Although the poem was not published until 1988, with the second edition of *Tree and Leaf*, containing "On Fairy-Stories" and "Leaf by Niggle," it reflects allegorically a debate between the two types of men embodied in Tolkien and C.S. Lewis, with

C.S. Lewis the dedicatee—the man who calls myths "worthless lies" even when myths are "breathed through silver."[7]

This monstrous critic in the *Beowulf* lecture and the adult and scientific fairy-story collector in the fantasy lecture find satiric expression in the mock translator of a supposed obscure Latin work, Tolkien's medieval parody *Farmer Giles of Ham* (1949). As a critic, the mock translator defends his decision to translate the "curious tale" into English for a historical reason: it provides a glimpse into "life in a dark period of the history of Britain, not to mention the light that it throws on the origin of some difficult place-names."[8] As an afterthought the translator adds a lesser, literary reason, probably one that would appeal to a child interested in marvels but certainly not to an educated adult: "Some may find the character and adventures of its hero attractive in themselves." The translator's interest is literary only in the sense that discussions of sources and influences are literary; he disparages the sources of the tale "derived not from sober annals, but from the popular lays" (*Farmer Giles*, p. 7). Superior in his respect for and fidelity to the fact and truth of geography and history, the translator denigrates the author's skimpy geographical knowledge ("[I]t is not his strong point") and his acquaintance with recent contemporary history ("For him the events that he records lay already in a distant past"). Ironically, he exposes his own supercilious ignorance of truth when he grudgingly admits that this author's voice must be authentic and the account true, for "he seems . . . to have lived himself in the lands of the Little Kingdom." Medieval literature, much of it anonymous, highly stylized, and conventional, rarely reflected the autobiographical experience of any writer.

This critic's instructive and apologetic preface smacks of presumption. He seeks to guide the reader's response to the work and to interfere with the artist's relationship with his reader. Given Tolkien's distaste for the role of critic, what role does he assume in the prefaces and forewords to his own editions and translations of medieval works and to his own artistic works, especially *The Lord of the Rings*?

II. THE PREFACES AND THE FOREWORD: TOLKIEN AS MONSTER

As an artist Tolkien portrays himself as a hero and the artistic process as a journey-quest very like that of the *Beowulf* poem in the first exemplum of the *Beowulf* article or like Frodo's in *The Fellowship of the Ring*. In the introductory note to *Tree and Leaf* (written when "On Fairy-Stories" and "Leaf by Niggle" were published together in 1964–65), Tolkien identifies himself as a childlike but heroic Hobbit who wrote these two works "when *The Lord of the Rings* was beginning to unroll itself and to unfold prospects of labor and exploration in yet unknown country as daunting to me as to the Hobbits. At about that time we had reached Bree, and I had then no more notion than they had of what had become of Gandalf or who Strider was; and I had begun to despair of surviving to find out" (*Tree and Leaf*, p. 2). This analogy between the role of the artist in the primary world and the role of the hero in the secondary world continues in the foreword to *The Lord of the Rings:* "In spite of the darkness of the next five years [1939–45], I found that the story could not now be wholly abandoned, and I plodded on, mostly by night, till I stood by Balin's tomb in Moria. There I halted for a long while."[9] The artist is the hero, especially a medieval romance hero.

If so, then the artist's editor and translator, like Sam, must serve as a kind of squire or yeoman to this knight. In prefaces to editions and translations of medieval works by others, Tolkien performs such service by rendering the text accurately or translating the work faithfully. He refuses to interject any interpretation of the work that might interfere with the relationship between artist and reader and contribute to misunderstanding—he refuses to act like a critic. In the preface to *Sir Gawain,* Tolkien and E.V. Gordon stress the importance of reading the poem "with an appreciation as far as possible of the sort which its author may be supposed to have desired."[10] This goal may be attained by establishing a pure text with a full glossary that determines, "as precisely as possible, the meaning of the author's actual words (in so far as the manuscript is fair to him)" (preface to *Sir Gawain,* p. vii). In the prefatory note to Tolkien's own edition of the Corpus manuscript of the *Ancrene Wisse* (his former student Mary B. Salu also translated the poem in an edition with his preface), Tolkien explains with a minimum of critical fuss only those editorial notations necessary for the reader's benefit (retention of manuscript punctuation, changes in the treatment of abbreviations, acknowledgments, etc.).[11] Such self-effacement remains necessary because critical assertions may divert the reader from the poem itself, a warning presented in Tolkien and Gordon's preface to the *Sir Gawain* edition: "Much of the literature that begins to gather about *Sir Gawain and the Green Knight,* though not without interest, has little bearing on this object, and many of the theories held, or questions asked, about the poem have here been passed over or lightly handled—the nature and significance of the 'test'; the sources, near and remote, of the story's elements and details; the identity, character life and other writings of the author (who remains unknown); his immediate motive in writing this romance; and so on."[12] Tolkien wants the poem itself and not the scholar's discussions of anthropology, archaeology, or history to remain at center stage.

Translations in this light become more problematic because of the danger of misreading and thereby incorrectly rendering the text; the possibility of subverting the reader—and the artist—increases. Thus, the first task of the translator must be the ascertainment of meaning in the original. In his preface to the translation of *Sir Gawain and the Green Knight, The Pearl, and Sir Orfeo,* Tolkien declares that "a translator must first try to discover as precisely as he can what his original means, and may be led by ever closer attention to understand it better for its own sake" (preface to translation of *Sir Gawain,* p. 7). So, in his preface to Mary B. Salu's translation of the Corpus manuscript of the *Ancrene Wisse,* Tolkien first certifies the authenticity of the manuscript used in the translation and its value for the translator and reader (here, few scribal alterations because of the scribe's familiarity with the language ensure the possibility that the original intention of the artist will be preserved in this translation), and then applauds the success of the translation in rendering idiom, that mixture of "cultivated speech" and "colloquial liveliness" characteristic of its author.[13] The translator does not compete with the artist but collaborates; in this manner, valuable works in unknown languages can be given continuing "life," as is *The Pearl* in Tolkien's posthumously published translation. Translation is justified in the preface because "*The Pearl* certainly deserves to be heard by lovers of English poetry who have not the opportunity or the desire to master its difficult idiom" (preface, Tolkien's translation of *Sir Gawain, Pearl, and Sir Orfeo,* p. 7).

Yet earlier, in the 1940 prefatory remarks to the Clark Hall translation of *Beowulf,* Tolkien cautioned that no translation is "offered as a means of judging the original, or as a substitute for reading the poem itself,"[14] especially if the poem, like *Beowulf,* is "a work of skilled and close-wrought metre" (Clark Hall, *Beowulf,* p. ix). Such a translation helps a student only by providing "an exercise for correction" rather than "a model for imitation" (Clark Hall, *Beowulf,* p. xvi). If a student does not return to the original, s/he risks misunderstanding and even disliking the poem, like the critic who condemned *Beowulf* as "only small beer" because s/he had used an incompetent translation (Clark Hall, *Beowulf,* p. ix). Thus, while a "translation may be a useful form of commentary" on the poem, as Tolkien admits in the preface to his *Pearl*-poet translations (preface, Tolkien's translation of *Sir Gawain, Pearl, and Sir Orfeo,* p. 7), it still remains a commentary by the critic and not necessarily by the artist and can become an act of presumption. Tolkien confesses that his own continued close study of poems like *Sir Gawain, Pearl,* and *Sir Orfeo* allowed him to learn more about them "than I knew when I first *presumed* to translate them" (preface, Tolkien's translation of *Sir Gawain, Pearl, and Sir Orfeo,* p. 7; my italics).

Although Tolkien's editions and translations attempt to render the original as closely as possible with the greatest respect for the artist and his work of art, his early scholarly articles seem to ignore the literary merits of the medieval work under discussion and focus on its philological and historical features. In the 1929 essay on "*Ancrene Wisse* and *Hali Meiðhad,*" Tolkien confesses that "my interest in this document [*Ancrene Wisse*] is linguistic."[15] Like the "translator" of *Farmer Giles,* Tolkien disparages the literary interests of other students of the work and rather defensively if modestly defends his decision to focus on its extraliterary features: "[I]t is very possible that nothing I can say about it will be either new or illuminating to the industrious or leisured that have kept up with it [literature surrounding the *Ancrene Wisse*]. I have not" ("Ancrene Wisse," p. 104). A judgmental and defensive critic here like some of the scholars lambasted by Tolkien in the *Beowulf* article, Tolkien is also an analyst of sources and influences in the introduction to the volume containing his translations of two of the *Pearl* poet's poems and *Sir Orfeo*. Here Tolkien reveals that research into the sources of *Sir Gawain* "interests me" although "it interested educated men of the fourteenth century very little" (introduction, Tolkien's translation of *Sir Gawain, Pearl, and Sir Orfeo*, p. 17). In short, Tolkien perfectly fulfills the role of the critic he so cleverly denigrates in the *Beowulf* and fairy-story lectures (themselves, by the way, for all their support of the creative process and art for art's sake, as critical, analytical, and interpretive as any work of literary criticism).

Tolkien displays a fictional self, a persona, divided by two different interests, art and philology (or literary criticism), which tug him first one way, then another. This figuration of the philologist posturing as an artist (or vice versa) has been described, by one of his students, S.T.R.O. d'Ardenne, in commenting on Tolkien's being awarded the C.B.E. "for services to literature," as part of the humorist's strategy: "[Tolkien's] literary works and fiction, quite unique in English Literature, brought something new into English letters: a humorist caught at his own trick!"[16] This type of split self also emerges in the personae dramatized in all three of Tolkien's mock prefaces to creative works— one by an "editor" in *The Adventures of Tom Bombadil,* one by a "translator" in *Farmer Giles of Ham,* and one by an "artist" in *The Lord of the Rings.* The "editor" of Hobbit songs by Bilbo, Sam, and their descendants in the first preface traces the chronology of the songs (based on historical evidence from the trilogy) and notes linguistic peculiarities of these songs as would any editor (in particular, strange words and rhyming and metrical tricks absorbed from the Elves). In addition, as a literary critic, Tolkien denigrates individual songs: "[S]ome are written carelessly in margins and blank spaces. Of the last sort most are nonsense, now often unintelligible even when legible, or half-remembered fragments."[17] By stressing the value of these songs *only* as historical and linguistic documents, the "editor" uses the poems as a means to his own end.

That this "editor" is actually the artist Tolkien himself parallels the concept of the split self that also appears, with greater subtlety, in *Farmer Giles of Ham.* The critic in *Farmer Giles of Ham* is a "translator" rather than an editor and hence capable of even greater acts of presumption against the artist's tale. Throughout the preface this *Farmer Giles* "translator" makes mistakes in his scholarship that undermine his authority and reveal his human flaws. When he analyzes the character of the age with which the Latin work deals, he says that his information comes from "historians of the reign of Arthur," presumably from a "sober annal"; but, in fact, instead of "history," he paraphrases a "popular lay" by the fictional artist (in fact, also Tolkien) at whom he scoffs throughout. Compare the "translator's" *Gawain*-poet-like remark, "What with the love of petty independence on the one hand, and on the other the greed of kings for wider realms, the years were filled with swift alternations of war and peace, of mirth and woe" (*Farmer Giles,* p. 7), with scholar Tolkien's own translation of the introductory lines of *Sir Gawain and the Green Knight:* "where strange things, strife and sadness, / at whiles in the land did fare, / and each other grief and gladness / oft fast have followed there" (Tolkien, trans. *Sir Gawain,* lines 15–18, in Tolkien's translation of *Sir Gawain, Pearl, and Sir* Orfeo, p. 25).

As "translator" and artist of *Farmer Giles,* Tolkien, of course, is appropriating the posture (and the lines) of the *Gawain* poet, who appears in the guise of a "historian" to talk about the founding of Britain. A borrower and imitator like many medieval artists, ironically this "translator" of *Farmer Giles* also functions like the modern literary critic he reproaches when he unknowingly disparages Aeneas, the lord of "well-nigh all the wealth in the Western Isles" in *Sir Gawain* (Tolkien, trans. *Sir Gawain*, line 7), by attributing the instability of the years to "the greed of kings for wider realms." The translation's inaccuracies and self-deceptions transcend the useful if unfactual fancies of the artist: the critic becomes a mirror-image of the artist he denigrates. When the critic attempts to undercut the false fiction and the pride of his medieval artist ("the original grandiose title has been suitably reduced to *Farmer Giles of Ham*" [*Farmer Giles*, p. 8]), his own falsity and pride are themselves undercut by the real artist, Tolkien, in this superb satire. The humble vernacular title and the crude subject matter ascribed to this "curious tale" reflect not only the true character of the artist but also that of the critic. Both actually project the two sides of Tolkien.

In Tolkien's own foreword to *The Lord of the Rings*, the artist and the critic initially seem to alternate voices, first one addressing the reader, then the other. Professor Tolkien the historian in the appendices and prologue to *The Lord of the Rings* also acts like an Andrew Lang in collecting, classifying, and organizing historical and philological information about a nonexistent species and world—but ones created by J.R.R. Tolkien the artist. Such a mask enhances the verisimilitude of the secondary world of Middle-earth, very like the mask of Gulliver provided by Swift in the preface to *Gulliver's Travels* as a kind of passport authenticating the travels of the central hero. In this case, because there are two "masks," the artist and critic clash dramatically with one another or battle as do hero and monstrous adversary in *Beowulf*. If the artist in his creative travails may be described as a Hobbit-like romance hero on a journey-quest to the Crack of Doom, then the critic in his interruptions of the artist's work may be described as a Sauron-like monster jeopardizing the quest.

Initially the professor of Old English and the artist were the same. Just as Tolkien the man in the primary world became attracted to an earlier age—the Middle Ages—instead of finding interest in the twentieth century, so Tolkien the sub-creator in the secondary world became attracted to its earlier age: of *The Lord of the Rings* Tolkien confesses that "the story was drawn irresistibly towards the older world, and became an account, as it were, of its end and passing away before its beginning and middle had been told" (*LR*, 1:viii). The problem in both worlds is that the Sauron-like critic or scholar in Tolkien interferes with artistic progress—a moving *forward* on the quest for completion. In the primary world the teaching and re-search of Professor Tolkien prevented much artistic progress on the sequel during the years 1936–45.[18] In the secondary world, creation halted altogether after the completion of *The Hobbit* while Tolkien the philologist attempted to complete the mythology and legends of the Elder Days, although "I had little hope that other people would be interested in this work, especially since it was primarily *linguistic* in inspiration and was begun in order to provide the necessary background of '*history*' for Elvish tongues" (*LR*, 1:viii; my italics).

In the foreword Tolkien's critical voice insists on ana-lyzing very rationally the artistry of *The Lord of the Rings* in opposition to the simple, humble, and emotional artist's voice that refers the reader to the text itself rather than to any critical assertions. For example, the critic asseverates that the events taking place in the primary world, specifi-cally the Second World War, had no impact on those in the secondary world of the trilogy: "If it had inspired or directed the development of the legend, then certainly the Ring would have been seized and used against Sauron; he .

would not have been annihilated but enslaved" (*LR,* 1:x). Certainly the fantasy with its secondary world boasts a happy ending alien to the reality of the primary world, but that does not mean the artist can protect the secondary world he creates from any contamination by the primary world. The critic's voice seems to grow more shrill, more dictatorial: "[I]t has been supposed by some that 'The Scouring of the Shire' reflects the situation in England at the time when I was finishing my tale. *It does not.* It is an essential part of the plot, foreseen from the outset, though in the event modified by the character of Saruman as developed in the story *without, need I say, any allegorical significance or contemporary political reference whatsoever"* (*LR,* 1:xi; my italics). This voice of the rational man so concerned with truth warns the reader not to "define the process" wherein an author is affected by his own experience because such hypotheses constitute mere "guesses from evidence that is inadequate and ambiguous" (*LR,* 1:xi).

Yet on the same page, Tolkien quietly reveals that "[b]y 1918 all but one of my close friends were dead" (*LR,* 1:xi)—as a consequence of the First World War instead of the Second World War, true, but also a fact that startles and moves the reader. While the critic may reject haphazard guesses about the artist's life and its relation to his work because of inadequate evidence, the artist elicits directly the irrational, speculative, imaginative response from his reader. The latter is the same speaker who wishes to "try his hand at a really long story that would hold the attention of readers, amuse them, delight them, and at times maybe excite them or deeply move them" (*LR,* 1:ix), no doubt as we are moved by the revelation about the loss of youthful friends in the war. Like Beowulf, portrayed in Tolkien's essay as a medieval hero battling dragonlike scholars who refuse to read it as a work of art, Tolkien the artist must rely on what might be termed the equivalent of the poem's godfather, named Poesis, which Beowulf's false allegorical guides spurn: "As a guide I had only my own *feelings* for what is appealing or moving" (*LR,* 1:ix; my italics).

The conflict between the two voices intensifies, with the reader caught in the middle, for the critic adopts the rhetorical mask of the artist in order to sway the reader and, in a sense, triumphs over the artist. Tolkien announces that *The Lord of the Rings* cannot be allegory, first, because "I cordially dislike allegory in all its manifestations"; second, because "I think that many confuse 'applicability' with 'allegory'"; and, third, because "the one resides in the freedom of the reader, and the other in the purposed domination of the author" (*LR,* 1:xi). It is ironic, then, that Tolkien as artist employs not just a metaphor but an extended metaphor, an allegory, when, in the foreword, he compares his writing labors to those of Frodo the quest-hero; he has also confessed his domination by his critic-self during the years 1939–45. It is perhaps a similar domination by this critic that forces the persona to announce that "this paperback edition and no other has been published with my consent and co-operation. Those who approve of courtesy (at least) to living authors will purchase it and no other" (*LR,* 1:xiii). In fact, it was because Houghton Mifflin had violated a legal provision limiting the number of copies of proof sheets that could be brought into the country that Ace had issued its unauthorized edition; further, according to Kilby it was this unauthorized edition by Ace that made Tolkien famous.[19] Of course, in the primary world Tolkien the man suffered financially from the unauthorized publication of the trilogy by Ace Books, even though Ace finally tendered remuneration to him,[20] but, in this fictional projection of the "drama" of the real or primary world, the heroic artist is overcome, so to speak, by the monstrous avarice of the critic.

As he often did in person, Tolkien in this foreword is trying to say several things at the same time, often appearing to contradict himself, a mode of behavior that Clyde Kilby has labeled (as we have seen) as "contrasistency." Underlying this polysemous manifestation by Tolkien in conversation was, first, Tolkien's perception of some underlying idea or relationship that his listener did not grasp, but often failing to be fully communicated;[21] second, as Kilby puts it, "I became convinced that Professor Tolkien was suffering in an accentuated way, because of his genius, from some of the inner conflicts belonging to us all."[22] One such conflict was Tolkien's own insecurity about his work: "I have never had much confidence in my work," he writes to Kilby, and even now when I am assured (still much to my grateful surprise) that it has value for other people, I feel diffident, reluctant as it were, to expose my world of imagination to possibly contemptuous eyes and ears"; at the same time, Kilby remarks on his perfectionism: "But if Tolkien was critical of others he was even more critical of his own writings. Few authors ever denigrated their own works more than he."[23]

So also Tolkien, behind the mask of his persona, wishes to alert the reader to a key theme of *The Lord of the Rings* without actually saying so. He does this in a very clever way. At the end of his long and difficult journey-quest Frodo suddenly refuses to relinquish the Ring to the flame—he clings, Gollum-like, to his Precious. He has been affected by his long possession of this material object created by the Dark Lord, and it makes him selfish. Similarly, at the end of *his* quest in the foreword, the artist succumbs to *his* dark side, of which the critic is an emblem, and in a sense refuses to give up *his* own creation: "Nonetheless, for all its defects of omission and inclusion, [*The Lord of the Rings*] was the product of long labor, and like a simple-minded hobbit I feel that it is, while I am still alive, my property in justice unaffected by copyright laws" (*LR*, 1:xii). As a Hobbit he accordingly compares the pirate publisher to "Saruman in his decay." In the secondary world of the fantasy, Gollum unintentionally saves the fallen Hobbit from himself by biting off his ring finger and forcing him to give up that Ring he loves most in an act that also saves Middle-earth. But who saves the fallen artist in the primary world? As Tolkien the critic noted, the Ring would never have been destroyed in the real world, hence the fallen artist might never be saved. Perhaps the critic saves the artist from himself by biting off *his* ring finger: by interpreting the trilogy specifically as nonallegory, he alerts the reader to possible "purposed domination" by the *critic* in the foreword and forces him to read the text more carefully to see if it is indeed allegorical. (That is, just as the author may guide the reader's response by creating an allegory, as Tolkien has in the foreword, so the critic may guide his response by claiming that it is *not* an allegory.) Fortunately, the reader's quest does not end on the last page of the foreword when the artist-Hobbit seems to succumb to his own greed, nor at the end of the Ring's life at the Crack of Doom in the trilogy when the hero-Hobbit succumbs to *his* greed, but instead at the end of *The Lord of the Rings* when the servant-Hobbit Sam returns to the Shire and announces simply, in the last words of the work, "Well, I'm back." The real hero spurns the Ring out of love for and obedience to his master, Frodo, and demands neither "courtesy" nor "payment" because, unlike fallen man, Sam suffers neither the sin of pride nor the sin of avarice. In this secondary world the innocent artist in Tolkien can also come "back" like Sam and be reborn as the author of Hobbit song. At the end of his own journey-quest the reader realizes the artist has triumphed over the critic at last.

As a Frodo-like Hobbit on the way to Mount Doom,

the reader must exercise his own free will when tempted by others—such as the Dark Lord or Gandalf or the critic—to guide his responses when he puts on the Ring (that is, when he reads *The Lord of the Rings*). Only the reader can decide whether the work has "inner meaning," despite the critic's proclamation that "it has in the intention of the author none. It is neither allegorical nor topical" (*LR*, 1:x). By so doing the reader helps to rescue the artist from the critic.

That the artist and critic may be the same figure in the dramatic foreword or the same man in the real world is an idea rehearsed for Tolkien in *Beowulf,* where the hero Beowulf never fully realizes his most awesome adversary is the monster of pride within himself, and by Tolkien in the *Beowulf* essay in which the critic never fully realizes he himself is a monster like the irrelevant monsters he ignores. Many of these ideas derive from the Christian culture imbuing those medieval works of literature Tolkien loved and studied all his life.

III. God's Word: Satan as Critic

For Tolkien, the critic figure based upon the monster Grendel or the dragon typifies Satan, as the artist figure based upon the hero Beowulf typifies the Creator. This myth of literary roles springs from the book of Genesis as a preface or foreword to the Word of God and the book of Revelation, the "rising" and "setting" aspects of the Bible related to the "rising" and "setting" moments and balanced structure of *Beowulf.* Paradoxically, the rising of the first book actually involves a fall—of man—as the setting of the last book involves his rising—or redemption. Because of the Fall instigated by Satan, humankind suffers a split self, with one side a monster and one side a hero—one side a child and one side an adult ("growing up" is necessary only in a world subjected to mutability, sickness, and death, all consequences of the Fall). So divided, humankind longs for another world where all may be whole. This world we experience only briefly on earth when a godlike sub-creator fashions a secondary world analogous to the Other World. In this secondary world of art, the word, like the Word of God (the Bible, especially Revelation), provides redemption ("recovery" through joy) for the world-weary fallen adult. Unfortunately, the critic attempts to interfere by guiding the reader away from fantasy and literature toward Drama, a form that mirrors the reality and sorrow of the primary world, just as Satan tries to lure humankind away from the eternal good of the Other World by offering the temporal good of this world. Satan also tries to dominate the free will of the reader by imposing his own interpretation of that literature or drama. This myth Tolkien constructs in the two lectures, his "Genesis" and "Revelation," and applies in the foreword to *The Lord of the Rings* in particular.

The concept of Satan as critic first surfaces in the *Beowulf* article. Just as God in Genesis first creates Eden as a paradise arousing Satan's envy, so in *Beowulf,* Tolkien notes, the artist as tower builder (that is, Hrothgar) constructs Heorot so that "its light spread over many lands" ("lixte se leoma ofer landa fela") in parody of "fiat lux" in Genesis, arousing the envy of the monster Grendel: "Grendel is maddened by the sound of harps" ("Beowulf," p. 88). This music signals the peace and joy of community denied to that exile suffering the mark of Cain. Grendel is the critic of light as Hrothgar and the *scop* are its artists: "[T]he outer darkness and its hostile offspring lie ever in wait for the torches to fail and the voices to cease" ("Beowulf," p. 88).

Similarly, the human *Beowulf*-critic arrogantly tries to muffle the artist's voice by using the poem as a means to an end—as a demonstration of his superior understanding of Old English history and linguistics. Preferring knowledge to wisdom, the critic resembles the monstrous serpent who tempts Eve with the desire to be Godlike by eating of the Tree of Knowledge of Good and Evil. Such knowledge is pursued in *The Lord of the Rings,* for example, by Saruman, the perverted Wizard (teacher? sage?) who gazes myopically into the *palantír* (ironically meaning "far-sighted") in a vain attempt to boost his own knowledge and power and to emulate the Dark Lord Sauron. Saruman exchanges for his previous wisdom mere knowledge ("all those arts and subtle devices, for which he forsook his former wisdom"), never realizing those "which fondly he imagined were his own, came but from Mordor."[24] Appropriately Saruman inhabits the citadel named Orthanc, "Cunning Mind" in the language of the Mark but in Elvish the monstrous name "Mount Fang," to underscore the exact nature of the Wizard's perversion or "fall." (Even Sauron originally misused Elven wisdom in creating the rings as a means to the end of self-aggrandizement.) Saruman, like the wily serpent of Eden, uses his own voice to dissuade others from courses of action not beneficial to him, literally when challenged by Gandalf and his followers on the steps of Orthanc, but more figuratively through his surrogate voice, "*Wormtongue,*" when his evil counsel demoralizes Théoden in the hall of Rohan. Significantly, by the end of the trilogy Saruman has become "Sharkey" and Wormtongue his beast "Worm," both names connoting the cold-blooded and animal nature of the monster.

To the portrait of Satan as a critic of the creation God's work, Tolkien adds the portrait of Christ as its heroic defender—the Word of God, or the archetype of the human artist—in the paired works "On Fairy-Stories" and "Leaf by Niggle" that comprise *Tree and Leaf.* Tolkien even mentions the Fall in the former through the "Locked Door" theme: "Even Peter Rabbit was forbidden a garden, lost his blue coat, and took sick. The Locked Door stands as an eternal temptation" ("On Fairy-Stories," p. 33). The critic longs to explore the "Tree of Tales" like the Tree of Knowledge of Good and Evil—with its "intricately knotted and ramified history of the branches" related to the philologist's study of the "tangled skein of *language*" ("On Fairy-Stories," p. 19; my italics). Unlike the critic, the artist Niggle in "Leaf by Niggle" merely wishes to portray accurately a single leaf. The humble, self-effacing, and imaginative artist contrasts with the proud, ambitious, and analytic critic. This is one reason why Tolkien dramatically combines the analytic and ambitious prose essay of the critic, "On Fairy-Stories," with the humble, self-effacing, and imaginative prose tale of the artist, "Leaf by Niggle," in one volume entitled *Tree and Leaf*. In the introductory note to *Tree and Leaf*, Tolkien claims there are three additional reasons for the two works to be combined in one book: their common leaf/tree symbolism, their interest in the theme of sub-creation, and their dates of origin, 1938–39, concurrent with the beginning of *The Lord of the Rings* (*Tree and Leaf*, p. 2).

The title of *Tree and Leaf* appropriately mirrors the mythological difference between the two works and their genres and roles, one an essay, written by a scholar, and one a fairy-story, written by an artist. For there were two trees in Eden, the Tree of Knowledge of Good and Evil and the Tree of Life. The wood of the latter was used for the cross upon which Christ was crucified to redeem humankind. And "Leaf by Niggle," as Tolkien explains in the introductory note to *Tree and Leaf*, was inspired by the felling of a great tree by its owner, "a punishment for any crimes it may have been accused of, such as being large and alive" (*Tree and Leaf*, p. 2). The tree destroyed wantonly by its equally fallen owner in our fallen world suggests the loss of the Tree of Life, a metonymy for Eden, by its gardener, Adam; it also reminds us of the similar destruction of the trees of Fangorn by Saruman, in the second volume of *The Lord of the Rings*, *The Two Towers*, although he does not own them, to use the wood in scientific experiments and to build machines for future destruction. Saruman's destructive act provokes the wrath of the Ents and thus leads to his "fall," as they attack and imprison him, symbolically, in Orthanc ("Cunning Mind"). But the loss of Tolkien's beloved tree in *Leaf by Niggle* leads to its artistic resurrection as a leaf by the artist Niggle (or, in other words, leads to the story entitled "Leaf by Niggle," by the artist Tolkien), who eventually creates or restores a whole tree, then a "sub-creation," or another world. This is the Tree of Life, a metonymy for the paradise Niggle is permitted to inhabit eternally by the story's end.

The distinction between the two trees and between Satan and Christ was amplified in the Middle Ages to include as well a distinction between the Old Man and the New Man, or the child, a typology Tolkien also uses in "On Fairy-Stories" to distinguish the adult-critic from the child-reader. For example, in the *Cursor Mundi*, Christ, the Second Adam, rests as a newborn child on the top of a faded tree (the Tree of Knowledge around which an adder is wrapped) reaching to the sky, at whose roots is buried Abel, slain by Cain who resides in Hell.[25] This image of the New Man, the *novus homo*, underscores the idea of rebirth and spiritual regeneration, which Saint Augustine in *De Doctrina Christiana* describes as the new skin of the snake revealed after it has wriggled out of its old skin, of the *vetus homo*, or the Old Man. Saint Augustine means that we should exchange the life of the senses, of the body or the Old Law, for the life of the spirit, of the soul or the New

Law of Christianity.[26] That Saint Augustine's Old Man and Tolkien's old, wary critic might be the same becomes more convincing within the context of the same passage, wherein Saint Augustine also blames the Old Man for adhering to the letter in reading the Bible instead of preferring the spirit, or an understanding of figurative signs and expressions of allegory.

Interestingly, Tolkien as a reader (or critic) refers to himself as an "old" and "wary" man in the foreword to *The Lord of the Rings:* "I cordially dislike allegory in all its manifestations, and always have done so since I grew *old and wary enough* to detect its presence" (p. xi; my italics). Elsewhere in his letters Tolkien defines allegory as the "particular" and "topical." It is clear that "allegory" for Tolkien is an elastic term that can be stretched to include any story, including that narrative of our own lives in which we participate: "In a larger sense, it is I suppose impossible to write any "story" that is not allegorical in proportion as it "comes to life": since each of us is an allegory, embodying in a particular tale and clothed in the garments of time and place, universal truth and everlasting life" (letter 163, to W.H. Auden, p. 212). If so, then why does Tolkien as critic condemn the use of allegory in his foreword to *The Lord of the Rings?*

Throughout Tolkien's works the concept of oldness is linked with literalness and knowledge as an end in itself. First, like this Old Man, Tolkien's critic in the foreword to *The Lord of the Rings* prefers "history, true or feigned, with its varied applicability to the thought and experience of readers" (*LR*, 1:xi), to allegory. Second, Tolkien also condemns the Old Man, or the adult, in his essay "On Fairy-Stories," whereas he glorifies that symbolic child, or New Man in each human being still able to receive "grace"—to be transported by the "word" of the sub-creator to the other world of Faërie, where the reader experiences the eucatastrophe of the happy ending of fantasy. Tolkien does caution that "[t]he process of growing older is not necessarily allied to growing wickeder, though the two do often happen together" ("On Fairy-Stories," p. 44). Finally, in *The Lord of the Rings* the old and wary Saruman disintegrates into dust at death, whereas the aged Gandalf, his good counterpart, dies as the Gray (puts off the Old Man) so as to be reborn as the White (puts on the New Man).

The New Man, as the archetype of Christ, symbolizes the incarnation of the Word of God in human form, a divine communication by the penultimate artist, God, to his "reader," fallen or Old Man, a metaphor, made explicit by Saint Augustine: "How did He come except that 'the Word was made flesh, and dwelt among us'? It is as when we speak. In order that what we are thinking may reach the mind of the listener through the fleshy ears, that which we have in mind is expressed in words . . . by means of which it may reach the ears without suffering any deterioration in itself. In the same way the Word of God was made flesh without change that He might dwell among us" (Augustine, *De Doctrina*, 1.13, p. 14). Elsewhere in *De Doctrina* Saint Augustine reveals that the often allegorical Word of God is incarnated in the "flesh" of parable[27] as is perfect love and truth in Christ the Word. This Word corresponds to the word of man, especially when the latter communicates the truth hidden in that parabolic Word eloquently and clearly by using the tropes, styles, and rules of rhetoric. The reader discerns the truth by applying the four-fold allegorical method of exegesis to the text.

Just as Tolkien's critic in the foreword cannot abide allegory—a sign of his "oldness"—Tolkien himself in the *Beowulf* article associates allegory (as distinct from myth) with that abstraction and rational analysis of which the critic, rather than the artist, is fond. Further, the bad artist in both the foreword and the *Beowulf* article is accused of dominating the reader by using allegory instead of myth. This does not mean Tolkien disliked figurative expression, of which allegory is one kind. Indeed, he constructs the central fantasy of the *Beowulf* article through the use of figurative expressions—allegorical and metaphorical exempla. Defining allegory very narrowly, Tolkien notes that *The Pearl,* for example, is not an allegory but is allegorical, a differentiation hotly debated by *Pearl* critics in the past.[28] Allegory must be confined (as Tolkien reveals in the introduction to his translation of *The Pearl*) to "narrative, to an account (however short) of events; and symbolism to the use of visible signs of things to represent other things or ideas. . . . To be an 'allegory' a poem must *as a whole,* and with fair consistency, describe in other terms some event or process; its entire narrative and all its significant details should cohere and work together to make the end. . . . But an allegorical description of an event does not make that event itself allegorical" (introduction, Tolkien's translation of *Sir Gawain, Pearl, and Sir Orfeo,* p. 18). This distinction between symbolism and allegory remains a modern one; Saint Augustine would not have quarreled with Tolkien. Note also that Tolkien's fellow Inkling C.S. Lewis knew of his friend's dislike of allegory but preferred to define the word in a wider sense: "I am also convinced that the wit of man *cannot* devise a story in wh. the wit of some other man cannot find an allegory. . . . Indeed, in so far as the things unseen are manifested by the things seen, one might from one point of view call the whole material universe an allegory. . . . It wd. be disastrous if anyone took your statement that the Nativity is the greatest of all allegories to mean that the physical event was merely *feigned.*"[29]

It is interesting to note that Tolkien's conception of the secondary world created by the artist in his fantasy depends upon allegory: human art corresponds to the art of God and the secondary world of Faërie resembles the other world of Heaven. In "On Fairy-Stories" Tolkien shows that the process of reading a fantasy imitates the process of reading (and living by) the Word of God. The Christian experiences joy in "reading" the happy ending or eucatastrophe of human history in the birth of Christ just as s/he enjoys the "happy ending" of the story of the Resurrection. Similarly, s/he "escapes" from this world into the "secondary world" of fantasy to experience as a child the joy of Recovery, as the Christian escapes from this world after death into the other world of Heaven to experience as a child eternal joy: for the Christian, life with its happy ending is a Divine Comedy, as Dante shrewdly noted. This message is imparted to the grieving father of *The Pearl* in a dream in which he confronts his lost child (or soul), after which his spirits are themselves lifted in a happy ending that invokes Revelation. It is a work Tolkien chose appropriately to translate into modern English. The child must be the *novus homo* or the New Man, a type of Christ, who is lost and then found by the Old Man, the father, as a type of Adam. Art then heals the split in the self by renewing the fallen individual. Just as the Old Man puts on the New Man, so the adult regains the child by reading fantasy and the critic becomes the artist by creating art, as Tolkien himself did. Indeed, about him S.T.R.O. d'Ardenne notes: "Tolkien belonged to that very rare class of linguists, who like the Grimm Brothers could understand and recapture the glamour of 'the Word,' 'In the beginning was the Word, and the Word was with God, and the word was God.'"[30] Unfortunately, in the primary world humankind is neither wholly critic nor artist, linguist or literary interpreter, adult or child, but both.

A metaphor for the loss of unified sensibility caused by the Fall, the split self or the antithetical pair reflects that rivalry—even fratricide—between the sons of Adam, Abel and Cain, that results in the murder of Deagol by Sméagol. The split self, division, homicide, symbolizes the quality of existence in the land ruled by Sauron, Mordor or Morðor, the Anglo-Saxon word for murder or slaying. The split self and the pair link many of Tolkien's fictional characters: Tídwald the old churl argues with the young minstrel Torhthelm in "The Homecoming of Beorhtnoth Beorhthelm's Son"; Niggle the artist is irritated by his neighbor Parish the gardener in "Leaf by Niggle"; Alf the humble apprentice serves Nokes the arrogant Master Cook in "Smith of Wootton Major"; and, of course, Théoden and Denethor rule as good and evil leaders, opposites like Denethor's good and evil sons, Faramir and Boromir, in *The Lord of the Rings*. The divided self of Bilbo—half Baggins, half Took—cannot decide whether to act as a grocer or a burglar in *The Hobbit*, just as Gollum argues with his other self, Sméagol, in the trilogy.

Within the context of medieval Christianity, then, the split self constitutes a badge of fallen human nature as both good and evil. But this favorite theme of Tolkien's art finds other contexts: in that of medieval literature, the conflict can be sketched as a Germanic heroic battle that can also be interpreted as a Christian allegory. Within the context of twentieth-century literary history in the twenties and thirties, the conflict projects the support of one school of artists for the art-for-art's-sake movement and one school of literary critics for the New Criticism in reaction to the nineteenth-century view of art and criticism as socially, historically, linguistically, culturally useful, both views Germanic in nature.[31]

Within the context of the "history" of Tolkien's own life, the war between the critic and the artist or the professor of Anglo-Saxon and the Christian reflects antithetical interests never completely reconciled. As his biographer

Carpenter admits, "There were not two Tolkien's, one an academic and the other a writer. They were the same man, and the two sides of him overlapped so that they were indistinguishable—or rather they were not two sides at all, but different expressions of the same mind, the same imagination."[32] This quality of "contrasistency" was (as noted above) also acknowledged by scholar Clyde Kilby, who came to know Tolkien in the last years of his life. It is possible that the two sides did meet only in the fantasy world of Tolkien's art, where the critic is redeemed by the artist and the best warrior is the most sacrificial and gentle. So *Beowulf*—a poem Tolkien greatly loved that depicted clashes between Germanic and Christian values, battles between hero and monsters, and a contrast between the "rising" and "setting" moments of the protagonist's life— remains amazingly and joyfully a single, unified, and balanced poem.

Chapter 2

THE KING UNDER THE MOUNTAIN

Tolkien's Children's Story

For in effect this is a study of a simple ordinary
man, neither artistic nor noble and heroic (but not
without the undeveloped seeds of these things)
against a high setting—and in fact (as a critic has
perceived) the tone and style change with the
Hobbit's development, passing from fairy-tale to
the noble and high and relapsing with the return.
                                    —J.R.R. Tolkien
                Letter 131, to Milton Waldman of Collins
                                           (c. 1951)

A good fairy story by a Christian for a twelve-year
old.
                            —J.R.R. Tolkien to C. S. Lewis
                     (cited by Clyde Kilby, *Tolkien and "The
                                      Silmarillion,"* p. 75)

A story about growing up or maturation, *The Hobbit* has
been regarded by some critics as merely a work of
children's literature[1] and by others as a badly muddled mix
of children's literature and adult literature.[2] In part readers' confusion over its genre and meaning may have

48

stemmed from its changing form, in that Tolkien revised *The Hobbit* three times: first in 1937, the year it was published in Great Britain; then in the second edition of 1951, with chapter 5—when Bilbo finds the Ring and participates in the riddle game with Gollum—having been revised earlier, in 1947, to create a transition to the "sequel" of *The Lord of the Rings;* and again for the third edition of 1966.[3] Bonniejean Christensen notes that the alterations in the character of Gollum between the edition of 1937 and that of 1951 "clearly increase Gollum's role and remove the story from the realm of the nursery tale," in preparation for his "expanded role" later in *The Lord of the Rings.*[4]

Nevertheless, while other critical interpretations have revealed the psychological and literary underpinnings of the adult level of the work,[5] they rarely justify or even account for the children's level, specifically, the reason for the narrator, who sounds suspiciously like Professor Tolkien himself, and the children's story framework.[6] Tolkien himself has admitted that his own children disliked the tone and style in which it was written: "'The Hobbit' was written in what I should now regard as bad style, as if one were talking to children. There's nothing my children loathed more. They taught me a lesson. Anything that was in any way marked out in 'The Hobbit' as for children, instead of just for people, they disliked—instinctively. I did too, now that I think about it."[7] It is precisely the voice of the narrator of *The Hobbit* that Tolkien tried at first to recreate in "A Long-Expected Party," the first chapter of *The Fellowship of the Ring,* as a sequel to *The Hobbit;* in Paul Thomas's examination of the various drafts of the first chapter, it is clear that the narrator ultimately (and appropriately) vanishes altogether in the final revision.[8]

The reason, then, that Tolkien employed the children's story frame in *The Hobbit,* along with the patronizing adult narrator that offended even his own children, has to do with the *adult* level of the work: Tolkien's narrative technique constitutes part of the work's fiction, in the manner of Chaucer's *Canterbury Tales*. The narrator, like a tale-telling pilgrim, must be regarded as one additional character. The arrogant, unimaginative, and very "adult" narrator assumes this story about little Hobbits must be relegated to an audience of little creatures—children. The narrator's pride, patronizing attitude, and literalism betray his "oldness," in the Augustinian sense. So *The Hobbit* is a children's story only in the sense expressed in the 1938 Andrew Lang Lecture on fairy-stories, that fantasy appeals to the child in every adult; otherwise it is a genre as fictional and false as its narrator. As a critic who denies the artist's intention by deliberately misunderstanding the story and its characters, the narrator also personifies the critic whom Tolkien views as a monster in the *Beowulf* essay and against whom Tolkien, as heroic defender of the poem as a work of art, must battle.

In the seminal *Beowulf* essay, as we have seen, Tolkien revolutionized *Beowulf* scholarship by interpreting its previously ignored monsters as central thematically and structurally to the meaning of the poem; in addition, he poked fun at the critical "monsters"—the scholars—who had dismissed it as a work of art in their eagerness to trumpet its historical, philological, and anthropological importance. The essay also serves as a guide to how Tolkien reads *The Hobbit* and many of his other works, for there are many other ideas and concepts in it that he fictionalizes in *The Hobbit*. The *Beowulf* lecture had been published as an article one year before *The Hobbit* (1937), indicating that Tolkien had been thinking about and teaching or writing about both works for some time.[9] Indeed, in a letter to the *Observer* on 20 February 1938, Tolkien admits that, for *The Hobbit*, "*Beowulf* is among my most valued sources;

though it was not consciously present to the mind in the process of writing, in which the episode of the theft arose naturally (and almost inevitably) from the circumstances."[10] In this same letter Tolkien also admits, "My tale is not consciously based on any other book—save one, and that is unpublished: the 'Silmarillion,' a history of the Elves, to which frequent allusion is made."

The parallels between the two works have not been generally recognized, even though scholars may have related the work to other medieval concepts, especially of Northernness.[11] Bonniejean Christensen comes closest to recognizing the parallelism between Tolkien's children's story and his scholarly lecture when she notes that *The Hobbit* can be interpreted as a retelling of *Beowulf*, "from a Christian rather than a pagan point of view."[12] However, Tolkien scholar Christensen prefers the idea of *Beowulf* editor Friedrich Klaeber about the poem's four-part structure to Tolkien's own interpretation of *Beowulf*'s dual structure, to show that *Beowulf*'s sections (comprising the monsters, the descendants of Cain, the episodes and digressions, and the dragon) parallel *The Hobbit*'s.[13] The uncomfortable result is that Grendel in *Beowulf* shares the same structural position as that of the Trolls and Goblins in the first section of *The Hobbit,* and Unferth and Grendel's Mother as that of Gollum in the second section.

The view of the structure of *Beowulf* in the lecture that seems more closely linked to that of *The Hobbit* perceives the poem as portraying two moments, rising and falling, in the hero Beowulf's life, with three adversaries— Grendel and Grendel's Mother in the first part, and the dragon in the second—battled by the hero. Tolkien describes the poem as "a contrasted description of two moments in a great life, rising and setting; an elaboration of the ancient and intensely moving contrast between youth and age, first achievement and final death. It is divided in consequence into two opposed portions, different in matter, manner, and length: A from 1 to 2199 (including an exordium of 52 lines); B from 2200 to 3182 (the end)."[14] In the similarly structured *Hobbit,* Bilbo also battles with his two adversaries, Gollum and Smaug the dragon, at various rising moments only, for it is a story of spiritual maturation and not of spiritual death.[15] If, instead, *Beowulf* is understood to have a tripartite structure, focusing on the monstrous adversaries of Beowulf rather than the hero—Grendel, Grendel's Mother, and the dragon—then it can be said to be more focused on monstrous failure (as represented by the three monsters) than Bilbo's heroic maturation. Indeed, it is also possible to recognize a tripartite structure in *The Hobbit,* or even a six-part structure.[16]

The major difference, then, between Tolkien's conception of Beowulf as hero in the essay and his conception of Bilbo as hero in *The Hobbit* is Bilbo's success in combating literal and internal monsters, in contrast, at least for Tolkien, to Beowulf's final failure. This difference affects the genres of the two works. Tolkien regards *Beowulf* explicitly as an elegy, defined as "tragedy" in the 1938 Andrew Lang Lecture on fairy-stories because of its unhappy ending (dyscatastrophe) and hence its link with the primary world, and *The Hobbit* implicitly as a "fantasy" because of its happy ending (eucatastrophe) and hence its link with the secondary world of sub-creation.[17] Their different genres affect the nature of the dual levels in each: the explicit Germanic-heroic ethic and culture of *Beowulf* masks a very Christian purpose, just as the explicit children's story framework of *The Hobbit* masks a more "adult" and serious purpose.

The monsters Grendel and the dragon were for Tolkien not only fierce enemies of the Danes and Geats against whom Beowulf fought but also, in a more symbolic fashion, projections of spiritual and political flaws in

Beowulf himself. Aged and yet still boasting of his youthful prowess in battle, King Beowulf fights the dragon in an ill-advised move that will result in his death and the betrayal of his people, for the Swedes among other tribes will attack the leaderless Geats after he dies. Beowulf manifests that same pride in his own ability and greed for dragon gold as does the dragon, and although he wins the battle with the monster (with the help of Wiglaf), he loses the one with himself. "For it is true of man, maker of myths," Tolkien declares, "that Grendel and the dragon, in their lust, greed, and malice, have a part in him" ("Beowulf," p. 76 note 23).

Tolkien's ideas about kingship in *Beowulf*, which he also employed in *The Hobbit*, were perhaps influenced by a scholarly study of the poem published in 1929 by Levin L. Schücking, "The Ideal of Kingship in *Beowulf*."[18] Schücking defines the true and wise king and his antithesis, the false and tyrannical king, by using Augustinian terminology: "In contrast to such a 'rex justus' [just king] who always appears as a *good shepherd* and with the *qualities of a father*, is the 'tyrannus' or 'rex iniustus,' who is ruled by the 'radix vitiorum' [root of vices], 'superbia' [pride] or 'amor sui' [love of self]. . . . Out of *amor sui* spring all other vices, such as 'invidia, ira, tristitia, avaritia, and ventris ingluvies' [envy, wrath, sadness, avarice and gluttony]" (Schücking, p. 39). The vices of the bad king can be recognized as five of the seven deadly sins—pride, envy, wrath, avarice, and gluttony.

More generally Tolkien's ideas about the sins of the king find expression in the thirteenth-century *Ancrene Wisse*, "Guide for Anchoresses," a work that first captured Tolkien's interest in a 1929 linguistic study and later in the preface to Mary Salu's translation in 1956 (of which he approved) and in his own critical edition of 1962.[19] These sins assume the shape of animals and monsters in the

Ancrene Wisse; wild beasts inhabit the wilderness we must all travel on the way to the Heavenly Jerusalem, or the Kingdom of the Elect: "But go with great caution, for in this wilderness there are many evil beasts: the Lion of Pride, the Serpent of venomous Envy, the Unicorn of Wrath, the Bear of deadly Sloth, the Fox of Covetousness, the Sow of Gluttony, the Scorpion with its tail of stinging lechery, that is, Lust. These, listed in order, are the Seven Deadly Sins" (Salu, *Ancrene Wisse,* p. 86).

The connection between the sinful king and the monster in *Beowulf* and the *Ancrene Wisse* reappears in *The Hobbit.* Tolkien calls his dragon Smaug "King under the Mountain" because under a mountain he guards a treasure that he wrongfully stole from previous Dwarf-kings. The epithet serves to link this inhuman monster with similar monsters—and monstrous kings or leaders—elsewhere in *The Hobbit* through four major significations. First, it refers to the monsters of the work as a whole: Smaug guards his treasure under the Lonely Mountain while Gollum hides his magic ring under the Misty Mountains. In addition, there are other monsters like the Trolls, Goblins, Wargs, and giant spiders. Second, there also exist Elf, human, Dwarf, and Hobbit "kings" or leaders who, like Beowulf, succumb to various monstrous vices, chiefly pride and greed. These include the Elvenking, the Master of Dale, the Dwarf-king Thorin, and even Bilbo, who rules Bag End located in Underhill, Hobbiton. Third, the epithet symbolizes the position of the narrator who dominates the narrative through his frequent, usually critical interjections intended to undermine the artist's tale. Finally, the phrase suggests the children's game of "King of the Mountain," in which various combatants try to topple a hill's resident "king." The epithet appropriately evokes the children's level of the novel used by Tolkien to mask his more serious purpose.

Furthermore, the idea of the good prince that Schücking sees in the Germanic and heroic Old English *Beowulf* resurfaces in the modern English *Hobbit*. Eventually Bilbo develops into a type of the good "king" when he tests his courage, justice, prudence (wisdom and intelligence but also awareness of moral good), and finally temperance or *mensura* (the bridling of emotions by moderation) in battles with those monsters. For Schücking, an exemplar of such a king is the hero Beowulf, as when he humbly and wisely refuses the crown offered by Hygd "in favor of his relation; thus, he becomes a member of the virtuous society which supports the ideal of temperance" (Schücking, p. 48). But Tolkien, as we have seen, perceives Beowulf, and hence Bilbo, whom he models in part upon this king, as more flawed and monstrous than does Schücking. For Tolkien, the ultimate model of the good king that Bilbo must become, after vanquishing his internal monsters of the deadly sins of pride and greed, is Christ. This king's monstrous adversary is the Devil, whose role in perverting humankind from good is "to incite us to the venomous vices such as pride, disdain, envy, and anger, and to their venomous offspring," according to the *Ancrene Wisse* (Salu, *Ancrene Wisse,* p. 85). In this same work Christ as a "good shepherd" with the "qualities of a father" is portrayed as a true and good king or knight of the Kingdom of the Elect. When the soul is attacked by demons and devils, Jesus proves his love and performs chivalric deeds in tournament play so that his shield (his body, which disguises his Godhead) is pierced on the cross. The parallel continues: "[A]fter the death of a brave knight, his shield is hung high in the church in his memory. And so is this shield, the crucifix, set in the church, where it may be most easily seen, that it may remind us of Jesus Christ's deed of knighthood on the cross. Let His beloved see by that how He bought her love, allowing His shield to be pierced, His side open, to show her His heart, to show her how completely He loved her, and to win her own heart" (Salu, *Ancrene Wisse,* p. 174).

Christ's love for humankind surpasses the four kinds of human love—friendship, sexual love, mother-child love, and love between the body and the soul. It also suggests the love of God *(amor Dei)* that Saint Augustine contrasts with the self-love *(amor sui)* of the tyrant. It is this love that Bilbo emulates as he completes his spiritual maturation in the course of *The Hobbit* through the tests with the monsters.

We turn now to a closer examination of these ideas, beginning with the monsters in *The Hobbit,* turning next to Bilbo, and concluding with the narrator—all "Kings under the Mountain."

I. THE MONSTERS: KINGS UNDER THE MOUNTAIN

If *Beowulf* is understood to have a two-part structure, then the hero basically clashes with two different monstrous adversaries: Grendel (and his mother) at the "rising moment" of Beowulf's life, during his youth, and the dragon at the "setting moment," in his old age.[20] Further, if the balanced two-part structure of *The Hobbit* (Chapters 1–8 and 9–19) mirrors that of *Beowulf,* then its two parts must differ in emphasis because the two monsters differ. In the *Beowulf* lecture Tolkien explains: "If the dragon is the right end for Beowulf, and I agree with the author that it is, then Grendel is an eminently suitable beginning. They are creatures, *feond mancynnes* [foe of humankind], of a similar order and kindred significance. Triumph over the lesser and more nearly human is cancelled by defeat before the older and more elemental" ("Beowulf," p. 86).

In *The Hobbit,* Gollum assumes Grendel's place and, thus, epitomizes the "lesser and more nearly human" vices, as Smaug assumes the dragon's place in the second part and thus epitomizes the "older and more elemental" vices. It is the *Ancrene Wisse* that characterizes the inward temptations as "bodily in the case of lechery, gluttony, and sloth, spiritual in the case of pride, envy, and anger, and also of covetousness" (Salu, *Ancrene Wisse*, p. 85). The lesser sins are certainly the "bodily" ones, which Gollum represents, just as Smaug represents the "old and more elemental" spiritual ones.[21]

Gollum, who enters the story in the middle (chapter 5) of the first half (chapters 1 to 8), expresses "bodily sin" chiefly through his perpetual hunger. Gluttonous even when young, Gollum taught his own grandmother to suck eggs.[22] His name resembles the sound of swallowing associated with gulping food. Because his stomach remains in his mature years his sole concern, Gollum values himself above all, addressing himself as "My Precious." He represents that love of self (*amor sui*) specifically directed toward lower or bodily functions. The ring (not yet the Ring) as a birthday present to himself symbolizes the narcissism of the self turned too much inward. It produces an invisibility of self in the external world as if the self had been pushed one step past mere isolation into nonbeing.

This ring links Gollum with the dragon Smaug in the second part when Bilbo uses the ring to burgle the dragon's hoard of a cup, the loss of which arouses Smaug's anger (p. 208). But here the invisibility caused by the ring allows Bilbo to function as a better burglar: for Bilbo, the alter ego of the perverted Hobbit Gollum, invisibility symbolizes that self-effacement requisite in loving one's neighbor for the sake of God. Thus, he forgets his own fears, remembers the Dwarves' mission, bravely steals the cup, and even tricks the dragon into revealing his vulnerable spot.

Smaug enters the story near the middle (chapters 11 to 13) of the second part (chapters 9 to 19) and expresses "spiritual sin" chiefly through his pride, although he also manifests wrath, avarice, and envy. After Bilbo has stolen his cup Smaug nurses his avarice with the thought of revenge. Unfortunately, Smaug's pride leads to his fall. When Bilbo unctuously flatters him with the admission, "I only wished to have a look at you and see if you were truly as great as tales say" (*Hobbit,* p. 212), Smaug begins showing off. He inadvertently reveals his vulnerable spot along with his diamond-studded underbelly while Bilbo exclaims, "Dazzlingly marvellous" (*Hobbit,* p. 216). The dragon's avarice leads to his death, just as the *revelours'* search for the treasure leads to death in the *Pardoner's Tale:* "Radix malorum est cupiditas" (The root of all evil is avarice), as Chaucer's Pardoner tells it. Gold is death: in *The Hobbit,* when the fools of Dale spot a heavenly light, they assume the gold is on its way as legends had predicted and rush forward to—their deaths. For it is the fiery dragon himself, in a highly symbolic scene, who lights up the heavens.

The two monsters Gollum and Smaug are set apart from the other monsters by their isolation in central chapters within each of the two parts. Nevertheless, the adversary in the first part derives its essential nature from Gollum as bodily sin as the adversary in the second derives its essential nature from Smaug as spiritual sin. The "bodily sins" of gluttony and sloth (lechery omitted because this is a children's story) plus the sin of anger are portrayed in the monsters of the Trolls, Goblins, Wargs, and giant insects and spiders. The more "spiritual" sins of pride, envy, covetousness, and again anger are portrayed in the "monsters" of the Elvenking, the Master of Dale, and the Dwarf-king. In each part the hierarchy of monsters begins with the least dangerous and evil and climbs to the most dangerous and evil.

In the first part, the Trolls resemble Cockney-speaking humans, followed by the Goblins or Orcs who pervert the species of Elves, the wolflike Wargs, and on the least rational level, the insects and spiders. The Trolls introduce the theme of gluttony in the appropriately entitled chapter "Roast Mutton." The mutton they roast on spits illustrates as well their laziness, for they actually detest it but are too lazy to seek out the "manflesh" they prefer. When Bilbo's carelessness allows them to capture the Hobbit and the Dwarves, they quarrel angrily over the best cooking method for Dwarf flesh and forget that dawn is nigh. The coming of the sun turns them to stone as if to symbolize their spiritual numbness and "death."[23] The Goblins are the second monstrous adversary, encountered in chapter 4, "Over Hill and under Hill." As interested in food as the Trolls ("they are always hungry" [*Hobbit*, p. 70]), they even capture the Dwarf ponies lodged in one of their caves. But they seem less civilized than the Trolls, possibly because of their greater anger and sadism. They savagely flick whips as they herd the captured Dwarves into the hall of the Goblin-king, and they build cruel machines of torture for innocent victims. The Wargs[24] of chapter 6, "Out of the Frying Pan," resemble wolves in their shape and their brute anger. The night when they surround the Dwarves they intend to kill whole villages of woodmen except for a few prisoners left alive for their Goblin allies, merely because these woodmen had encroached upon their forests. Finally, the "Flies and Spiders" in chapter 8 exemplify uncontrolled gluttony and anger on the lowest level. After tying the Dwarves up in trees, one spider notes that "the meat's alive and kicking" (*Hobbit*, p. 156). Their gluttony is used by Bilbo to trick them: he lures them away from the captured Dwarves by describing himself as "far more sweet than other meat" (*Hobbit*, p. 158). Bilbo also invokes their anger. By calling them insulting names like "Attercop" and "Tomnoddy," he makes them so "frightfully angry" that they follow the sound of his voice while the invisible

Hobbit doubles back to untie the Dwarves and then battle with the returning, stupidly angry giant pests.

The "chain of evil being" traced in this first part is also used in the second. In the second part, the less physically dangerous "monsters" threaten instead the various societies surrounding them through their obsession with treasure and social position, in effect revealing the flaws of avarice, envy, and pride. Hence they operate behind the mask of the king or leader who occupies the highest social and political position in the community. It is for this reason that the chain of evil being in this part is one of individuals, rather than of species as in the first part. It begins with the most noble and least dangerous, the Elvenking, and progresses to the most ignoble and dangerous, the Dwarf-king Thorin, with Man—the Master of Dale—occupying a medial position. Interestingly, their dwelling places reflect this hierarchy through their distance from the earth—the Elven treehouse, the human house, the Dwarf hall under the mountain.

The Wood-Elves and the Men of Dale team up like the Wargs and Goblins of the first part to fight the Dwarves; both are inordinately fond of gold. When the Elvenking "strongly suspected attempted burglary or something like it" from the Dwarves (*Hobbit*, p. 192), he imprisons them. The Master, less generously, "believed they were frauds who would sooner or later be discovered. . . . They were expensive to keep, and their arrival had turned things into a long holiday in which business was at a standstill" (*Hobbit*, p. 193). The pragmatism of the Master reflects the concerns of trade and business that preoccupy Dale, for in the distant past, "they had been wealthy and powerful, and there had been fleets of boats on the waters" (*Hobbit*, p. 185). If the Wood-Elves with their king and ceremonious feasting function as an aristocracy, the Men of Dale with their master and practical gatherings of townspeople function instead as a bourgeoisie. The lowest social class of criminals and thieves in one sense is comprised of the Dwarves—but all of these kings and leaders spiritually, if not socially, betray avarice and pride that group them together as sinners. The Elvenking as a burglar steals the Dwarves from Bilbo just as the Master of Dale as a fraud steals from his own people many years later. Each suspects the Dwarves of that crime of which he and his people are most guilty.

Yet Thorin, king of the Dwarves, does reveal most blatantly the sins of avarice and pride. He fulfills the predisposition of his people to such flaws: "[D]warves are not heroes, but calculating folk with a great idea of the value of money; some are tricky and treacherous and pretty bad lots; some are not, but are decent enough people like Thorin and Company, if you don't expect too much" (*Hobbit*, p. 204). Like the greedy dragon whose role as "King under the Mountain" he assumes after his death, Thorin refuses to share the hoard with "thieves" and "enemies" such as the deserving Men of Esgaroth or even his own comrade Bilbo: "[N]one of our gold shall thieves take or the violent carry off while we are alive!" (*Hobbit*, p. 245). In addition, Thorin's pride leads him into error. He ignores the wise raven Roäc who advises him that "[t]he treasure is likely to be your death, though the dragon is no more!" (*Hobbit*, p. 253). The treasure *is* his death. Indeed, Thorin refuses to listen to anyone else but himself, although his apology to Bilbo at the moment of death rejuvenates him spiritually if not physically.

In a sense, the last "King under the Mountain" is a legal trio introduced at the end of the novel. The tunneling names of Grubb, Grubb, and Burrowes illustrate their literal and figurative positions as "kings" or monsters under the mountain, in this case the comfortable tunnel belonging to Bilbo in Underhill. These dragonlike lawyers guard a treasure appropriately named Bag End that they intend to auction. A less frightening adversary than the others and therefore more easily overcome, nevertheless this Hobbit trio forces Bilbo to realize that a "King under the Mountain" may be a neighbor Hobbit—or even oneself.

II. BILBO: BAGGINS OF UNDERHILL

At the very beginning of *The Hobbit* Bilbo acts as a "King under the Mountain" when he hoards his wealth—food in the Hobbit world—against depletion by strange intruding Dwarves. Later, in a cryptic riddle, Bilbo will describe himself as a foil for Smaug: "I come from under the hill, and under the hills and over the hills my paths led" (*Hobbit*, pp. 212–13). Because this "King under the Mountain" must defeat himself before attempting to defeat other monsters, the real battle in *The Hobbit* might as well take place at home in the Shire. It is for this reason Tolkien subtitled the work "There and Back Again," to draw attention to the geographical location of the major battle: not the Lonely Mountain, as a careless reader might assume, but "There"—the Shire—and "Back Again," as the first and last chapters precisely indicate.

That is, in the first chapter, the Dwarves and Gandalf arrive at the Shire to interrupt an irritable host for an "Unexpected Party"; in the last chapter the Dwarf Balin and Gandalf return to the Shire to interrupt a pleased host for a smaller but still unexpected party in "The Last Stage." It is Bilbo's attitude toward food that changes: at the beginning he complains to himself about the amount of food Dwarves require, but at the end he generously and unasked hands Gandalf the tobacco jar, laughing because he now realizes the joy of community and the love of neighbor. For food provides not only physical sustenance and continued life but also on a higher level the renewal of spiritual life, as in the Christian Mass of the Eucharist. The absence of food, the interruption of feasting, or the refusal to feast with others—all communicate interference with the life force, the life of the community, and symbolically spiritual life, or virtue. On the Germanic level, as in *Beowulf,* feasting celebrates the concern of warrior for warrior and lord. The raids on Heorot by Grendel symbolize the dark forces on earth against which man must fight to preserve his hall-joy and brotherhood. Tolkien describes the situation beautifully in the *Beowulf* essay: "A light starts . . . and there is a sound of music; but the outer darkness and its hostile offspring lie ever in wait for the torches to fail and the voices to cease. Grendel is maddened by the sound of harps" ("Beowulf," p. 88). Thus, Bilbo's attitude toward the food used in feasting and the money used to buy that food becomes important in resolving his own inner conflicts and in battling against his monsters.

The contrast between feasting and battle, or the hero and the adversary, is incorporated into *The Hobbit* in three ways: thematically through the confrontation between Bilbo and various monsters, structurally through an alternation of party chapters with battle chapters, and symbolically through the internalization of the conflict within the hero. Structurally, the alternation of feasting with battling chapters begins with "An Unexpected Party," followed by the more unpleasant interruption of the Trolls' "party" in "Roast Mutton." In chapter 3, "The Short Rest" at Elrond's Last Homely House enables them to battle with Goblins, Gollum, and Wargs in the next three chapters until they rest at Beorn's "Queer Lodging" in chapter 7. Battles with flies and spiders, Wood-Elves, and Raft-Elves leave them grateful for the "Warm Welcome" by the feasting Men of Dale in chapter 10. Subsequent battles with the dragon, the Dwarves, and then of the Five Armies weary them until the last two chapters where they return to

Beorn's and Elrond's houses in "The Return Journey" and to Bilbo's Bag End in "The Last Stage."

Symbolically, the conflict between the hero and adversary is internalized within the split self of the protagonist. Bilbo, for example, is both Baggins and Took: he "looked and behaved exactly like a second edition of his solid and comfortable father," a Baggins, but he had "got something a bit *queer* in his makeup from the Took side, something that only waited for a chance to come out" (*Hobbit*, p. 17; my italics). The chance is provided by the visiting Dwarves, who invite him to accompany them on their adventure as a professional burglar. The Tookish imagination in Bilbo, which is inherited from renegade Hobbits who have themselves experienced adventures sporadically (*Hobbit*, p. 16), is swept away by the sound of Thorin's harp "into dark lands under strange moons" (*Hobbit*, p. 26), so that he begins to yearn for the adventures he has earlier in the evening spurned (*Hobbit*, p. 18). His dormant imagination, expressed previously only through a love of neat smoke rings, flowers, and poetry (*Hobbit*, pp. 26, 19), awakens completely: "As they sang the hobbit felt the love of beautiful things made by hands and by cunning and by magic moving through him, a fierce and jealous love, the desire of the hearts of Dwarves. Then something Tookish woke up inside him, and he wished to go and see the great mountains, and hear the pinetrees and the waterfalls, and explore the caves, and wear a sword instead of a walking-stick" (*Hobbit*, p. 28).

This adventuresome imaginative self fully dominates Bilbo by the novel's end, for when he returns to the Shire, "[he] was in fact held by all the hobbits of the neighborhood to be 'queer'" (*Hobbit*, p. 285). But the conflict between the Tookish side and the Baggins side begins much earlier. When he is accused of looking more like a grocer than a burglar by Gloin the Dwarf on this same night, he realizes, "The Took side had won. He suddenly felt he would go without bed and breakfast to be thought fierce" (*Hobbit,* p. 30). It is indeed the grocer side of him he has defeated: the solid comfortable side appropriately named "Baggins" as if in description of "The Bag," both a pouch for storage of money or food and, of course, the stomach, which Bilbo will later call an "empty sack" (*Hobbit,* p. 103). Even Bilbo's house is called "Bag End." It is almost as if the Baggins side represents the temptations of the body as the Took side represents the desire for fulfillment of the soul. This desire is expressed through the image of the burglar that the Took side of Bilbo is asked to become.

Because burglars usually take things unlawfully from others, it is at first difficult to see how burglary will fulfill the spiritual or Took side of Bilbo. Yet it is more than a pun ("take"/"Took") for Bilbo: to steal requires physical dexterity and courage, some cunning and forethought, and in this particular case a love of his fellow creature. For Bilbo as burglar will merely retrieve for the Dwarves that treasure that has been previously stolen from them by Smaug. Thus, the dying Thorin will describe Bilbo as possessing "[s]ome courage and some wisdom, blended in measure" (*Hobbit,* p. 273). The quality the Dwarf-king admires is temperance, that Augustinian moderation that almost seems Virtue itself. Indeed, when Bilbo renounces the arkenstone he has stolen, he resembles the greatest burglar, the *rex justus* Christ who gave up that humanity he had appropriated in order to redeem humankind.

Although Christ never actually appears in *The Hobbit,* still, a type of Christ is provided in the figure of Gandalf. In *The Lord of the Rings* Gandalf dies as the "Gray" and is reborn as the "White" to suggest through color imagery a parallel with Christ's own death and Resurrection. In *The Hobbit* Gandalf acts as a guide and teacher for Bilbo. Leading them through Rivendell and over the Misty Mountains up to Mirkwood, the Wizard protects them all from danger by supernatural means, mainly fire and magic wand, and encourages Bilbo by sparking the Hobbit's enthusiasm for the adventure with a few tales. Like any good parent, though, Gandalf realizes he must depart (in chapter 7) in order for Bilbo to develop his own physical, intellectual, and spiritual qualities as a burglar. When Bilbo achieves these, Gandalf returns as a deus ex machina (in chapter 17) to congratulate his pupil and to aid in the great Battle of the Five Armies.

Bilbo learns his trade as a burglar by defeating various monsters who collectively represent *amor sui,* but individually "bodily" temptation and "spiritual" temptation, as we have previously seen. In the process his initial physical bumbling changes to real dexterity, then skill, and is finally aided by the courage of the newly confident Hobbit. The way that Bilbo defeats these adversaries in almost every case involves a type of burglary, as if in practice for the final and most crucial theft of the arkenstone. The first phase begins in the Troll episode of the second chapter and concludes with his maturation as a brave burgling warrior in chapter 8, "Flies and Spiders."

In the first phase, Bilbo fails as a burglar in the Troll episode because of poor timing and clumsiness. "'Silly time to go practising pinching and pocketpicking,' said Bombur, 'when what we wanted was fire and food'" (*Hobbit,* p. 52). Bilbo was asked by the Dwarves to investigate the source of the light shining among the trees, not to put on the magic ring and pick the Trolls' pockets. Still, the Hobbit does "steal" by accident the key to the Troll cave. This shelter will afford them food and treasure (scabbards, hilts, sheaths) that they will "steal" as they will later steal the cup and arkenstone from the dragon. In the second (Gollum) episode Bilbo is slightly more successful. He "steals" Gollum's ring, again by accident, and he withstands Gollum's efforts as a mental burglar to discover "What have I got in my pocket?" (the ring, of course [*Hobbit*, p. 85]). This theft is important because it provides Bilbo with the means to perform the burglary of the dragon's hoard—the invisibility caused by the ring. In addition, it heightens Bilbo's confidence in his new vocation. This allows the Hobbit to demonstrate real heroism and leadership as a "burglar" in chapter 8, "Flies and Spiders." Bilbo first shows purely physical skills: his keen sight spots a hidden boat that will let them cross the magic water; he prevents the other Dwarves from falling in the water by snatching the rope they have been pulling; he climbs a tree to determine their location, thereby displaying his farsightedness and his light feet. But then Bilbo manifests more abstract qualities like courage. Asked to investigate a fire in the forest, he eventually saves his friends not from the Elves whose festivities they have spotted but from the giant spiders who capture the Dwarves while he sleeps under the Elven spell. The first battle changes Bilbo: "Somehow the killing of the giant spider, all alone by himself in the dark without the help of the Wizard or the Dwarves or of anyone else, made a great difference to Mr. Baggins. He felt a different person, and *much fiercer and bolder in spite of an empty stomach*" (*Hobbit*, p. 154; my italics). With this new boldness, Bilbo "steals" the captured Dwarves, untying them after using his voice to lure the spiders away. He has learned from Gandalf's ventriloquism in the Troll episode. Bilbo also kills six of the spiders with his sword, Sting, while rescuing Bombur—its new name a projection of the spiderlike quality he now possesses after defeating the giant spider.

In chapters 9 to 13, Bilbo's burglaries depend more on his intellectual efforts than on his physical ones. After he becomes invisible to enter the Elvenking's castle where the Dwarves are imprisoned, he devises the ruse of shutting them in wine barrels to allow his "booty" to escape in the underground stream. Later, in chapter 11, "On the Doorstep," Bilbo can be a burglar only after he figures out a way of breaking into the tunnel leading to the dragon's lair. Much thinking and sitting take place before the thrush knocks at the gray stone, reminding Bilbo of the rune letters on the map that explain the setting sun on Durin's Day that will illuminate the keyhole into the rocky door. Finally, Bilbo uses both his imagination and his wit to trick the dragon into revealing its only vulnerable spot. After the Hobbit steals the cup from the hoard he realizes that he "had become the real leader in their adventure. He had begun to have ideas and plans of his own" (*Hobbit,* p. 211). Part of these ideas involves posturing as a wise riddling poet to the dragon, for "[n]o dragon can resist the fascination of riddling talk and of wasting time trying to understand it" (*Hobbit,* p. 213). Further, Bilbo's flattery diverts the dragon so that the monster even shows off his magnificent diamond-studded waistcoat with its bare patch when the Hobbit wonders whether dragons are softer underneath.

Now both courageous and wise, the Hobbit becomes a burglar in the third and spiritual sense when he battles against that proud and avaricious monster inside himself. The dragon tempts Bilbo as Smaug's serpent forefather tempted Adam in Eden: the dragon intimates that the Dwarves will never pay Bilbo a "fair share." Bilbo succumbs, stealing the precious arkenstone to ensure that he is paid for his work: "Now I am a burglar indeed!" he cries (*Hobbit,* p. 226). Only in chapter 16, "A Thief in the Night," does he forget about himself in his concern for others—the Elves, Men, and Dwarves who may die from the approaching winter, starvation, or battle. Bilbo then relinquishes to the Dwarves' enemies (the Elves and Men) the arkenstone he has stolen from them so that the

Dwarves may bargain with Thorin and end the dispute. This highly moral act redeems Bilbo: "I may be a burglar— . . . but I am an honest one" (*Hobbit,* p. 257). The Hobbit acts like the *Pastor bonus* Saint Augustine describes as the true king. Indeed, Bilbo now renounces all he has previously demanded in payment, taking away only two small chests of treasure and even making reparation to the Elvenking whose Dwarf prisoners he has stolen and whose bread he has eaten: "[S]ome little return should be made for your, er, hospitality. I mean even a burglar has his feelings" (*Hobbit,* p. 277).

In giving to his "host," Bilbo proves himself more than a guest, and the opposite of the burglar. In fact he becomes a host as well as an artist when he returns to the Shire, each role an expression of one of two sides, Baggins and Took. As the Baggins-grocer has demanded good financial terms for his work and his food in the very first chapter, so the new Baggins-host offers freely his tobacco and fire, physical commodities, to his friends. And as the Took-burglar has taken what is not his but also given it to someone else who needed it, so the new Took-artist offers freely what is never his to keep (experience and talent as expressed in poems and memoirs) to his future readers. The artist as hero is ultimately typified in Bard the Bowman, who saves Esgaroth by bravely killing the dragon but who continues to subordinate himself to the Master of Dale (*Hobbit,* p. 240). So Bilbo unifies his selves.

When Gandalf declares at the end that Bilbo has succeeded not because of personal luck but because of the general scheme of things—"You are only quite a little fellow in a wide world after all"—Bilbo exclaims, "Thank goodness!" (*Hobbit,* pp. 286–88). In this last line of the novel Bilbo thanks the goodness of God as a universal and providential force for his selflessness, his littleness. The Hobbit is indeed a "child of the kindly West" living that life of the spirit characteristic of the Augustinian New Man, or *novus homo*. Bilbo has progressed from the chronological maturity of a fifty-year-old "grown-up" (*Hobbit*, p. 17) to the state of wonder and joy common to the child—and the Christian. The cranky "adult" Bilbo at the beginning snaps at Gandalf for interrupting his tea party and chastises his "child" Thorin once he emerges from his closed barrel: "'Well, are you alive or are you dead?' Bilbo asked quite crossly. . . . 'If you want food and if you want to go on with this silly adventure—it's yours after all and not mine—you had better slap your arms and rub your legs'" (*Hobbit*, pp. 186–87). At the end this cranky adult is transformed into the joyful, laughing, childlike Bilbo who welcomes his visitors Gandalf and Balin with a round of tobacco. As a child or childlike Hobbit Bilbo must resemble those comprising the audience of *The Hobbit*—literal children, if the narrator's patronizing remarks are any indication.

III. THE NARRATOR: THE CRITIC UNDER THE MASK OF THE CHILDREN'S STORYTELLER

The narrative intrusions—direct addresses to children, use of the first person singular, foreshadowing of later events, joking tone, plot clarifications, and sound effects intended for entertaining children[25]—have annoyed readers and critics. Yet they all constitute devices to create a narrative persona that functions as a character himself. Primarily the character personifies the critic of the *Beowulf* lecture, or the adult or fairy-story teller (that is, Andrew Lang) in the fairy-story lecture. This critic assumes that fairy-stories attract only children and probably function best as a bedtime narcotic to quiet restless boys and girls. As a tale-teller the critic contrasts sharply with the wonderful Gandalf ("Tales and adventures sprouted up all over the place wherever he went, in the most extraordinary fashion" [*Hobbit*, p. 17]) and with the artist Tolkien, who is analogous to Chaucer the poet creating the character of Chaucer the pilgrim to introduce the Canterbury pilgrims—themselves tale-tellers.

As a narrator the critic patronizes his audience. He reminds them of details they may have forgotten, as when Bilbo crosses "the ford beneath the steep bank, which *you may remember*" (*Hobbit*, p. 282)—but probably have forgotten, as it was crossed two hundred and fifty pages back. Like a literary critic the narrator helps them understand the characters by delving beneath the surface: "[Y]ou will notice already that Mr. Baggins was not quite so prosy as he liked to believe, also that he was very fond of flowers" (*Hobbit*, p. 46). This narrator adopts a falsely jovial tone, as when Bilbo has difficulty guessing Gollum's riddle: "I imagine you know the answer, of course, or can guess it as easy as winking, since you are sitting comfortably at home and have not the danger of being eaten to disturb your thinking" (*Hobbit*, p. 83).

As a character the critic prides himself on his superior wisdom and status as an adult. He is too busy to tell them even one or two songs or tales the Dwarves heard at Elrond's house (*Hobbit*, p. 61). He belittles the silliness of legends like the one announcing a Took Hobbit marriage to a fairy wife (*Hobbit*, p. 16). He expects the characters to emulate his adult wisdom and social decorum. Thus, the critic applauds Bilbo's intelligent handling of Smaug by speaking riddles, but he criticizes Bilbo's growing reputation for queerness that results from visits to Elves and poetry writing (*Hobbit*, p. 285). A conformist socially, the critic especially dislikes signs of immaturity: when the Dwarves ring the doorbell energetically he compares the action pejoratively to the mischievous pulling-off of the handle by a "naughty hobbit-boy" (*Hobbit*,

p. 22). The critic automatically assumes that his audience is the same size and shape as he, rather than four feet tall and light-footed like Hobbits. He describes the Hobbits, for example, as a "little people, about half *our height*" who "disappear quietly and quickly when *large stupid folk like you and me* come blundering along, making a noise like elephants which they can hear a mile off" (*Hobbit*, p. 16; my emphasis). To be smaller than the critic is to be abnormal: "You must remember it [Gollum's tunnel] was not quite so tight for him [Bilbo] as it would have been *for me or for you*. Hobbits are not quite like ordinary people" (*Hobbit*, p. 77; my emphasis).

As a tale-teller the narrator also behaves more like a critic when he laughs at or disapproves of his characters, expressing neither pity nor terror at the plights that he relives vicariously. First he criticizes Bilbo's unprofessional burgling in the Troll episode: "Either he should have gone back quietly and warned his friends that there were three fair-sized trolls at hand in a nasty mood, quite likely to try toasted dwarf, or even pony, for a change; or else he should have done a bit of good quick burgling. A really first-class and legendary burglar would at this point have picked the trolls' pockets—it is nearly always worthwhile, if you can manage it—pinched the very mutton off the spits, purloined the beer, and walked off without their noticing him" (*Hobbit*, pp. 46–47).

In this critical attack and avaricious advice the narrator resembles the Dwarves who initially disbelieve in Bilbo's capabilities as a burglar, unlike Gandalf who trusts him implicitly from the beginning. When Bilbo does not see the edge of the forest as he peers from a tall tree just before they are captured by spiders, the narrator accuses him of lacking sense (*Hobbit*, p. 148). And when the Dwarves worry about finding the entry to the Lonely Mountain and become depressed and demoralized—only

Bilbo has more spirit than they have—the narrator finds this "strange." He even underestimates the Dwarves by labeling them as "decent enough people . . . if you don't expect too much" (*Hobbit*, p. 204). For this reason he is not prepared for Thorin's charitable retraction at the moment of his death.

Perhaps most terribly, the narrator lacks compassion for and understanding of others. He reveals his cruelty when he confides that "[y]ou would have laughed (from a safe distance), if you had seen Dwarves sitting up in the trees with their beards dangling down" (*Hobbit*, p. 104). For the narrator, the Dwarves ready to be eaten are chiefly sources of amusement, not objects of pity. He also imagines that the audience laughs at the weak spot in Bilbo's plan when the hero forgets there is no one to place the lid on his barrel so that he too can escape the Wood-Elves (*Hobbit*, p. 177). The narrator's lack of compassion renders him cruel and mean.

Loving only himself, in this pride and lack of charity the narrator becomes a monster like the dragon Smaug and the critic, who desires to be godlike in his acquisition of knowledge. This last King under the Mountain, under the mask of the storyteller, seems to triumph, undefeated by any Hobbit hero. Yet Bilbo does have the last word, when Gandalf reminds him at the end that he is "only quite a little fellow in a wide world" (*Hobbit*, pp. 286–87), and Bilbo thanks goodness for this. Perhaps the reader now notices the difference between the unobtrusive Hobbit and the usually obtrusive narrator. Or perhaps the wordy and pompous narrator himself has learned something from this mere "children's story." So quiet now, maybe the narrator is mute with wonder at the humiliating possibility that the small, childlike, queer Bilbo is "right," after all.

Chapter 3

THE CHRISTIAN KING

Tolkien's Fairy-Stories

> Myth and fairy-story must, as all art, reflect and
> contain in solution elements of moral and
> religious truth (or error), but not explicit, not in
> the known form of the primary "real" world.
> —J.R.R. Tolkien
> Letter 131, to Milton Waldman
> of Collins Publishers (c. 1951)

> God is the Lord of angels, and of men—and of
> elves. Legend and history have met and fused.
> —J.R.R. Tolkien, "On Fairy-Stories"

In the nineteenth century, fairy tales were regarded as fantastic and trashy and found little support from moralists and educationalists concerned with informing young minds: "[I]t would be absurd in such tales to introduce Christian principles as motives of action."[1] In the twentieth century, in part due to the efforts of the Victorian compiler of fairy tales Andrew Lang, fairy-stories became for many parents and educators acceptable entertainment for children, but received little support from critics concerned with analyzing great literature, if only because such stories were intended for children and not for adults.

Tolkien attempted to change this modern view by providing a literary aesthetic linking the fairy-story to Christian morality in his 1938 Andrew Lang Lecture, "On Fairy-Stories," and by implementing that literary aesthetic in his own two fairy-stories, "Leaf by Niggle" (written 1937–38 and published 1945) and "Smith of Wootton Major" (published 1967 but written years earlier).[2]

Considered by scholars not "strictly a work of Faërie," these two Tolkien stories have been criticized because they include "a framing device set in the Primary World" and also "a closely worked allegory": "True fantasy, according to Tolkien's own rule, takes place *inside* Faërie; there is no going to and from. . . . In both works Tolkien is presenting a message not a work of Faërie; true fantasy is nought but pure narrative, potent enough in the telling only and requiring no overlay of 'meaning.' Tolkien uses other devices to have his say about Faërie, and it seems that allegory is for him a favorite."[3] In addition, the message conveyed by these two supposed non-fairy-stories has been subject to critical dispute. "Leaf by Niggle" has been viewed as a fictionalized version of "On Fairy-Stories"[4] but also as "deeply Christian"—unlike "Smith of Wootton Major," which is not "overtly religious."[5] In contrast, the latter has been perceived as autobiographical—reflecting the value of his art to Tolkien.[6]

Yet *both* of the stories outline in fiction the literary and moral aesthetic described in "On Fairy-Stories"; *both* rely upon either an implicitly or explicitly Christian allegory that conjoins the primary to the secondary world. As I shall argue in this essay, the secondary world of Faërie resembles the Other World of Heaven, literally or figuratively, just as the primary world is our real world—that "underworld" described by medieval writers as Hell. The frame of the primary world remains necessary because both stories trace the transportation of the individual from this world to the other world. Such a need to contrast the two worlds in the fairy-story originated in Tolkien's early childhood: "Quite by accident, I have a very vivid child's view, which was the result of being taken away from one country and put in another hemisphere—the place where I belonged but which was totally novel and strange. After the barren, arid heat a Christmas tree."[7] The "barren, arid heat" of Africa in December, Tolkien's early "primary" world, resembles the dazzlingly fiery inferno of the medieval underworld, in contrast to the joyous, cool "other world" of England; the mention of the Christmas tree in this paradise also hints at Eden's Tree of Life, and the cross signifying Christ's salvation of humankind, to underscore the religious symbolism. Tolkien's traumatic journey from one world to another so impressed the three-year-old boy that the contrast informed his literary aesthetic long after he had matured, and he continued to use the tree as a major symbol of life—as opposed to death, aridity, barrenness—throughout his literary career.

This new "genre" of Tolkien differs from his previous accomplishments—his very scholarly editions, prefaces to editions, his lecture on *Beowulf,* and other medieval articles—as well as from *The Hobbit,* a children's story more "scholarly" and academic than these stories in that it incorporates Germanic heroic ideas included in the *Beowulf* lecture, in addition to Christian notions of temptation and sin delineated in the *Ancrene Wisse* (the "Guide of Anchoresses" discussed by Tolkien in a 1929 article and in 1962 edited critically for the Early English Text Society). Still, both *Beowulf* and Tolkien's *Beowulf* lecture continued to influence this newly shaped literary aesthetic despite the marked departure from past accomplishments, as the discussion of the lecture "On Fairy-Stories" and the two fairy-stories implementing the ideas contained in that lecture will show.

I. "ON FAIRY-STORIES": CHRIST AS ELF-KING

"Beowulf: The Monsters and the Critics," Tolkien's Sir Israel Gollancz Lecture of 1936, defines the poem's central concern as this (primary) world—specifically, the forces of chaos and death on the Germanic level and of sin and spiritual death on the Christian level. These forces are epitomized in the two monsters, Grendel and the dragon, as Beowulf's chief adversaries, descended from Cain and Satan, respectively.[8] In contrast, "On Fairy-Stories," in 1938, defines the fairy tale's central concern as what Tolkien names "Faërie"—a secondary world or Perilous Realm, whose magic (unlike the sorrow, chaos, and unreason of Beowulf's primary world) satisfies the deepest human desires. Such desires include, first, the exploration of time and space; second, communication with other beings; and third, but most important of all, "the oldest and deepest desire, the Great Escape: the Escape from Death. Fairy-stories provide many examples and modes of this which might be called the genuine escapist, or I would say *fugitive* spirit. . . . Fairy-stories are made by men not by fairies. The Human-stories of the Elves are doubtless full of the Escape from Deathlessness."[9]

In addition to the satisfaction of these desires, the fairy-story also supplies what Tolkien identifies as the "Recovery" of clear-sightedness and "Consolation," or joy. The fairy-story's generic antithesis is *Beowulf*. Because the Anglo-Saxon epic ends with the hero's death, the sorrow of his tragedy overwhelms the mood: the work imitates the dyscatastrophic tragedy discussed in "On Fairy-Stories" and has been termed an elegy by Tolkien in the *Beowulf* lecture. But if the elegiac *Beowulf* ends with the triumph of chaos and death over the mortal, then the fantastic fairy-story ends with the triumph of the mortal over death and the escape into the other world.

The agent of such triumph over death in fantasy is the supernatural guide, analogous in role to the death-allied monster of the elegy or tragedy. For Tolkien this guide is usually an Elf or fairy. The Elf (or fairy—the terms are used equivocally in modern times, according to "On Fairy-Stories" [p. 9]) is listed as an incubus or succubus, a demon, or a malignant being, in the *Oxford English Dictionary,* in whose compilation Tolkien assisted (he worked on the *w*'s). [10] Like the *Beowulf* monsters, the Elf can threaten human spiritual well-being. In "On Fairy-Stories" the Elves and fairies represent tempters: "[P]art of the magic that they wield for the good or evil of humankind is power to play on the desires of his body and his heart" ("On Fairy-Stories," p. 8). Yet elsewhere in "On Fairy-Stories" and in Tolkien's own tales, the Elves appear as guides of goodwill toward others, a nobler and wiser species than any other. Tolkien fondly cites Spenser's use of "Elfe" to characterize the worthy and good knights of Faërie in *The Faerie Queene:* "It [the name] belonged to such knights as Sir Guyon rather than to Pigwiggen armed with a hornet's sting" ("On Fairy-Stories," p. 9). Like Sir Guyon in his bravery and virtue, the Red Cross Knight in the first book of *The Faerie Queene* battles with the dragon in an allegorical three-day encounter complete with a Well and Tree of Life, after which he releases the king and queen of Eden (Adam and Eve). This "Elfe" repeats the redemptive efforts of Christ as the second Adam.

The tie between the Elf-Prince and Christ is a strong one for Tolkien, who had read in the *Ancrene Wisse* that Jesus in His love for our soul functions as a king and noble knight in love with a lady: Christ "came to give proof of His love, and showed by knightly deeds that He was worthy of love, as knights at one time were accustomed to do. He entered the tournament, and like a brave knight had His shield pierced through and through for love of His lady. His shield, concealing His Godhead, was His dear body, which was extended upon the cross."[11] For this reason the birth of Christ in the Gospels is the penultimate fairy-story and the greatest fantasy of all time: "The Gospels contain a fairy-story, or a story of a larger kind which embraces all the essence of fairy-stories . . . and among the marvels is the greatest and most complete conceivable eucatastrophe. . . . The Birth of Christ is the eucatastrophe of Man's history. The Resurrection is the eucatastrophe of the story of the Incarnation" ("On Fairy-Stories," pp. 71–72). Reading about the "character" Christ in this fairy-story of the Gospels allows humankind to experience escape from the sorrow of this world and recovery and joy in the hope of another world—the Other World. All secondary worlds, all realms of Faërie in such fairy-stories ultimately are modeled upon Heaven. Entering paradise remains the deepest human fantasy because it constitutes the most important escape from death and from the stranglehold of this world on life.

The difference between God's "fairy-story" of the Gospels and fallen-human fairy-stories is that in the Gospels the primary world converges with the secondary world and creation becomes sub-creation: "Art has been verified. God is the Lord, of angels, and of men—and of elves. Legend and History have met and fused" ("On Fairy-Stories," p. 72). For once, the happy ending has actually occurred in the normally tragic primary world; death has indeed died, in John Donne's words. But fallen humankind stains its own creation with the sin that darkens its glimpse of reality, so that its view of the happy ending may be limited and even false. Just as the *Beowulf* poem displays two distinct levels, the Germanic and the Christian, because its author found himself caught in transition between two different ages, so the fairy-story similarly caught between two worlds possesses both a fallen and a redeemed (or perfect) form. For Tolkien, "All tales may come true; and yet, at the last, redeemed, they may be as like and as unlike the forms that we give them as Man, finally redeemed, will be like and unlike the fallen that we know" ("On Fairy-Stories," p. 73). If human fantasies that construct an imaginary secondary world could be "redeemed" or realized, they might indeed come true.

The fairy-story as a projection of hope, desires, and fantasies embodies the ideals of the human behind the sub-creator. Similarly, the fairy-story of the Gospels about the Word of God is itself the Word of God and thus represents God Himself. Christ's "fairy-story" traces the happy turn of his life as human fairy-stories trace the imagined happy turns of mortal life through *aventures* in perilous realms. For such reasons these tales must often become autobiographical, although only in the Bible is the "autobiography" true: "For the Art of it has the supremely convincing tone of Primary Art, that is, of Creation" ("On Fairy-Stories," p. 72). If the stories often take the form of eucatastrophic legends not realizable in this world, then their sub-creation imitates in more humble form that of the Gospels: "The Evangelium has not abrogated legends; it has hallowed them, especially the 'happy ending'" ("On Fairy-Stories," p. 73). What this means is that the Christian who experiences joy and consolation after reading the fairy-story of the Gospels hopes for a similar happy ending to his life: "The Christian has still to work, with mind as well as body, to suffer, hope, and die; but he may now perceive that all his bents and faculties have a purpose, which can be redeemed" ("On Fairy-Stories," p. 73). When as sub-creator the Christian projects this hope into fantasy, the subsequent fairy-stories assume a religious and also a very personal cast.

Thus, as a genre the fairy-story presents a "sudden glimpse of the underlying reality or truth" ("On Fairy-

Stories," p. 71). This reality is perceived by the heart or imagination rather than by the head; Tolkien reveals an Augustinian bias toward faith and revelation, "the eye of the heart," instead of the Aristotelian's "eye of reason."[12] As Colin Duriez also notes, "Tolkien's natural theology is unusual in that his stress is with the imagination, rather than with reason. It is by imagination that there can be genuine insight into God and reality independently of the specific revelation of scripture. However, he emphasizes in his essay, 'On fairy-stories,' that any such insights are acts of grace from the Father of Lights. . . . Whereas traditional Roman Catholic thought emphasizes the rational and cognitive in natural theology, Tolkien links it with imaginative meaning."[13] Tolkien finds that the fantasy offers "not only a 'consolation' for the sorrow of this world" (like the consolation of Philosophy to Boethius for the sorrow produced by a world in which nothing lasts and in which all seems to be subject to Fortune's whims) but also a "satisfaction, and an answer to that question, 'Is it true?'" ("On Fairy-Stories," p. 71). Tolkien suggests that fantasy will be true for the reader if the secondary world it describes has been fashioned well and truly to inspire *belief.*

Tolkien's prose nonfiction essay on fairy-stories is itself structured, however, like the *Consolation of Philosophy,* through the use of questions and answers, a technique that at first glance seems to appeal more to reason than to imagination and belief. The essay answers three questions: in the first section, "What are fairy-stories?"; in the second, "What is their origin?"; and in the following four, "What is the use of them?" Yet in the initial sentences of this essay, Tolkien cautions potential explorers of fairy-stories (he himself is a "wandering explorer" and not a "professional") *not* to "ask too many questions, lest the gates should be shut and the keys be lost" ("On Fairy-Stories," p. 3). The truth of which Tolkien speaks here springs from magic and cannot be captured by the scientist's question-and-answer techniques. The scientist's tendency to reduce the whole by analyzing it into parts in this manner clashes with the artist's tendency to see the whole and with the reader's tendency to ask of the whole story, Is it real? The scientist's studies of fairy-story elements are "the pursuit of folklorists or anthropologists: that is of people using the stories not as they were meant to be used, but as a quarry from which to dig evidence, or information, about matters in which they are interested" ("On Fairy-Stories," p. 18).

What Tolkien has written in this essay is certainly not a fairy-story or a fantasy but its opposite. As what Tolkien calls Literature (essentially fantasy) "sub-creates" a secondary world with its characteristic eucatastrophe, so what he calls Drama mirrors the primary world with its characteristic dyscatastrophe. This essay, dramatic nonfiction portraying those clashes between Tolkien as artist-hero or lover of fairy-stories and the critic-as-monster, reflects the battling and sorrow common to the real world. In the introduction Tolkien sides with the lover of fairy-stories against the question-asking professional scientist. In section 1, he argues with an invisible critic who believes fairy-stories concern diminutive creatures conceived by limited imaginations. In section 2, "Origins," he traces the convergence of history and myth in the "Soup" of tales, frustrating the scientist and compiler interested in identifying the ingredients of the Soup. In section 3, "Children," Tolkien opposes Lang and similar educationalists and parents who intend the fairy-story for the child and not the adult, the latter of whom in many cases desires more than the child to escape from this world and to believe in another: "Let us not divide the human race into Eloi and Morlocks: pretty children—'Elves' as the eighteenth century often idiotically called them—with their fairy tales (carefully pruned), and dark Morlocks tending their machines" ("On Fairy-Stories," p. 45). In section 4, "Fantasy," Tolkien analyzes the differences between Literature and Drama, the latter the especial province of the critic. In section 5, "Recovery, Escape, Consolation," Tolkien contrasts the secondary world with the primary and the effects of both on humankind. Only in section 6, "Epilogue," does a "eucatastrophe" occur, a happy ending that reveals that a fairy-story (the Gospels) is true and provides the model for all other fairy-stories. But the Christian alone will believe in Tolkien's eucatastrophe because such belief is a matter of faith and not of reason. And perhaps the Christian alone will perceive the genre of this nonfiction "fairy-story" as eucatastrophic, with the monstrous clashes between the critic and the artist in this work triumphantly resolved.

The accompanying fairy-story, "Leaf by Niggle," with which the essay appeared in 1964–65 in *Tree and Leaf,* and "Smith of Wootton Major" more clearly embody the aesthetic principles and genre discussed in "On Fairy-Stories." These fairy-stories also more clearly illustrate, as fictional autobiography, those central Christian truths and joys projected into his fantasy by Tolkien the sub-creator. Indeed, these two incarnate the "description of two moments in a great life, rising and setting; an elaboration of the ancient and intensely moving contrast between youth and age, first achievement and final death," which Tolkien had clarified as the structure of *Beowulf* in his lecture ("Beowulf," p. 81). "Leaf by Niggle" was written first in 1938–39 and projects the fears of the "rising" artist-as-hero (Tolkien had just finished *The Hobbit* and had recently started "The New Hobbit") that worldly demands might frustrate the completion of his work before his death. Second, "Smith of Wootton Major," which was published in 1967 although written years earlier, as a "setting moment" in the career of an artist who had finally finished the mammoth epic of *The Lord of the Rings,* projects his final, peaceful acceptance and even his joy at the relinquishing of his artistic gift. Because both fairy-stories end in eucatastrophic turns, neither can be considered a work of "setting," of death, even though the second work describes the end of the artist's career and the first describes the younger artist's imagined "death." Both attempt to portray the Great Escape from Death.

If *The Hobbit* constitutes Tolkien's attempt to rewrite *Beowulf* as a fairy-story fantasy with a eucatastrophic ending rather than as a heroic elegy,[14] then "Leaf by Niggle" and "Smith of Wootton Major" provide the next step in the fictional metamorphosis of his literary aesthetic. Using the Andrew Lang essay as a springboard, Tolkien rewrites his own life as a fairy-story, moving backward from the true secondary world of the Hobbits to the traumatic and awkward convergence of primary and secondary worlds in his own life. Not his aspirations as a medieval scholar, philologist, and teacher but his hopes and fears as a man, an artist, and a Christian surface in these two stories. Put another way, his interest in philology and the meaning of words informs the leap of his imagination. Anthony J. Ugolnik identifies the source of Tolkien's fantasy in his linguistic aesthetic, which manifests his medieval interests: working from Old English, Old Norse, and Gaelic (Celtic), Tolkien depended on the "attributive power of language, freed from the tyranny of imposed causality," so that the fantasist might have power over his secondary world.[15] It is appropriate that the synthesizing and harmonizing art of Tolkien, which sought always to wed his diverse sides, depicted in these stories a sub-creation in which angels and Elves, Christ and fairy kings, meet. True, the *Beowulf* monsters reappear—but depicted as *human* characters, flawed, suffering from various sins and subordinated to the Christian savior-heroes. The monster in "Leaf" is Parish and also Tompkins, the critical neighbor and councillor, like the destructive critics Tolkien denigrates in his *Beowulf* lecture; the monster in "Smith" is Nokes, the proud, critical Master Cook who reigns over the kitchen as evilly as the various "kings under the mountain" in *The Hobbit*.

But Tolkien's real interest in these joyous fairy-stories centers on the figure of the Elf, a Christ-like figure and agent of good. The merciful Second Voice in "Leaf" allows the artist Niggle to enter a consoling secondary world or the Other World; Alf the King of Faery in "Smith" similarly provides consolation to the artist Smith who must give up his visits to the secondary world. Mortals caught between this and the Other World, divided between their Niggle and their Parish sides (in the medieval sense, between the angel and the beast), ultimately freely choose the good, as does Smith when confronted with the choice by Alf—at least, in Tolkien's own autobiographical, heavily Christian and allegorical fairy tales.

II. "LEAF BY NIGGLE":
THE SECOND VOICE AND NIGGLE

That "Leaf by Niggle" is the most heavily Christian and allegorical of any of Tolkien's fiction is clear; exactly how Christian, despite the vestigial Germanic concepts inherited from the *Beowulf* lecture–*Hobbit* phase of his career, has not been fully revealed. Along with "Smith of Wootton Major," the fairy-story forms a Christian parable that neatly exemplifies those basic concepts illustrated, for example, in the *Ancrene Wisse*. In this "Guide for Anchoresses," or conduct book outlining the process of self-discipline for the Christian, eight major sections emerge that the translator (but not the medieval author in the manuscript Tolkien edited) has labeled appropriately "Devotions,"

"Custody of the Senses," "Regulation of the Inward Feelings," "Temptations," "Confession," "Penance," "Love," and "External Rules." Earlier, Tolkien used some of these sections to guide Bilbo's transformation into a Christian-like artist-hero in *The Hobbit,* specifically the sections "Custody of the Senses," "Regulation of the Inward Feelings," and as the culmination of the disciplinary process, the withstanding of "Temptations" both bodily and spiritual. Now in "Leaf" he seems to use the next sections, "Confession" and "Penance," especially: as a "rising moment" in Tolkien's literary autobiography the story dramatizes the Roman Catholic sacrament of Penance through the hard work justly warranted by Niggle's artistic inadequacies, followed only much later by the merciful "Gentle Treatment" Niggle receives. In contrast, in "Smith" Tolkien seems to use the next-to-last section of the *Ancrene Wisse,* "Love," as a "setting moment" in Tolkien's life: the story celebrates fully the power of Smith's love or *amor Dei* rewarded by the gift of grace.

The title of "Leaf by Niggle" possesses two significations that unify the major themes of the tale. First, referring to the torn fragment of canvas adorned by the single leaf created by Niggle and discovered by Atkins the schoolmaster, who hangs it in the museum, which along with the Leaf burns down later, the title emblematizes the effects of the primary world on all material things. Second, the title refers to Niggle's original impulse to create a single, perfect leaf on canvas, but one that he accomplishes only in the secondary world he enters after leaving the "Workhouse"; as such it emblematizes the changelessness and absolute perfection or the eternal "Idea" of all matter in a very Neoplatonic other world—"All the leaves he had ever labored at were there, as he had imagined them rather than as he had made them."[16]

Moreover, these associations typifying the two worlds

are inexorably linked in Christian tradition through the symbol of the tree. Because our first parents ate of the fruit of the Tree of Knowledge of Good and Evil, they were expelled from paradise, forced to wander the wilderness in exile, and condemned like their descendants to suffer the effects of sin, or death and mutability. So it is ironic that Niggle captures in oils a single leaf that is eventually destroyed by that mutability that resulted from their original sin. The cross, too, on which Christ, the second Adam, was crucified was frequently regarded in the Middle Ages as a "tree" constructed from the same wood as the Tree of Life, the other tree appearing in paradise, in order to anticipate the power of His love in overcoming the sin of Adam and redeeming all humankind. And in medieval representations of the Garden of Eden a Tree of Life also appears.[17] Again ironically, just as the torn leaf connotes Niggle's failure as an artist to complete his life's work because of constant interruptions for menial reasons, so the ideal leaf parallels the Gentle Treatment offered to him as a reward for his charity, or success as a human being in helping his neighbor in this world even though his own ambitions as an artist are thwarted. Niggle is permitted to enter a paradise where his travails as an artist are not only perfectly conceived but perfectly implemented. The two worlds in which the torn and the ideal leaves have their beings are drawn from Neoplatonic as well as Christian commonplaces.

The Neoplatonic Macrobius in the fourth century and his commentators in later centuries, especially the twelfth, conceived of our world (Tolkien's primary world) as an "abode of Dis," the lower regions of the universe, or the *infernum* (both the inferior and fallen regions and the underworld, or Hell).[21] But there was a second underworld, equally fallen and inferior—the body in which the soul after journeying through the spheres of the supernal regions was incarcerated. Like the underworld, the body was regarded as tomblike or prisonlike because it forced the soul to endure the corruption of corporeality in this world.

This prisonlike underworld dominates both "Leaf by Niggle" and Tolkien's conception of the primary world. In "On Fairy-Stories," Tolkien vehemently condemns the twentieth-century world for its burgeoning technology and dehumanized values and promotes the idea of "Escape" by the return to the past or to another world: "Why should a man be scorned if, finding himself in prison, he tried to get out and go home? Or if, when he cannot do so, he thinks and talks about other topics than jailers and prison-walls?" (p. 60). The prison metaphor picks up the Neoplatonic and Macrobian associations of the under-world—a metaphor Tolkien also uses in "Leaf by Niggle" to characterize the Purgatory-like Workhouse and, through the rigidity and sternness of the many jailerlike officials governing the primary world, the actual world in which Niggle must struggle as an artist.

The Neoplatonists also conceived of an overworld— a superior Aplanon called "paradisus" in Greek, "ortus" in Latin, and "Eden" in Hebrew—from which souls de-part at birth and to which they return at death. In this world all exists to be transformed by the World Soul into fallen and earthly living images destined for life on earth.[22] It is this superior Aplanon to which Niggle proceeds for Gentle Treatment and where he locates the perfect leaf that his earthly artistry only imperfectly copied. The major idea of Niggle that metamorphoses into image on earth is the idea of the leaf: he is his art, or his self as an artist is one with his artistic ideas (just as "Tolkien" refers both to the man and to his works). Only in the other world can Niggle "be" himself ideally. Further, what he has accomplished on earth as an artist constitutes his reward in the other world:

Tolkien reworks the Christian convention of good works into a fairy-story framework.

Tolkien has also reworked the Christian convention of the earthly conflict between soul and body into his fairy-story. Niggle and Parish personify the two sides of humankind that inevitably clash in this world because each is pulled in a different direction, although they eventually enjoy a harmonious "collaboration" (resurrection) in the other world after the fantasy equivalent of "death." Etymologically their names reflect their natures as personifications of the complementary sides of the macrocosm and of the microcosm of humankind. The verb "niggle," apparently derived from Scandinavian, means (according to the *Oxford English Dictionary*) "to work, or do anything, in a trifling, fiddling, or ineffective way; to trifle (*with* a thing); to spend work or time unnecessarily on petty details; to be over-elaborate in minor points." The ineffective worker Niggle suggests the microcosmic counterpart of the parish, or Parish, that, again in the *Oxford English Dictionary*, refers not necessarily only to the charge of a bishop or presbyter but also to a county subdivision used for civic and local government, that geographical area dependent upon the work of its governing officials. If "Parish" personifies the practical and economic needs of a geographical area, then "Niggle" personifies the earthly failure to supply those needs, a failure overseen and condemned by various Inspectors of Houses and Gardens and various government officials who seem to make Parish's interests their business.

In the other world, however, these two eventually harmonize their efforts in a change reflected through the names of the geographical areas they inhabit, construct, and control. Although Niggle first arrives at a place called "Niggle," after he gardens and builds, "Niggle" becomes "Niggle's Country," then, given the burgeoning of Parish's

garden, "Niggle's Parish." The last name perfectly epitomizes the harmony between the artist and the gardener,
the sub-creator and sub-creation, that results in this paradise. Truly a whole and single world as well as a whole and
single self emerges, rather than a primary world divided
and warring and a self fragmented and divided as they
have been on earth. More microcosmically the names illustrate these complementary sides of the self. "Niggle"
also means "to trot about, keep moving along" in a fiddling or ineffective manner, which perfectly describes his
activity as "legs" or "messenger" for the lame Parish and
his bedridden, ill wife. Finally, the names echo the complementary roles of the artist and the gardener used by
Tolkien as metaphors for the soul and the body. Thus,
Niggle means "to cheat, trick," plus, in its nominative
form, someone who "niggles," especially in artistic work:
he resembles as a niggling or cheating artist the artist-as-
burglar embodied in Bilbo of *The Hobbit.* The Parish who
prunes real flowers, plants, and trees represents the opposite of the artist who draws or paints on canvas a single leaf.

On earth Niggle the kindhearted artist and Parish the
critical gardener struggle for mastery as do soul and body,
one against the other. Niggle—lazy, kindhearted, imaginative and giving—portrays the heart itself: "He could not
get rid of his kind heart. 'I wish I was more strong-minded,'
he sometimes said to himself, meaning that he wished
other people's troubles did not make him feel uncomfortable" ("Leaf by Niggle," p. 89). Faced with interruptions
by visitors, friends, and Parish, Niggle dares not say no (p.
90). In contrast, Parish lacks warmth and imagination: he
is practical, commonsensical, and rational. Critical of
Niggle's garden and what he sees as "green and grey
patches and black lines" in Niggle's paintings, Parish dis-
misses them as "nonsensical" ("Leaf by Niggle," p. 91). A
gardener who tends to the raising of food rather than spir-

its and who is excessively concerned about house repairs and illnesses, Parish demands help from his neighbor the artist, who cares primarily about "work" only in the sense of art.

Parish also symbolizes the Macrobian underworld as Niggle symbolizes the overworld. As the name of a place, "Parish" suggests the inferior, infernal regions of the earth; as the name of a person, he symbolizes the underworld of the inferior body into which the superior soul is plunged. In "Leaf by Niggle" Tolkien recognizes this idea by making the lower primary world in character like Parish, just as Niggle in his character symbolizes the soul journeying to the Other World, an idea underscored by the initial naming of the overworld "Niggle." Material good becomes an end in itself because of the nature of this world, imbued with sickness and death for the individual, storm and catastrophe for the larger world, the macrocosm. Parish criticizes Niggle's efforts as an artist to the point where Niggle wishes that Parish would provide "help with the weeds (and perhaps praise for the pictures)" ("Leaf by Niggle," p. 91), instead of ignoring his painting and criticizing his garden.

Similarly, the human officials governing this world ignore spiritual or imaginative activities and criticize, through the enforcing of rigorous laws, infractions of their concern with material goods like the garden produce that serves to feed the body, if not the soul. Such stern laws so dominate all human life—"The laws . . . were rather strict" ("Leaf by Niggle," p. 90)—that when Niggle has to serve on a jury (an emphasis upon law, once again) and thereby neglects his own garden his visitors warn him of a probable visit from the Inspector. Providing for the needs of the body—such as food to satisfy hunger, a house to shelter, medicine to quell illness—is the usual human activity; inactivity in this sense invites punishment. Individual freedom of choice is lacking because neighbor must help neighbor no matter what personal feeling dictates. When Parish's house is deemed unsatisfactory, Niggle is blamed for not helping him roof it with his canvas: "houses come first. That is the law" ("Leaf by Niggle," p. 95). Like Parish, who regards painting as having no practical or economical use, the House Inspector looks at Niggle's painting workshop and sees only things: "There is plenty of *material* here: canvas, wood, waterproof paint" ("Leaf by Niggle," p. 95; my italics). Parish goes lame, his wife catches a fever, and Niggle experiences chills and fever before dying: Niggle's garden needs tending, Parish's house needs repairs, and the storm both damages the house and causes Niggle to become ill. The house constantly requires repair and the Museum is lost through fire; the body, similarly, succumbs to illness, dies, and is forgotten after death. Things do not last.

Even more Parish-like than inspectors who check for violations of the law are the human "judges" who comment after his death on Niggle's worth as a man, for they carry Parish's perceptions and criticisms to an extreme. Condemning Niggle's art ("private day-dreaming"), the literalistic and materialistic Councillor Tompkins sees in Niggle's painting only the "digestive and genital organs of plants"; he totally misunderstands the spiritual value of the painting and its restorative effects. Because Tompkins's judgment is impaired and blinded, this human "king" or "councillor" wrongly condemns Niggle as a "footler" who should have been relegated either to "washing dishes in a communal kitchen or something" or to being "put away" before his time ("Leaf by Niggle," p. 110). Tompkins is blinded in his judgment by his own selfish greed, or his *cupiditas:* because he has always wanted, and eventually obtains, Niggle's house for his own, he must rationalize this action by dismissing the man as insignificant. Even though

Atkins the schoolmaster sees great value in Niggle's paint-ing—"I can't get it out of my mind" ("Leaf by Niggle," p. 111)—and goes so far as to rescue and then frame and hang the surviving leaf in the local museum, it is Tompkins's view that dominates the dialogue—just as mutability obliterates all trace of Niggle and his art from existence in this world as if he were indeed insignificant and inconsequential.

If Niggle while on earth does not measure up to the expectations of his neighbor Parish, the Inspectors, and Councillor Tompkins because he is not interested in gardens and houses, neither does he measure up to the expectations of the Workhouse Infirmary doctors and to a certain extent the members of the Court of Inquiry convened after he recuperates in the Infirmary, but for a very different reason. On earth Niggle has been distracted by the requests of his neighbor and of his community from preparing for his "Journey" (presumably after death), which incurs the wrath of the Workhouse officials. As a consequence, like the somewhat distracted Christian who sins too often during life in this world, Niggle must endure the rigors of the harsh, prisonlike purgatory of the Workhouse infirmary.

Niggle's status almost resembles that of the first and lowest class of the Elect described in "The Penance" section of the *Ancrene Wisse*. In this class, the good pilgrims are "sometimes pleased by what they see on their way, and they pause a little, while not quite stopping, and many things happen to them to hinder them, and this is the worse for them, for some arrive home late and some never at all" (Salu, *Ancrene Wisse*, p. 155). While Niggle is not pleased at all by Parish's interruptions of his work, still he is hindered in arriving "home" and is punished accordingly for it, making his "Escape" from the prison of this world very late and very badly.

In a sense Niggle makes it not at all—for this new world he inhabits resembles the worst of the old world. Because Niggle has prepared inadequately for his "Journey," without packing any luggage or finishing his work, he is confined to the Workhouse Infirmary, given bitter medicine and unfriendly, strict ministrations by attendants and a severe doctor—"It was more like being in a prison than in a hospital" ("Leaf by Niggle," p. 97)—and denied any freedom of choice to work at his own leisure, or even any leisure. The emphasis on law here is similar to that in the real world but understood more abstractly: Niggle does not have to complete a specific task like that of preparing for a journey, but he does have to discipline himself or to subordinate desire and the self to law, duty, and reason. Niggle must manage to keep "Custody of the Senses" as demanded of the recluse in the *Ancrene Wisse* and become "dead" to the world, feeling neither sorrow nor joy, as if he had risen to the status of the second class of the Elect (described in "Penance"). He carpenters and paints houses "all one plain color" without feeling any joy: "[P]oor Niggle got no pleasure out of life. . . . But . . . he began to have a feeling of—well, satisfaction: bread rather than jam" ("Leaf by Niggle," p. 98).

Now self-disciplined, in contrast to his previous procrastination and inefficiency on earth, "Niggle had 'no time of his own' (except alone in his bed-cell), and yet he was becoming master of his time" ("Leaf by Niggle," p. 98). He suffers the hardship of plain digging instead of the luxury of plain carpentry and painting, and this breaks him physically—"his back seemed broken, his hands were raw" ("Leaf by Niggle," p. 98)—but cures him spiritually. Niggle worries about what he might have done better for Parish, he learns peace, rest, and satisfaction from doing work well and efficiently, and eventually he so forgets previous curses and gripes as to achieve a total serenity of mind and love of Other. He comes ultimately to resemble members of the third class of the Elect in the *Ancrene Wisse*, those "hung with consent on Jesus' cross" (Salu, *Ancrene Wisse*, p. 154) who experience joy in suffering. What this suffering involves in the *Ancrene Wisse* is climbing the ladder of Penance with "*Dishonor and hardship* . . . the two sides of the ladder which go straight up to heaven, and between these sides are fixed the rungs of all the virtues by which men climb to the happiness of heaven" (Salu, *Ancrene Wisse*, p. 157). Specifically, hardship occurs "in the face of injustice when one suffers the ignominy of being accounted worthless" (Salu, *Ancrene Wisse*, p. 157). After Niggle endures the labor (or physical hardship) of the Workhouse, he indeed suffers so: counted a "silly little man," "Worthless, in fact; no use to Society at all" by Councillor Tompkins on earth, he is also regarded as "only a little man . . . never meant to be anything very much" by the Second Voice in the dark outside his Workhouse room ("Leaf by Niggle," pp. 110, 99).

Yet Niggle reveals perfect humility when he voices his concern for his former neighbor Parish before the Second Voice and when he feels shame over being singled out for Gentle Treatment—"To hear that he was considered a case for Gentle Treatment overwhelmed him, and made him blush in the dark. It was like being publicly praised, when you and all the audience knew that the praise was not deserved. Niggle hid his blushes in the rough blanket" ("Leaf by Niggle," p. 101). But this very humility has earned him Gentle Treatment. Labor and humility, "in which all penance consists," allow these third members of the Elect to receive in the Other World the joy of honor for dishonor or humility and delight and eternal rest for suffering or hardship. Interestingly, Tolkien echoes this very Christian sentiment in "On Fairy-Stories" when he indicates that "fairy-stories are not the only means of recovery, or prophylactic against loss. Humility is enough" ("Leaf by Niggle," p. 58).

Niggle's "education" as a "Christian" has involved passing through the three stages described in the *Ancrene Wisse* and dominated by the three classes of Elect who undergo the rigors of Penance. His progress or lack of it at every level has been evaluated by various judges, human and superhuman. Niggle is first judged inconsequential by a human judge (Tompkins) because he ignores worldly concerns and is then judged as a partial failure in completing his own duties to himself (preparing for the journey by finishing his artistic rather than his worldly work—this is, after all, a Workhouse, where how one performs one's job, whatever it may be, even painting, does count). But he is finally judged in the more important Court of Inquiry as deserving Gentle Treatment. A failure as a gardener and as an artist, he succeeds as *a good man* when judged by the Two Voices. It is partly as a result of the mercy of the Second Voice and not as a result of the justice of the First Voice that he is accorded Gentle Treatment, or grace.

The "severe" First Voice, of course, represents the fantastic equivalent of God the Father, the First Person of the Trinity, suggesting Old Testament wrath. Such justice contrasts with the New Testament Mercy characteristic of the "gentle" God the Son, the Second Person of the Trinity. The dialogue between the two in the Workhouse world of Purgatory echoes the dialogue between their foils, Tompkins and Atkins, the practical politician and the wise, gentle schoolmaster, in the primary world—or even between Parish and Niggle, personifications of the two sides of each individual. The First Voice denigrates Niggle's various moral weaknesses, as the Second Voice, whose role it is to "put the best interpretation on the facts" ("Leaf by Niggle," p. 101), finds, in contrast, his moral strengths.

When the Second Voice declares, "His heart was in the right place," the First Voice counters, "Yes, but it did not function properly. . . . And his head was not screwed on tight enough: he hardly ever thought at all" ("Leaf by Niggle," p. 99). Even though the First Voice, in the best Old Testament fidelity to the letter, accuses him of neglecting "too many things ordered by the law" ("Leaf by Niggle," p. 100), the Second Voice's defense wins Gentle Treatment for him because he stresses his humility and service to his neighbor Parish. Niggle has portrayed beautiful leaves in paint but "never thought that that made him important" and has served Parish by answering many appeals for which "he never expected any Return" ("Leaf by Niggle," p. 100). His greatest sacrifice occurred during the wet bicycle ride, when he realized that he was relinquishing his last chance to finish the picture and that Parish did not really need him that desperately. He sacrificed himself for his neighbor in the most Christ-like fashion.

The mercy of the Second Voice permits Niggle to enter Niggle's Country for an eternity of rest and convalescence, wherein he eventually enjoys the pleasure (and grace) of coming "home" to his painting. Tolkien here illustrates the virtues of Faërie's secondary world in this "world" called Niggle, the virtues of Escape, Recovery, and Consolation. Usually entry into a secondary world occurs for Tolkien through the reading of fairy-stories whose fantasy guarantees a sub-creation that offers these three virtues. In "Leaf," Niggle "dies" and because of his Christian humility—a second means of entry into a secondary world—"recovers" or is reborn and redeemed. His recovery follows the pattern outlined by Tolkien in his definition in "On Fairy-Stories": "Recovery (which includes return and renewal of health) is a re-gaining . . . of a clear view . . . 'seeing things as we are (or were) meant to see them'—as things apart from ourselves" ("On Fairy-Stories," p. 57). The first step is physical, the renewal of health, followed by the second, more figurative and spiritual step, recovery of true vision.

Thus, after Niggle in the Workhouse Infirmary heals with the help of the doctor's medicines, he is then offered Gentle Treatment (the term "treatment" itself implies a remedy for an illness), and he and Parish drink from a bottle of tonic that eases the tiredness experienced soon after their arrival. Most of all it is the place, "Niggle," that restores them through its sub-creative gifts "as a holiday, and a refreshment. It is splendid for convalescence. . . . It works wonders in some cases" ("Leaf by Niggle," p. 112). The metaphor of sickness on earth (fever, lameness, chills) and of recovery of health in the secondary world is beautifully handled in the story.

Niggle's recovery and that of Parish include as well the clearing of vision. When Niggle first enters "Niggle's Country" he *perceives* immediately that some of the most beautiful leaves "were seen to have been produced in collaboration with Mr. Parish." This fact surprises him ("Leaf by Niggle," p. 104) because he always considered that "collaboration" as interruption. Now he realizes that Parish remains very necessary to his work, for "[t]here are lots of things about earth, plants, and trees that he knows and I don't" ("Leaf by Niggle," pp. 105–6). Similarly, Parish sees his former neighbor clearly and finally understands and appreciates his artistry as restorative: "Did you think of all this, Niggle? I never knew you were so clever" ("Leaf by Niggle," p. 109).

Both men escape as well from suffering the "hunger, thirst, poverty, pain, sorrow, injustice" and death characteristic of the primary world ("On Fairy-Stories," pp. 65–66), to receive Consolation in the secondary world. The usually kindhearted Niggle in this world grumbled and complained to himself after Parish made his requests; even

Parish was a critical, sour, grim-mouthed neighbor. Once Niggle reached the Workhouse he became "quieter inside now"—less angry and more tolerant and gentle. Now in "Niggle," both men alter their moods tremendously. They sing merrily while they plan and plant gardens; eventually, having arrived at the uppermost reaches of the Mountains, they fully reveal their joy when they learn of the "happy catastrophe," the name of their country being Niggle's Parish: "They both laughed. Laughed—the Mountains rang with it!" ("Leaf by Niggle," p. 112). Recovery, Escape, Consolation—such fantastic virtues transform, even redeem and resurrect, Parish and Niggle as opposites and collaborators. The Gospels relay a fairy-story, after all. And the artist as sub-creator, the "practical" architect of the secondary world as is Niggle of Niggle's Country, desperately needs the lover of art or the reader of fairy-stories, who is liberated by the fantasy of fairy-stories to escape his real-life function and character, or his Parish-side, in order to complete him.

III. "SMITH OF WOOTTON MAJOR": ALF THE ELF-KING AND SMITH

While less obviously Christian and allegorical than "Leaf by Niggle," "Smith of Wootton Major" still emphasizes Christian themes and concepts. As a "setting moment" describing what must have seemed like the end of Tolkien's career as a writer, "Smith" provides the ultimate consolation for the good Christian—the reward of grace for humility and suffering. Unlike "Leaf," in "Smith" no punishment or stern, literalistic judging of the individual occurs. Here suffering is valuable because God may reward it—may (in the words of the *Ancrene Wisse*) "turn towards it with His grace, and make the heart pure and clear-sighted, and this no one may achieve who is tainted with vices or with an earthly love of worldly things, for this taint affects the eyes of the heart so badly that it cannot recognize God or rejoice in the sight of him" (Salu, *Ancrene Wisse*, p. 170).

This quotation from "Love," the seventh section of the *Ancrene Wisse*, beautifully summarizes the pure spiritual condition of the child Smith. Because free of vice and filled with charity, Smith is "graced" with the gift of the star, his passport into the other world of Faery (what Tolkien usually calls Faërie), but one which simultaneously endows him with a recovery of insight and perception because of his visits to the other world. And the love of Smith for his family and for his fellow man and ultimately for God stems from a pure heart, an Augustinian pronouncement springing from the pages of the *Ancrene Wisse:* "A pure heart, as Saint Bernard says, effects two things: it makes you do all that you do either for the love of God alone, or for the good of others for His sake" (Salu, *Ancrene Wisse*, p. 170).

Humility and love find expression in Smith's behavior both before the star is bestowed upon him and at the moment he must return the star. While children in Wootton Major seem in general more likely to appreciate the magnificent Master Cakes baked every twenty-four years, only a child graced with charity (Saint Augustine's true New Man) receives the gift of insight. Smith, who has given up the silver coin he found in his piece of cake to the luckless Nell who discovered nothing in hers, manifests that fine charity that enables him to qualify for the fairy star.[20] When the time comes for him to relinquish the star, Smith also gives it up because someone else needs it ("Smith," pp. 41, 44). His lifelong concern for others earns him the right to choose the new recipient of the star— Nokes of Townsend's Tim, the great-grandson of Master Cook Nokes. Such a choice well illustrates Smith's insight into human nature but also a markedly Christian attitude of beatitudinal meekness and love of those who are different—"[Nokes]'s not an obvious choice," says Smith ("Smith," p. 47). Even Tim himself portrays the same humility and selflessness: he requests only a very small piece of cake ("Smith," p. 57) without demanding more than he can eat.

Such humility and love motivate Alf's behavior as well: he endures quietly the chagrin of being Nokes's apprentice and receiving no recognition for his work. Alf's love is manifested toward others: he gives up years in Faery for the opportunity to be the insignificant Prentice in the primary world. Here he patiently waits for the opportunity, first, to slip the fairy star into Nokes's cake and, then, years and years later, to slip it into his very own last Great Cake for Tim. Alf or Elf typifies the apprentice to the master whose humility leaves him always ready to learn and whose selflessness and love make him ready to serve others. That is, Alf signifies the eternal youth, or *novus homo*, the youngness of the spirit rather than the oldness of pride and the senses. After living in Wootton Major a short time as an apprentice, "[he] had grown a bit taller but still looked like a boy, and he had only served for three years" ("Smith," p. 13). Ironically, it is because of Alf's youth that the townspeople do not regard him as an obvious choice to replace the old master, and instead they choose Nokes. Generously lending his great skill to the proud and ambitious Nokes, Alf serves the community humbly and well for years. Even at the very end, long after Smith has aged, Alf remains youthful: he "looked like the apprentice of long ago, though more masterly" ("Smith," p. 40). (The Queen also appears to be a "young maiden" when first espied by Smith.)

But the opposites of humility and love—arrogance and selfishness, or *cupiditas*—are exemplified in Nokes.

While the zeal of Faery is directed toward the higher imaginative and moral pursuits of art and immortality, the zeal of the primary world—here, Wootton Major—is directed toward material goods, specifically as symbolized by cooking. Appropriately, excessive interest in physical sustenance, the senses, literalness, leads to a spiritual oldness characterized by greed, pride, or *cupiditas* in general. About gluttony the *Ancrene Wisse* (which Tolkien edited and his student Mary Salu translated) speaks in terms of a cooking metaphor: "The greedy glutton is the devil's manciple, but he is always about the cellar or the kitchen" (Salu, *Ancrene Wisse*, p. 96). Nokes insists on being if not performing as the Master Cook and similarly puts himself before others because he lacks both humility and charity. A literal "old man" by the end of the story, Nokes remains interested in the mystery of food but misunderstands or totally ignores higher forms of sustenance. His clashes with Alf dramatize the Christian confrontation between Satan (or a Satan-figure) and the Second Person of the Trinity.

Called eventually a "vain old fraud, fat, idle and sly" by Alf, in his size and age Nokes illustrates gluttony, materialism, and the oldness of literalism. At the beginning of the story he patronizes the children at the Feast by giving them what he thinks they deserve: "Fairies and sweets were two of the very notions he had about the tastes of children. Fairies he thought one grew out of; but of sweets he remained very fond" (p. 14). Like Andrew Lang and the narrator of *The Hobbit*, Nokes assumes that "small" and "young" signify "inferior." So Nokes similarly misunderstands the deceptive youthfulness of Alf: "You'll grow up someday" ("Smith," p. 16). To Nokes, growing up involves the development of a materialism similar to his "adult" values. Thus, he regards the unusual and different fay star, the passport to Faery, as "funny," something intended to make the children laugh. Nokes lacks imagination as well

102

as the youthfulness characterizing the life of the spirit. Puzzled by the seeming disappearance of that fay star, Nokes projects a practical and materialistic interpretation of the mystery onto the facts: so he imagines first that Molly has swallowed the star by mistake because she is greedy and bolts her food; or that Cooper's Harry, with his froglike mouth, has it; or else Lily, with her capacity to swallow large objects without harm. All of these children display physical attributes that might explain the disappearance of the sharp trinket, but they also typify Nokes's greed (Molly) and literalism (Harry and Lily).

Finally, Nokes promotes spiritual oldness as he condemns spiritual youngness. Because he is himself a "burglar"—he "stole" Alf's skill long ago by pretending it was his own—Nokes views Alf as a burglar who probably stole the star himself, given his "nimble" dexterity. When confronted by reality rather than its earthly shadow (when Alf appears to him as the King of Faery—a spelling preferred by Tolkien in this story), Nokes refuses to believe Alf's admission that the star came from Faery and went to Smith. He also refuses to accept Alf's accusation that Nokes is a "vain old fraud" whose work was actually performed by Alf. Alf grants him the "miracle" of transformation into a thin man but he still does not believe in the king: "He was artful. Too nimble," he declares ("Smith," p. 59), construing art and miracles to be manipulation and tricks, the devices of the burglar and the magician. Possessing free will like Smith, Nokes as freely chooses to reject the truth as Smith does to accept it when confronted by the king. He continues to suffer the effects of that pride and greed and literalism common to the *vetus homo.*

Tolkien carefully underscores the morality play of the story through the use and etymology of his characters' names. Nokes in the obsolete and rare sense, according to the *Oxford English Dictionary,* means "a ninny" or "fool."

"Smith," as a very common surname, suggests Everyman (or an Everyman who does not mind being common, as one expression of his humility) and also the artistry of the smith who works in iron. But Alf or Elf, more than the other two characters, possesses an unusual name: in mythology the name refers to the species of supernatural beings known as "Elves." Often implying a malicious being or demon, a succubus or incubus type of "monster," the name can also be attributed to any diminutive creature, especially a child. Often it is a "tricksy" (nimble?) creature, such tricks resembling the deceit implied by the etymology of the artist Niggle's name and by the burglar-artist Bilbo. Thus, the three characters in "Smith" through their names exemplify the roles of the monster-fool, the everyman-hero, and the divine or Elven savior-guide. Unlike *The Hobbit,* however, in this fairy-story it is the savior and not the hero who "battles" against the monster. The hero contrasts with the fool through his reaction when he encounters the savior.

The story is appropriately structured around the journeys from one world to another: Alf's journeys into the primary world, Smith's journeys into the secondary world. Smith's journeys end when he meets the Queen of Faery on his last trip and when on the way back he meets the King of Faery, Alf. (In contrast, Nokes the Master never meets or understands the Queen of Faery, envisioned by him as a sweet cake-icing doll, and even after meeting the king many times never recognizes him as king.) Thus, Alf enters the primary world *from* Faery and Smith enters the secondary world *of* Faery from the primary world: one is an apprentice-cook in appearance and an Elf-king in reality; one is a smith or artist in appearance and something far greater in reality ("The shadow was the truth," his son says, referring to the long shadow he cast upon one return from Faery).

Alf's roles as cook and king remind us of the Christian concept of the Incarnation of the divine Word in mortal flesh in Christ: he submerges his nobility beneath the humble guise of cook's help. Smith's role as artist allows him to journey to Faery like the Christian's soul journeying to the Celestial City, the Holy Jerusalem where he eventually meets Christ the King. Smith's passport from one world to the other is the star that allows him to be called Starbrow in reality and signals his rebirth or recovery like the star announcing the rebirth of humankind in the birth of Christ. Alf's passport, unlike Smith's, is his cooking ability, which suggests familiarity with the needs of the body rather than the soul.

Cooking provides physical sustenance and in itself is neither good nor bad. It thus serves a double symbolic purpose in this story. As Wootton Major is known for the excellence of its cooking, it is an appropriate place to test human values. Material good can become an end in itself, which can subvert the soul, in the medieval sense. So the Master Cook occupies the most important symbolic role: as the agent of life he functions as a liaison between the material and spiritual realms and between this world and the other world of Faery, because with his artistry and skill he can satisfy both the spirit and body of his fellow man. Alf the messenger to others, like the Word of God, brings Good News with him in his artistry—and "mortality"—as a cook, which Smith in his elaborate and beautiful ironwork emulates. Like Christ, eventually Alf must relinquish his mortality and his sojourn in the primary world in order to return to heaven (Faery) as Smith must relinquish his name Starbrow and his own star in order to return to the primary world.

Smith's visits to Faery eventually earn him Epiphany. In this case it is not the appearance of the Star of the King to the Magi but the "appearance" of the Queen and King to Smith and his recognition of them. In effect Smith sees the reality beneath the surface appearance and experiences true Escape, Recovery, and Consolation. If the King of Faery represents by analogy the Christian King, then the Queen of Faery by analogy represents the essence of Faërie suggested by sub-creation. Imagination and Love: the cardinal principles of Faërie, as enunciated in "On Fairy-Stories," stand revealed.

The Queen of Faery was envisioned by Nokes as a doll of sugar icing (a "Fairy Queen") and interpreted as "a tricky little creature" ("Smith," p. 20) so unscrupulous that she might not allow each of the twenty-four children to receive a trinket in the slice of Great Cake—only "if the Fairy Queen plays fair" ("Smith," p. 20). What seems tricksy and manipulative to Nokes seems artistic and alive to Smith, who swallows the fairy star. Every twenty-four years, or every generation, there exists a single child (or "reader") capable of receiving the fairy star and recognizing the Queen of Faery. The gift of the star acknowledges Smith's appreciation of Faery and also his artistic talent; it allows him to escape ("Escape") from the primary world into the secondary world of Faery. The escape occurs in two ways: first, Smith actually transports himself into the other world of Faery, another country, another world. But also this "reader" becomes himself an artist or a sub-creator and provides escape for others. Hence, on his tenth birthday Smith begins to "grow up" or mature spiritually and artistically by suddenly singing a beautiful song of Faery. Then as smith he fashions both those "plain and useful" objects needed by the people of the village and also beautiful iron objects wrought into "wonderful forms that looked as light and delicate as a spray of leaves and blossom" ("Smith," p. 23). Like Niggle, Smith creates a leaf-like object: his art imitates Nature and its life.

Smith's progress in art and in understanding—his

recovery (or "Recovery") of insight—parallels the progress of his journeys into Faery. At first he walks quietly along the outer peripheries; then he proceeds farther into Faery as time passes. He sees the Elven mariners returning from battle at the Dark Marches in a terrifying vision that compels him to turn away from the sea and the strand and toward the safer, inner Kingdom of Faery. Faery seems to embody in its life forms the mirror image of the strong iron leaf and flower objects that Smith creates: the King's Tree consists of "tower upon tower, into the sky, and its light was like the sun at noon; and it bore at once leaves and flowers and fruits uncounted, and not one was the same as any other that grew on the Tree" ("Smith," p. 28). Life is art in Faery. Both provide a recovery, physical and spiritual, for Smith. Note that he once encounters a lake of water unlike any natural lake he has ever seen, for it is "harder than stone and sleeker than glass," with flame and fiery creatures circling below. This unnatural lake is also a deathlike and death-dealing artifact: when Smith falls on it, a Wind "roaring like a great beast" hurls him away. He is saved by a birch, a natural object of life and life-giving power antithetical to the deadly lake that saves him at the cost of its own leaves: it wept, and "tears fell from its branches like rain. He set his hand upon its white bark saying, 'Blessed be the birch! What can I do to make amends or give thanks?'" ("Smith," p. 30). The birch suggests a tree of life like the Tree of Life whose spirit of rebirth and Recovery for Tolkien pervades fantasy.

Thus, Smith creates iron leaves and flowers of beauty and practical domestic implements but never weapons of war. He understands through the recovery of perspective or insight the difference between death and life, our world and Faery (Faërie). Knowing that the evils of Faery must be combated by weapons too dangerous for mortals, he knows also that "he could have forged weapons that in his own world would have had power enough to become the matter of great tales and be worth a king's ransom," even though in Faery they would have received little notice. Hence always in his sojourns he acts as a "learner and explorer, not a warrior" ("Smith," p. 24).

Eventually Smith earns not only Escape and partial Recovery but full Recovery and rebirth as well as Consolation, or Joy. He "sees" the Queen of Faery, although he does not recognize her in the first incident; and then he understands her and what she represents in the second, in both incidents experiencing feelings of joy and consolation. First appearing as "a young maiden with flowing hair and a kilted skirt," the Queen of Faery laughs and smiles at him while she chastises him for venturing here without the queen's permission. Joining with her in a dance, Smith experiences "the swiftness and the power and the joy to accompany her"—the joy or consolation of Faery (Faërie) incarnate in fantasy, in effect ("Smith," p. 33). The dance as an art form in itself suggests the paradox of art conjoined with nature, art alive. So the Queen of Faery lends him the symbol of Faery, a Living Flower that will never die. It emblematizes the eternal life of art like the flowers and leaves adorning the King's Tree and the "blessed birch." In the second encounter she appears as a queen, but without a throne, who seems to be crowned by a host glimmering like "the stars above" and with a white flame burning on her head ("Smith," pp. 36–37). This time she communicates with him without words. At first ashamed of Nokes's image of her, he is reminded by her, "Better a little doll, maybe, than no memory of Faery at all." Then to pinpoint the rebirth or recovery of vision possible to the explorer of Faery, she declares, "For some the only glimpse. For some the awaking" ("Smith," p. 37). *Seeing* the Queen has allowed Smith to *awaken*, to be reborn and Recover. And when the Queen of Faery touches his head, he experiences simultaneously primary-world sorrow coupled with secondary-world joy: "[H]e seemed to be both in the World and in Faery, and also outside them and surveying them, so that he was at once in bereavement, and in ownership, and in peace" ("Smith," p. 38). Once the "stillness" passes in a moment of joy and peace, he must return to the "bereavement" of the world.

Having returned to the "world," however, Smith must give up his star, signaling Epiphany, to the King. His quest is complete. But because this is itself a fairy-story, its ending also bestows a eucatastrophe upon its reader (who, like Smith, must return at its end to the bereavement of the world). Smith chooses the great-grandson of Nokes to be the next recipient of the star, and he and we now know that at least for those graced with goodness and imagination the future holds the possibility of a journey to Faery. The star resembles in this moral sense the Living Flower of art. The story ends as it has begun, with yet another great Feast of Good Children, and after yet another child, a "New Man," has been picked to continue artistic endeavors.

A new "son" will some day meet his spiritual parents, or the King and Queen of Faery, that is, of the secondary world embodied in fantasy, just as at the end the old father Smith returns to his physical family in the primary world and leaves his artistic heir Tim to the joy of Faery. The fairy-story concerns cycles temporal and spatial—the passing of one generation to another, the journey from one world to another. Nokes allows Alf to inherit his vocational role as Master Cook, Smith allows his son to inherit his vocational role as smith (once he too was Smithson), and Smith and Alf both allow Tim to inherit his former role as artist, explorer of Faery. Construction and creativity, whether material or imaginative, foster the continuation of such natural cycles; destruction denies life, perpetrates death, both materially and spiritually. It is the warrior,

especially the Germanic lord, who for Tolkien most frequently occupies the polar opposite of the human artist
and the Christian king. In Tolkien's medieval parodies such
a lord kills and maims and destroys civilization out of a
murderous self-aggrandizement. The Germanic lord represents a Nokes with power—and with weapons. This lord
or king is also constructed as a very medieval (if human)
"monster." We turn now to Tolkien's medieval parodies,
the formal antitheses of his Christian fairy-stories.

Chapter 4

THE GERMANIC LORD

Tolkien's Medieval Parodies

But an equally basic passion of mine *ab initio* was
for myth (not allegory!) and for fairy-story, and
above all for heroic legend on the brink of fairy-
tale and history, of which there is far too little in
the world (accessible to me) for my appetite. I was
an undergraduate before thought and experience
revealed to me these were not divergent interests—
opposite poles of science and romance—but
integrally related. . . . Of course there was and is
all the Arthurian world, but powerful as it is, it is
imperfectly naturalized, associated with the soil of
Britain but not with English; and does not replace
what I felt to be missing. For one thing its "faerie"
is too lavish, and fantastical, incoherent and
repetitive. For another and more important thing:
it is involved in, and explicitly contains the
Christian religion.

—J.R.R. Tolkien
Letter 131, to Milton Waldman
of Collins (c. 1951)

That Tolkien had a taste for parody is clear from the existence of thirteen early poems using medieval languages,
verse, and metrical forms, written at Leeds in the twen-

111

ties with E.V. Gordon and in 1936 appearing in an unpublished University College of London anthology of thirty pages entitled "Songs for the Philologists."[1] In part also an indication of Tolkien's propensity for satirizing his own field of English language and literature, these poems point to a direction he will pursue in other venues: humorous criticism of the eccentricities—particularly pomposity, intolerance, and pride—of those judgmental and narrow-minded professors and scholars who practice his own profession.[2] In relation to the first, medieval purpose, in the opening lines of one poem, "Across the Broad Ocean" (lines 5–7), Tolkien invokes the *Beowulf* poet's actual words in the first lines, about his having witnessed the past noble deeds of valor performed by the kings of the Spear-Danes: "Hwæt, wē Gār-dena in gēardagum, / þēodcyninga þrym gefrūnon, / hu ðā æþelingas ellen fremedon!" (Lo, we have heard how the kings of the Spear-Danes performed deeds of valor, the princes, noble [deeds], in days of old) (*Beowulf*, lines 1–3).[3] The mournful note of the passing of the great and a wistfulness for the glory that was is sounded in almost all of Tolkien's other medieval parodies.

The medieval parodies differ in genre or form and theme from Tolkien's earlier creative and critical efforts. Neither lecture, children's story, nor fairy-story, they consist of lay, romance, fabliau, alliterative-verse drama, "imram," and lyric. Such genres specifically derive from the Middle Ages. "The Lay of Aotrou and Itroun" (1945) is modeled upon the Breton lay of the twelfth to the fourteenth centuries characteristic of northern France but influenced by old Celtic tales.[4] *Farmer Giles of Ham* (1949) combines the late medieval forms of the fabliau and the romance.[5] "The Homecoming of Beorhtnoth Beorhthelm's Son" (1953) functions as an alliterative-verse drama continuation of the Old English heroic poem "The Battle of Maldon" written in 991, followed by "Ofermod," Tolkien's gloss on the sequel and its relationship to medieval hero-ism in "The Battle of Maldon," *Beowulf*, and *Sir Gawain and the Green Knight*.[6] "Imram" (1955), as an English poetic reworking of the Latin prose *Navigatio Sancti Brendani Abbatis*, parodies the medieval Irish genre of the "voyage" (known as the "imram").[7] Finally, the collection of sixteen poems entitled *The Adventures of Tom Bombadil* (1962) includes some lyrics strongly influenced by Old English principles of scansion. As a whole it is said to be derived from the Hobbit records in the Red Book of Westmarch and relates more to the developing mythology of Middle-earth than to the literature of the Middle Ages.[8]

The chief difference between these medieval parodies and Tolkien's other works exists in their formally mimetic nature. It is true that *The Hobbit* and *The Lord of the Rings* rely heavily upon medieval ideas and works for their shape and structure and their meaning, as we have seen in the introduction and chapter 2 and will see in chapter 5.[9] It is also true, as we have seen in chapter 3, that the fairy-story form of "Leaf by Niggle" and "Smith of Wootton Major" springs from and is heavily influenced by a Christian ethos predominant during the Middle Ages. However, a second and related difference involves Tolkien's distinction in the lectures on fairy-stories and on *Beowulf* between the el-egy, or what he calls "Drama," and fantasy, or "Literature." In the former lecture, Tolkien shows that the Drama, like the elegy, offers a dyscatastrophe, common to the primary world with its pervasive mutability and death, in contrast to the fantasy's eucatastrophe, common to the secondary world with its singular Joy, Consolation, and Recovery.[10] Tolkien defined *Beowulf* as an heroic-elegiac poem because "all its first 3,136 lines are the prelude to a dirge: "him þa gegiredan Geata leode ad ofer eorðan unwaclicne" (then the people of the Geats made ready for him a splendid pyre on the earth).[11] Tolkien's medieval parodies, with the possible exception of the fairy-story *Farmer Giles of Ham,* might all be characterized as elegies similar to *Beowulf.*

Specifically, all of the medieval parodies stress the difficulty of living in this primary (or real) world, whether that world is designated as England (Maldon, Ely, Mercia, the Little Kingdom) or Ireland. So also all of them, with the exception of "The Lay," a poem whose designated time period remains difficult to date precisely, but as a lay is probably set in the twelfth century, refer to periods or events historical or legendary occurring during the Middle Ages. *Farmer Giles* has as its subject a pre-Arthurian time (that is, before A.D. 600) but has as its imaginary author a fourteenth-century writer similar to the *Gawain* poet. "The Homecoming" pinpoints its time as exactly A.D. 991, the date of the Battle of Maldon. "Imram" deals with the last, legendary voyage of Saint Brendan in the years 565–73.

Further, all these elegiac works are imbued with a sadness that distinguishes them from the joyful, eucatastrophic fairy-stories and the happily-ended *Hobbit* and "New Hobbit." "The Lay" as an explicitly elegiac poem nears its end with these words: "Sad is the note and sad the lay, / but mirth we meet not every day" ("The Lay," p. 266). While *Farmer Giles* seems superficially to end happily, in fact its conclusion masks a profoundly disturbing realization about the cyclical nature of the reigns of kings and the sway of Fortune in this world, almost medieval in its similarity to the tragic stories of the fall of princes in Chaucer's *Monk's Tale* or to the medieval tragedy caused by the turn of Fortune's wheel in his *Troilus and Criseyde.*[12] "Homecoming" ends with monks chanting the Office of the Dead to mourn the death of Beorhtnoth. "Imram" concludes with the cold grim reminder that Saint Brendan died "under a rain-clad sky, / journeying whence no ship returns; / and his bones in Ireland lie" ("Imram," p. 1561). Even Saint Brendan's last words to his monastic brother can hardly be characterized as joyful in their admonishing tone: if the latter wants to know more about this paradisal land, "in a boat then, brother, far afloat / you must labor in the sea, / and find for yourself things out of mind: / you will learn no more of me" ("Imram," p. 1561). Learning and labor for the Christian remain arduous tasks. These stern endings differ radically from the cheery "Well, I'm back" of Sam at the end of the trilogy and the laughing "Thank goodness" of Bilbo in *The Hobbit*. That cheeriness belongs only to the secondary world of fantasy, extant in the imagination; indeed, as we have seen in chapter 3 of this study, fairy-stories trace the *relationship* between a primary and secondary world of which the latter, as Faërie, bears a strong resemblance to the analogous Christian Other World of paradise.

What interests Tolkien in these medieval parodies, in lieu of that spatial journey from a primary to a secondary world in the fairy-story or within a secondary world in *The Hobbit* and *The Lord of the Rings*, is the temporal shift from one phase to another in the United Kingdom's past. In a broader sense the passage of time and the change that accompanies it have always interested Tolkien: as a result of the meetings of the Inklings and his many conversations with C.S. Lewis, Tolkien had intended to write a narrative about time, as C.S. Lewis had intended to write (and did in fact complete, in the *Perelandra* trilogy) a narrative about space. But in a sense, he did: Bilbo and Frodo mature in microcosm as, in macrocosm, Middle-earth moves from its Third to its Fourth Age. The maturation of Niggle and Smith in the fairy-stories transcends the merely chronological passage of years. But in the medieval parodies the protagonist does not grow either chronologically or spiritually so much as degenerate, fall, or die like the knight in "The Lay," King Augustus in *Farmer Giles*, Beorhtnoth in "Homecoming," and the questing Saint Brendan in

"Imram." Further, these negative changes mark a time of dramatic change in the macrocosm, defined either as a family in "The Lay," a kingdom in *Farmer Giles,* a nation in "Homecoming," or the Christian community in "Imram." That is, in "The Lay," the father's desire for an heir leads to his wife's pregnancy, the birth of twins, his death followed by hers, then the end of his line and the ruin of his castle fiefdom. The fall of Augustus Bonifacius's old kingdom and the rise of Giles's new kingdom considerably alter the countryside and its community. The change from an older Anglo-Saxon-heroic culture to a newer romantic-chivalric and more Christian one is imminent in "Homecoming." Finally, in "Imram" the dialogue between monks of different generations (the "father" Brendan and his younger "brother") heightens the passage of one age (the age of paganism that regards the other world as Elven) to another (the age of Christianity that regards the other world as Christian) in the sixth century.

The child, nephew, or heir who matures into the hero dominates many of Tolkien's greatest descriptions of a secondary world; as we have seen previously, the child symbolizes the New Man, or *novus homo.* In contrast, the Old Man—uncle, father, representative of a dying culture—occupies the position of the head of the household or the head of state in a primary world setting such as England or Ireland. It is this figure Tolkien observes in the medieval parodies through the role of the knight or the king. The child, nephew, or heir occupies a complementary role, either literally as the king's heir or more figuratively as his subordinate warrior, knight, or servant. In every case the child's attempt to revitalize the community or culture dominated by the old knight or king fails or is marked by frustration and stultification. This occurs not through any fault of his own so much as through the debilitating consequences of the old king's behavior.

I. *"OFERMOD"*: THE MEDIEVAL KING

Tolkien outlines his conclusions concerning medieval ideas of kingship in the short third part of "The Homecoming" entitled *"Ofermod."* Using Beorhtnoth as an example of the bad lord, Tolkien specifies his chief flaw as *ofermod,* Old English for "pride." In lines 89–90 of "The Battle of Maldon," the Old English poet explains the reason for the loss of the battle: *ða se eorl ongan for his ofermode alyfan landes to fela la þere ðeode,* or "then the earl in his over-mastering pride actually yielded ground to the enemy, as he should not have done" ("The Battle of Maldon," p. 19). Because the *comitatus* ethic pervasive in Old English heroic poetry defines the lord's chief obligation to his tribe of warriors as that of wise leadership, protection from enemies, and food, shelter, and reward for valor in battle, such folly destroys the lord, Beorhtnoth himself, and most of his tribe. The reason for Beorhtnoth's pride is simple: "Yet this element of pride, in the form of the desire for honor and glory, in life and after death, tends to grow, to become a chief motive, driving a man beyond the bleak heroic necessity to excess—to chivalry" ("Ofermod," p. 20). When a chief considers his men as a means to the end of self-glorification, he suffers from the pride characteristic, according to Tolkien at least, of chivalry. Such excessive pride is not truly indicative of heroism. Beowulf, like Beorhtnoth, finds criticism from Tolkien because of his error in judgment in fighting the dragon alone, a man of fifty guilty of the same overweening pride: "He will not deign to lead a force against the dragon, as wisdom might direct even a hero to do; for, as he explains in a long 'vaunt,' his many victories have relieved him of fear" ("Ofermod," p. 21). Boasting he will rely only on a sword and on none of his subordinates, Beowulf nevertheless fails to kill the dragon alone and to lead his tribe wisely. It is his warrior

Wiglaf who finally helps him vanquish the dragon, but even this act of heroism, rather than chivalry, cannot save the leaderless tribe doomed to fall before the onslaughts of the Swedes and Frisians.

In "The Battle of Maldon," too, the subordinate warrior portrays the positive and heroic values of love and loyalty for his lord, as contrasted with the chief's negative and chivalric value of *ofermod*. The old retainer Beorhtwold, ready to lay down his life for his foolish lord, proclaims: "Hige sceal þe heardra, heorte þe cenre, / mod sceal þe mare þe ure mægen lytlað" ("Will shall be the sterner, heart the bolder, / spirit the greater as our strength lessens") ("The Battle of Maldon," p. 5).

Such love and loyalty in Anglo-Saxon heroic poems are expressed through acts of valor by a subordinate warrior; in a Christian medieval poem like *Piers Plowman* they are ultimately translated into the faith, hope, and charity represented by Abraham, Moses, and the Samaritan, all types of Christ as the *novus homo*. Tolkien anticipates this transformation without mentioning Christianity explicitly by designating for the subordinate warrior a position on the continuum at the opposite end to his lord: "Personal pride was therefore in him at its lowest, and love and loyalty at their highest" ("Ofermod," p. 20). What Tolkien does here, of course, is to reconcile Germanic heroic values with Christian ones in the same way the *Beowulf* poet does, if not Beowulf himself.

In the 1936 lecture on *Beowulf* Tolkien revealed its dual levels (Germanic and Christian) in the figures of its monsters. Representative on one level of the natural forces of chaos and death threatening humankind, on another level they signify the supernatural dangers of sin and spiritual death. Thus, the monsters Beowulf fights in the poem must be destroyed externally by heroism in battle; they symbolically project internal flaws in the nations and their lords that can be conquered only by wisdom and self-control. In short, the hero must display that *sapientia et fortitudo* characteristic of the Germanic warrior and the Christian leader. If Beowulf fails here, Bilbo and even Frodo do not—as we have seen and will see in the fiction published in the year after the *Beowulf* article (*Hobbit*, 1937) and continually revised throughout the ensuing years ("The New Hobbit," 1937–49).

But in his later fictional works, Tolkien's attention to the Germanic-Christian values splits. In the medieval parodies published during the years 1945 to 1955 ("The Lay," 1945; *Farmer Giles*, 1949; "The Homecoming," 1953; "Imram," 1955), Tolkien focuses primarily on the failure of Germanic values. In contrast, in the fairy-stories published during the equivalent period of 1945 to 1967 ("Leaf by Niggle," 1945; "Smith of Wootton Major," 1967), Tolkien focuses on the success of Christian values. In both groups he grows less interested in literal monsters and more interested in figurative ones. That monster in the medieval parodies assumes the familiar form of the Germanic lord, chief, or master suffering from an excess of *ofermod*. (Antithetically, in the fairy-stories the king of Faery resembles Christ the king.)

In the four works discussed in this chapter, the Germanic king is depicted as flawed in various ways. In "The Lay of Aotrou and Itroun" (1945), Aotrou is a Briton lord whose chief defect is an internal pride in his familial line that ironically leads to his death and the loss of his family. In *Farmer Giles of Ham* (1949), however, the king's pride stems from the cultural values of the aristocracy— from a flaw in the external social class rather than an internal spiritual deficiency. As such, King Augustus Bonifacius resembles the proud Beorhtnoth. In asking himself why Beorhtnoth committed such a grievous error, Tolkien concludes, "Owing to a defect of character, no doubt; but a character, we may surmise, not only formed by nature, but moulded also by 'aristocratic tradition,' shrined in tales and verse of poets now lost save for echoes" ("Ofermod," p. 21). So the pride and avarice of King Augustus (the spiritual equivalent of Beorhtnoth's figurative "death") lead to the fall of his kingdom and the rise of the hero (a farmer) from the lowest of classes. In "The Homecoming" (1953) the *ofermod* of the lord Beorhtnoth results in his death and those of his warriors at Maldon in 991, symbolizing the demise of Germanic heroic culture. At the end, the "Voice in the dark" (identified by Tolkien as that of the Danish king Canute) is heard admiring the monks' song; during Canute's reign, from 1016 to 1035, his Christianity allowed him to rule both Danes and English as a wise and strong king, the antithesis of the weak lord Beorhtnoth. Finally, in "Imram" (1955), because of its medieval Irish genre and Christian subject, heroic values are expressed only metaphorically in the role of Saint Brendan as a knight-militant, or superior "lord," to a youthful subordinate, in a clash of generations within a single social class—the clergy. In all four Tolkien moves backward in time gradually. The courtly "Lay" is followed by the mock-chivalric and very fourteenth-century *Giles;* then we encounter the late tenth century in "The Homecoming" and the late sixth century in "Imram." In this last medieval parody, set earliest in time and most Christian in bias, we can detect that transition to a form and a theme with which Tolkien would end his publishing career in his final years—the fairy-story detailing the hero's journey to another world through the employment of Christian virtues, chiefly charity.

II. "THE LAY OF AOTROU AND ITROUN": THE BRITON LORD

"The Lay" has been termed a poem with "an unusually

strong religious cast, which transforms the customary series of knightly exploits and amours into a story of temptation and fall."[13] But in addition and less obviously, there exists in this lay a delineation of familial pride in the knight Aotrou very similar to the tribal pride of Beorhtnoth resulting in the deaths of him and his warriors. If the latter abrogates his Germanic relationship with his men by using them as a means to an end, the former abrogates his feudal relationship with his wife by using her as a means to an end.

Beorhtnoth desired glory in battle in order to make immortal his name. Aotrou yearns not for glory in battle but for a child and heir, imagining "lonely age and death, his tomb / unkept, while strangers in his room / *with other names* and other shields / were masters of his halls and fields" ("The Lay," p. 254; my italics). That Aotrou's situation is worsening is clear from the key lines "his pride was empty, vain his hoard, / without an heir to land and sword" ("The Lay," p. 254). He resembles the old king Beowulf who, childless, faces the end of his family line and of his leaderless tribe. Tolkien's use of "pride" here indicates he intends it in the Germanic and racial and not the Christian and spiritual sense. Aotrou errs, then, in his use of his wife as a mere tool in implementing his ends and in the violation of her love and loyalty to him in a subtle parody of the chivalric code.

In return for wooing and wedding her with a ring, Aotrou receives her love in "board and bed." Tolkien likens the social bond joining lord and lady to the contract between lord and retainer by linking these two reciprocal gestures. Aotrou's economic and literal protection of the lady (the ring) complements her domestic and conjugal expressions of love (board and bed). Aotrou fails her when he finds inadequate that expression—when he yearns for a child "his house to cheer, / to fill his courts with laugh-

ter clear" ("The Lay," p. 254). His failure Tolkien underscores through the monstrous or supernatural female re-
placements for Itroun—Corrigan the witch and the
mysterious white doe that leads him to Corrigan. In effect Aotrou "mates" with the first and hunts the second
on two separate journeys, the first suggesting a perversion
of the Ovidian "soft hunt" and the second an inversion
of the "hard hunt" that medieval poets, especially Chaucer
in the *Book of the Duchess,* used to depict the bifold role
of the knight as courtly lover and skillful hunter in pur-
suing the heart/hart. That is, Tolkien symbolically depicts
Aotrou as mating with Corrigan as the monster of excessive familial pride, or pride in lineage. Corrigan, with her
"dark and piercing" eyes "filled with lies," gives him a vial
of magic fluid to rectify Aotrou's infertility and through
this Aotrou is able to father twins—and to deceive his wife
as darkly as Corrigan will deceive him. Aotrou deceives
Itroun, that is, by preferring to her himself (or Corrigan
the witch as monstrous alter ego). Specifically, Aotrou
deceives her by pretending the cause of the conception is
natural. Suggesting a merry feast so that they "will *feign*
our love begun / in joy anew, anew to run / down happy
paths" (my italics), he construes his motivation as an attempt to realize "our heart's desire" more quickly—as if
achieved because of their "hope and prayer" and not the
magic vial of Corrigan ("The Lay," p. 257; my italics). The
word "feign" is aptly chosen.

Throughout the "Lay" Aotrou supposes his own desires are those of Itroun. After the twins are born his mistake becomes more apparent. Having attained an heir and
proved his ability as lover Aotrou will now prove his ability as knight by journeying to fulfill his wife's least desire:

> Is it not, fair love, most passing sweet
> the heart's desire at last to meet?

Yet if thy heart still longing hold,
or lightest wish remain untold,
that will I find and bring to thee,
though I should ride both land and sea!
("The Lay," p. 259)

Aotrou pretends their children resulted from his virility, just as the satisfaction of her other desires will be similarly satisfied by his journeying and chivalric questing. But what Itroun wants is clear: "I would not have thee run nor ride / to-day nor ever from my side" ("The Lay," p. 259). True, she expresses a desire for cold water and venison, but she regards this as a "foolish wish," a hunger superficial in contrast to her need for him by her side—for his continued protection of her. Aotrou ignores her real desire in order to hunt the white doe and perform a chivalrous deed as he believes a true knight should. Tolkien, however, describes this hunt as a "reckless" and "vexed" pursuit of "deer that fair and fearless range" beyond the reach of most mortals ("The Lay," p. 260). In short, Aotrou's pride is excessive and, in Tolkien's pejorative sense, chivalric.

When the white doe leads Aotrou to Corrigan and her demand for love, he violates the terms of yet another contract, in addition to the marital one, by refusing Corrigan's fee and incurring thereby her condemnation to "stand as stone / and wither lifeless and alone" ("The Lay," p. 262); she takes back that life-giving fertility bestowed on him by the vial. Aotrou's spiritual "death" has already occurred; his physical one follows in three days. The water in the vial he hoped would rejuvenate his familial line, and also his marriage to Itroun, becomes instead the potion of death, sterility, darkness—of impotence, in effect. His excessive pride in himself and his desire for glory, the perpetuation of his name, cause two deaths and, appar-

ently, the end of his family and his estate, given the "ruined toft" described in the first lines of the lay.

The real "hero" of this lay is Itroun, the loving and
loyal wife whose subordination to her husband resembles
that of the servant or retainer to the master or king, like
that of Beorhtwold to Beorhtnoth, Wiglaf to Beowulf, Sam
to Frodo, and countless other servants in Old English and
Tolkienian fiction. Itroun's death, while useless, occurs after
she learns of his and expresses so well the extent of her
love for Aotrou. If he had pursued her true desire—to
remain by her side—he might have redeemed himself: if
he had understood her request for cold water figuratively
rather than literally, he might have lived, for the poem
concludes with a prayer to God, to keep them from evil
counsel and despair by dwelling near the "*waters blest* of
Christendom" until they come to Heaven and the "maiden
Mary pure and clean" ("The Lay," p. 266; my italics).

Just as the white doe leads Aotrou to Corrigan, Itroun
might have led him to the Virgin Mary, had he chosen to
"pursue" her. Itroun would have performed as a spiritual
guide on the journey to that forest and holy fountain tra-
ditionally associated with paradise. So she resembles
Beatrice in Dante's *La Vita Nuova* and *Divine Comedy* as
a guide to the Virgin Mary.

The child as heir, represented by the male and female
twins, never has a chance to mature into the hero. Aotrou's
vision of their laughter while they play "on lawns of sun-
light without hedge" is tinged with darkness—the "dark
shadow at their [hedges'] edge" ("The Lay," p. 258). Eventually the vision disappears altogether, both for Aotrou,
now dead, and also for the reader: "and if their children
lived yet long, / or played in garden hale and strong, / they
saw it not, nor found it sweet / their heart's desire at last
to meet" ("The Lay," p. 266). The only laughter remaining is "cold and pale," springing from Broceliande's own

"homeless hills," the habitat of Corrigan. The monstrous witch as Aotrou's dark alter ego replaces his heir and thus denies him immortality and "life." The lay ends, then, with a dirge that mourns the deaths of lord and lady as part of the tragedy inherent in this world and emphasizes the human need to transcend its evil through God's grace. The last line alludes fittingly to the joy of a heaven inhabited by "the maiden Mary pure and clean"—a miracle, a mother whose child left her still virgin, a mother whose heir redeemed and purified all of humankind unlike the heirs of Aotrou, who have disappeared without a trace. To seek a racial immortality through heirs as does Aotrou reveals a folly rectified only by the quest for spiritual immortality through God's Son. Aotrou's failure is clearly attributable to the chivalric code. It is matched by that of King Augustus Bonifacius in *Farmer Giles of Ham.*

III. *FARMER GILES OF HAM:* THE LATE-MEDIEVAL ENGLISH KING

Farmer Giles of Ham represents Tolkien's only medieval parody that both imitates a medieval form or genre and also burlesques medieval literary conventions, ideas, and characters drawn from fourteenth-century works, especially *Sir Gawain and the Green Knight* and Chaucer's *Canterbury Tales.* These two masterpieces of English literature are usually seen by Tolkien scholars—when they are considered at all—as having influenced *The Lord of the Rings* rather than *Farmer Giles of Ham.*[15] Published in 1949, this medieval parody marks Tolkien's completion of *The Lord of the Rings* and, as "a vacation from the 'things higher . . . deeper . . . darker' which these epics [*The Lord of the Rings* and *The Silmarillion*] treat,"[16] spoofs the epic through its mock-heroic style and the academic scholarship of its fussy, editorial preface by the pseudo-historian and linguist who "discovered" the original manuscript. In addition, *Farmer Giles* mocks Tolkien's own creative works and his scholarship, themselves indebted to the medieval literature from which so many of his ideas of heroism, chivalry, and kingship derive. It is no accident that Tolkien spent so many years of his life polishing texts and glossary for his edition of *Sir Gawain and the Green Knight* (1925), later publishing a critical essay, "Ofermod," to accompany his verse drama "The Homecoming of Beorhtnoth Beorhthelm's Son" (1953), and also his translation of two of the poems by the *Gawain* poet along with the Middle English poem *Sir Orfeo* (1975).[17] Tolkien also published two philological essays directly or indirectly involving language in Chaucer's *Canterbury Tales,* one short note ("The Devil's Coach-Horses," 1925) referring to the kind of horse the Shipman was riding on the pilgrimage, as described in his portrait in the *General Prologue,* and one long study ("Chaucer as Philologist: The Reeve's Tale," 1934) on the class and cultural difference of the two northern clerks in *The Reeve's Tale* and how their dialect reveals their place of origin to their disadvantage.[18]

The mock-heroic style reduces the grandiose and long Latin title of the work to the simple translation *Farmer Giles of Ham:* the serious is made trivial. So the hero and his chief adversary become a rude farmer and his domesticated pet. Giles never wants to slay monsters; his cowardly dog barks until he is roused from bed one night, sensing an intruder. This giant intruder turns out to be deaf and nearsighted, accidentally flattening Galatea the cow as he enters Giles's farm and mistaking his assailant's blunderbuss charge for a swarm of horseflies. The second monster, the dragon Chrysophylax, after defeat in battle becomes a large pet who, like Garm the dog earlier, protects Giles's farm and his acquired treasure. Tolkien's medievalized art undergoes a humorous reduction very similar to the squashing of Galatea the cow, named after Pygmalion's ivory statue brought to life as a woman. Suggesting the life-giving power inherent in the artist's function, the myth under mock-heroic treatment shows how life (the cow) is snuffed out by the artist (a deaf and shortsighted giant) and how myth (classical or medieval, but in this case from Ovid) is flattened into burlesque (modern, from Tolkien). Throughout *Farmer Giles* it is not the mythology of Ovid's *Metamorphoses* that Tolkien delights in flattening so much as his own mythology portrayed in *The Hobbit* and "The New Hobbit." These works were influenced by various medieval sources, including *Beowulf*, as understood in Tolkien's "Beowulf: The Monsters and the Critics," and *Sir Gawain and the Green Knight*, later discussed in the "Ofermod" section of "The Homecoming of Beorhtnoth Beorhthelm's Son."

That is, as we have seen in chapter 2, Tolkien fictionalizes ideas of monstrosity in *The Hobbit* also delineated in the *Beowulf* article. In *The Hobbit* the two primary monsters are Gollum in the first part and the dragon Smaug in the second; the first signifying the more physical sins of gluttony and sloth; the second signifying the more intellectual sins of wrath, envy, avarice, and pride. But these monsters merely externalize the evil present in Bilbo and other characters. So avarice and pride also trouble Thorin the Dwarf-king and the Master of Dale, expressed through their desire for kingship or mastery over others. Finally, the critic-as-monster is represented by the supercilious adult narrator of the children's story.

Tolkien parodies this same schema in *Farmer Giles*. One important clue to his intentions exists in the use of the phrase from the "Beowulf" essay, "until the dragon came," to mark the change in Giles's luck caused by the first appearance of the dragon (*Farmer Giles*, p. 22). Originally ending his *Beowulf* article, the phrase dramatized the universal threat of chaos and death to humankind. Further, the giant who stumbles onto Giles's farm mimics the monster Grendel, who deliberately attacked Heorot out of envy; the dragon Chrysophylax in the later parts who first attacks Ham and then is attacked within his lair by Giles plays the part of Beowulf's dragon who first ravages the Geat countryside because of the theft of a cup and then is approached in his barrow by Beowulf and Wiglaf. Farmer Giles also invites comparison with *The Hobbit*: its first monster, Gollum, exhibits inordinate gluttony and sloth (lower, physical sins) and its second monster, Smaug, exhibits avarice and pride (higher, more spiritual sins) in the same way that the giant is physically limited because deaf and nearsighted and the dragon is spiritually limited because greedy and conscienceless. In addition, the metaphor of kingship in *Farmer Giles* reiterates that of *The Hobbit*: Augustus Bonifacius is depicted as avaricious and proud as are both King Beowulf and Thorin the Dwarf-king. Finally, the pompous editor-translator who belittles the vulgarity of the manuscript resembles the narrator of *The Hobbit* who throughout belittles the childishness and stupidity of the halflings and Dwarves.

But this fictionalization of the *Beowulf* article differs from the original article and *The Hobbit* because it also fictionalizes the distinction between heroism and chivalry evidenced four years later in "Ofermod." In the latter essay Tolkien perceives that the excessive pride of king or knight stems from the chivalric code of the aristocracy as criticized in both *Beowulf* and *Sir Gawain and the Green Knight*. In "Ofermod" he uses these as exemplary works; in *Farmer Giles* he also introduces new material drawn from Chaucer's *Canterbury Tales*, especially the fabliaux of the Miller and the Reeve, to mock the heroic form of the romance. Just as the Miller tells a scatological tale to humiliate Chaucer's Knight, who has just narrated a long romance of lofty, appropriately aristocratic idealism and chivalry, so Tolkien's hero in this fabliau-romance, a crude farmer, will humiliate several knights and even a king. Their chivalry cannot be viewed as ideal because it distracts the aristocracy from protecting the lower classes for which it is responsible. Giles becomes a knight and then a king of his own realm because he does not fall prey to the excessive pride inherent in the chivalric code of the upper class. However, he also apparently lacks the manners and courtesy of the knight as defined in *Sir Gawain and the Green Knight.*

The testing of Sir Gawain's *cortaysye* occurs on the three days he is visited by his lord's lady, even while his allegiance to his host-lord and to God (through loyalty and through adherence to Christian virtue) is simultaneously tested. That he fails, even mildly, despite exemplary behavior, becomes clear by the end of the poem when he scandalously accepts the lady's magic girdle, deceives his host by refusing to give him this "winning" as he had promised, succumbs to cowardice in combat by flinching before the Green Knight's axe, and then blames his failure rather discourteously and rudely upon a woman. Tolkien terms the work, in "Ofermod," "in plain intention a criticism or valuation of a whole code of sentiment and conduct, in which heroic courage is only a part, with different loyalties to serve" ("Ofermod," p. 23). For Sir Gawain does risk death in order to support his lord and uncle, King Arthur, literally and courageously by accepting the challenge of the Green Knight and more figuratively and spiritually by showing his loyalty and love for him. He is a heroic figure here *because* he is a subordinate.

Tolkien deliberately invokes *Sir Gawain and the Green Knight* in *Farmer Giles* through humorous parallels. Specifically, the entry of the "rude and uncultured" giant (*Farmer Giles,* p. 10) into Giles's territory at the beginning mimics the boisterous arrival of the Green Knight—atop his green horse—in the midst of the king's Christmas feast. Unknowingly this giant does issue a "challenge" to the incipient knight Giles similar to that of the Green Knight—for thereafter Giles finds himself embroiled in knightly exploits fighting the dragon with the subsequent reward of the king's sword "Tailbiter" for his valor. Later in the work there is actually a Christmas feast during which the dragon, lured to the territory by the giant's idea that knights have become mythical, is ravaging the countryside as a rude "guest." And the king's knights, who in their cowardice resemble Arthur's, delay in fighting this dragon because of a tournament planned for Saint John's Day: "It was obviously unreasonable to spoil the chances of the Midland Knights by sending their best men off on a dragon-hunt before the tournament was over" (*Farmer Giles*, p. 28). Like Sir Gawain, Giles must defend his king's honor.

More generally the theme of cultural degeneration caused by an effete and selfish chivalry appears similar in the two works. When manners and etiquette supersede heroic courage and loyalty to lord, then a culture has become corrupt in the worst and most effetely chivalric sense. Augustus's knights have become literalists in their interpretation of the chivalric code: they are more interested in how they appear on the outside than in what they really are on the inside. When the king acknowledges Giles's retention of "the ancient courage of our race," his knights meanwhile talk "among themselves about the new fashion in hats" (*Farmer Giles*, p. 50). Forced to accompany Giles on his quest of the dragon's lair, they do not see dragon-marks on the trail because they "were discussing points of precedence and etiquette, and their attention was distracted" (*Farmer Giles*, pp. 57–58). Of course, they turn tail and run when confronted by the monster.

The king too seems to regard manners as more important than morals, just as he regards money as a greater good than love and loyalty. When Giles does not come to the king after being summoned upon his return with the treasure from the dragon's lair, the king scolds, "Your manners are unfit for our presence, . . . but that does not excuse you from coming when sent for" (*Farmer Giles*, p. 70). Yet the king himself reacts very coarsely when he first learns of Giles's recalcitrance: his "rage exploded," he "bellowed," he ordered Giles to be thrown into prison, and later he even demands the return of his gift of Tailbiter (*Farmer Giles*, pp. 69–70). Indeed, his greatest concern throughout the tale lies with the treasure rather than with Giles's bravery in battle: his "knight" becomes a means to a financial end. The dragon's promise to return with his treasure after his defeat by Giles "deeply moved" the king—"for various reasons, not the least being financial" (*Farmer Giles*, p. 49). And when the beast does not reappear on the designated day, Augustus rages because "the King wanted money" (*Farmer Giles*, p. 53). Caring only about his coffers, Augustus fails to treat Giles as a real person; such a failure results in his kingdom's downfall.

The well-mannered and fashionable knights and king in the tale contrast with the "rude and uncultured" giant and the merchantlike dragon who bargains with Giles over the price of his defeat—and with the coarse Farmer Giles. But the apparent heroes are revealed as adversaries, and the "monsters" become heroes (or the hero's pets) by the tale's end. Tolkien condemns the aristocracy throughout for its perpetration of the dehumanizing chivalric code and applauds the commons' heroic courage and love, which eventually triumphs over the former. Worthiness springs from good deeds and not fine clothes or ancestry or manners.

Giles, despite his uncouth behavior, does manifest heroism and courage. The dragon immediately recognizes

his true nature during their first meeting: "You have con-
cealed your honorable name and pretended that our meeting was by chance; yet you are plainly a knight of high
lineage. It used, sir, to be the custom of knights to issue a
challenge in such cases, after a proper exchange of titles
and credentials" (*Farmer Giles,* p. 43). He is actually what
a knight *should* be, despite his lack of a title. Tolkien agrees
with the dragon by providing an appropriate feast day for
the confrontation between hero and monster, the Feast of
the Epiphany on Twelfth Night, or 6 January, when Christ
was revealed to the Magi. The "epiphany" or revelation
here introduces the true knight to the dragon—and to the
reader.

As the true hero of the work is a churl, so its real form
or genre emerges as the low-styled, humorous fabliau that
Chaucer's Miller uses to *quyten* (or "repay") the high-
flown rhetoric of the Knight in his philosophical romance.
The style of the former involves a "bourgeois realism" in
contrast to the "aristocratic idealism" of the latter.[19] So, in
Farmer Giles, the villagers speak a rough and idiomatic
language very unlike that of the genteel and elegant aris-
tocrats. And indeed, these rural folk who establish themselves as Draconarii in league with Giles derive their
identities in part from Chaucer's low-life and poor Canterbury pilgrims. Not only is there Farmer Giles, reminiscent of the Miller, there is also a reeve who is as
antagonistic toward Giles as Oswald is toward the Miller
in the *Canterbury Tales.* The parson seems to combine
Chaucer's gentle and good Parson with his learned Clerk,
for he acts also as a grammarian in *Farmer Giles* and reveals the original name of Tailbiter as Caudimordax. Finally, there exists a blacksmith who favors Giles's cause by
providing him with steel chain-mail and helmet, possibly
a pale shadow of the blacksmith in the *Miller's Tale* who
gives Absolon the hot coulter with which to "battle" with

his adversary, *hende* Nicholas, as the latter plays his crude joke for the last time.

Tolkien's view of the subordinate as more admirable than the chief or king who employs his men as instruments to boost his name in battle is expressed in this fabliau-romance through a class struggle between the commons and the aristocracy: the *comitatus* ethic dividing Germanic society into subordinate warriors and king is metamorphosed into that division of late medieval society into two if not three estates (usually commons, clergy, and aristocracy). The triumph of commons over aristocracy, however, communicates a singularly unmedieval and very modern idea: it suggests a nineteenth- or twentieth-century revolutionary outlook, except that the leader of the commoners actually becomes king and a new aristocracy is created, presumably with its own new commons (note that when Giles becomes king the blacksmith engages in undertaking; the miller, given the royal monopoly on milling, serves the crown; and the parson advances to bishop). The old order is revitalized, but perhaps there is no real change except in the introduction of a bourgeoisie, yet another class. A similar consequence of the failure of the aristocratic code occurs after the death of Beorhtnoth in a work that deals with an even earlier medieval period—"The Homecoming," describing the events of 991.

IV. "THE HOMECOMING OF BEORHTNOTH BEORHTHELM'S SON": THE ANGLO-SAXON KING

In this alliterative-verse drama, a young man, Torhthelm, a freeman and the minstrel's son, and an old man, Tídwald the *ceorl,* search the battlefield at Maldon for the body of the dead Beorhtnoth to take to the monks of Ely. The young man in his idealism views the scene from a Germanic heroic stance; the old man in his pragmatic realism views it from a pre-Christian, moralistic stance. Their dialogue functions allegorically as a debate over the merits of the two views. Torhthelm sings of Beorhtnoth as a prince among men because of his courage and judgment:

His head was higher than the helm of kings
With heathen crowns, his heart keener
and his soul clearer than swords of heroes
polished and proven; than plated gold
his worth was greater. From the world has
passed a prince peerless in peace and war,
just in judgment, generous-handed
as the golden lords of long ago.
("Homecoming," p. 9)

But the shrewd Tídwald recognizes the true nature of this excessively proud *eorl:* he risked and lost the lives of his men to obtain greater glory. "Our lord was at fault, . . . / Too proud, too princely! But his pride's cheated, . . . / He let them cross the causeway, so keen was he / to give minstrels matter for mighty songs. / Needlessly noble" ("Homecoming," p. 14).

This pair functions in microcosm as those representative poor ignored by the aristocracy and the minstrels. Neither of these men belongs to the aristocracy: Torhthelm, although a freeman, is a minstrel's son and Tídwald is a farmer. Yet Torhthelm dreams of serving his lord as a warrior in battle—"I loved him no less than any lord with him; / and a poor freeman may prove in the end / more tough when tested than titled earls / who count back their kin to kings ere Woden" ("Homecoming," p. 8)—despite Tídwald's admonition that iron has, in reality, a "bitter taste," and that, when faced with the choice, often a shieldless man is tempted to flee rather than die for his lord. Too, Tídwald implicitly criticizes the aristocracy when he complains of the lot of the poor. The heroic earls die in battle, but poets sing their praises in lays. In contrast, "When the poor are robbed / and lose the land they loved and toiled on, / they must die and dung it. No dirge for them, / and their wives and children work in serfdom" ("Homecoming," p. 15).

Torhthelm perhaps learns something from old Tídwald on the journey back to the monks' abbey at Ely. In a dream of darkness he sees a lighted house and hears voices singing. The joyful song in the "Homecoming" (based upon the speech of the old retainer in "The Battle of Maldon") celebrates the love and loyalty of the subordinate rather than the pride of the lord:

> Heart shall be the bolder, harder be purpose,
> more proud the spirit as our power lessens!
> Mind shall not falter nor mood waver,
> though doom shall come and dark conquer.
> ("Homecoming," p. 12)

By switching emphasis from lord to followers Torhthelm reaffirms those values of love and loyalty to Lord God celebrated as well by Christianity that will make possible a transition from a dying Anglo-Saxon culture to a newly flourishing Christian one.

Yet it is only 991: "The Battle of Maldon," in terms of its criticism of the chivalric and praise of the heroic, as Tolkien admits in "Ofermod," occupies a chronologically medial position between the early *Beowulf* and the later *Sir Gawain and the Green Knight*. The date marks not only the ending of heroism but the beginning of the triumph of chivalry, set within the context of a Christianity more pervasive than that in the time of *Beowulf* (seventh to eighth century). Tolkien emphasizes this transition through the use of verse in the drama. The verse spoken by Torhthelm and Tídwald—"I've watched and waited, till the wind sighing / was like words whispered by waking ghosts" ("Homecoming," p. 6)—bears four stresses per line, three of which are linked by alliteration as in Old English verse. This changes to rhyming verse (a measure predominant in France in the thirteenth and fourteenth centuries), spoken somewhat anachronistically here by a "Voice in the dark" who comments upon the "Dirige" of the monks at the end: "Sadly they sing, the monks of Ely isle! / Row men, row! Let us listen here / a while!" ("Homecoming," p. 18). The voice presages events of the future (the lines from the *Historia Eliensis* actually refer to Canute, ruler of England from 1016 to 1035).

Sound is important in this drama, which should be staged to be fully understood.[20] Sound dramatizes the change in a culture from the primarily Anglo-Saxon to the Christian through the contrast between human words and the Word made flesh and between the chaotic noise of life and the silence of death. It begins with the sound of a man moving and breathing in the darkness; it ends with the sound of the monks' dirge as it "fades into silence" (p. 18). The first line introduces a suspicious voice crying "Halt!" in the dark, but in the last lines an admiring voice urges his rowers on in order to listen to the monks. Mostly, however, the heroic lay of Torhthelm contrasts with the Christian service of the monks.

The flawed human lord Beorhtnoth who sacrifices his men to his pride also contrasts with the good Lord Christ who sacrifices himself for his "men." So the title of "The Homecoming" refers specifically to the coming home of the corpse of the dead lord but also alludes more generally to the "homecoming" of the soul to its heavenly habitat. Thus, the Office of the Dead at the end of "The Homecoming" asks the Lord, "Guide my way . . . into your presence" ("Dirige, Domine, in conspectu tuo viam meam") and, further, into God's "house" or temple: "Introibo in domum tuam: adorabo ad templum / sanctum tuum in timore tuo" ("Homecoming," p. 18). The homecoming of the true subordinate (the Christian) is joyous because he relies solely on the Lord; the homecoming of the false lord (the proud earl) is funereal because he relies too heavily on himself. The notion of return here echoes Tolkien's usage in *The Hobbit* ("There, and Back Again") and in *The Lord of the Rings:* it usually signifies redemptive change and rebirth. Because of the chivalric code, however, this literal "return" ends only in death and darkness.

Yet there is hope. When Torhthelm ("Bright Helmet"), whose name invokes Germanic heroic values of an earlier period, fancies a barrow or pyre in the best heathen fashion for Beorhtnoth, Tídwald ("Time-Guardian") chides him realistically: that "Beorhtnoth we bear not Beowulf here: / no pyres for him, nor piling of mounds; / and the gold will be given to the good abbot" ("Homecoming," p. 11). His name, meaning "Time-Guardian," intimates his awareness of time and his earthbound values. Less imaginative and idealistic than his companion, he also advances a commonsense charity antithetical to the Germanic bloodlust of Torhthelm. When they hear corpse robbers moving around the bodies, Torhthelm wishes to "thrash the villain" (p. 13), but the wise Tídwald cautions, "Their life's wretched, / but why kill the creatures, or crow about it? / There are dead enough around" ("Homecoming," p. 12). Like Gandalf counseling pity and mercy in *The Lord of the Rings,* Tídwald views homicide as destructive and evil, not heroic. He sees these corpse strippers as hungry and masterless men deserving of pity.

But neither is Tídwald altogether Christian in his viewpoint. His *contemptus mundi* suggests a pre-Christian attitude transitionally similar to Torhthelm's post-Ger-

manic-heroic attitude at the end of the drama. Note that
he imagines the next morning as without hope: "more
labor and loss till the land's ruined; / ever work and war
till the world passes" ("Homecoming," p. 17). His is the
harsh First Voice of "Leaf by Niggle" that sought to measure justly by the Law, or the demanding voice of Parish
seeking practical aid and materials from his neighbor
Niggle. A *tertium quid* between the artist-minstrel and the
gardener-farmer or between the Germanic-heroic and the
pre-Christian is announced by a "third voice" from the
future belonging, appropriately, to a warrior and a Christian, a Dane and an Englishman, a king and a lover of
music.[21] Canute, as a Danish king ruling England from
1016 to 1035, commands both hard labor and also enjoyment of art: "Row men, row! Let us listen here a while."

The *tertium quid* is symbolically enhanced by light-
dark imagery. The monks' candles provide some light in
the darkness to brighten the way for those journeying
home, unlike the lanterns of Tídwald and Torhthelm light-
ing their search for corpses but similar to the hearth light
warming the dark for the loyal warriors of Torhthelm's
dream vision. Both forms of light provide hopeful consolation for those doomed to live in this primary world. True,
Torhthelm's ways lead eventually to darkness: as Tídwald
reminds us, "Dark is over all, and dead is master" ("Homecoming," p. 17). But all ends in silence anyway, like this
verse drama. Only in the Other World do light and true
vision occur: the Office of the Dead asks that the Lord lead
us into his presence or his vision ("in conspectu tuo").

The dialogue between artist and farmer here suggests
the conflict between Niggle and Parish in "Leaf by Niggle"
or between Frodo and Sam in *The Lord of the Rings*. Like
the divided self of Bilbo as both Took and Baggins, the
complementary pair also personifies the relationship between soul and body or between the *novus* and the *vetus*

homo. As the young monk and the older "saint militant," the latter couple resurfaces with even more Christian effect in "Imram."

V. "Imram": The Saint Militant

Like Beorhtnoth, Saint Brendan must return home, but "to find the grace to die" ("Imram," p. 1561) after performing heroically on his journey-quest for the Living Land. Mostly, the results of his "voyage" (as the poem is entitled) are described to a younger monastic brother who wants easy answers but who is told to "find for yourself things out of mind." The "king" here is no king at all but a Christian saint modeled upon the *miles Christi* described in Ephesians 6 who is functioning as a knight errant in his search for the home of Elvenkind. The only mention of kingship occurs when Saint Brendan describes the shoreless mountain stretching into what Tolkien terms "the Cloud" and resting on "the foundered land / where the kings of kings lie low" ("Imram," p. 1561). The "kings of kings" are mere mortals destined to die despite their desire for glory on earth, in contrast to this errant monk's desire for the glory of the other world "whence no ship returns"— even though his physical remains, like theirs, reside on earth ("his bones in Ireland lie") ("Imram," p. 1561).

As a saint, Brendan most resembles the Christian king found in the fairy-story, even though this short "imram" represents a parody of the medieval Irish genre and hence *should* invite comparison with the other medieval parodies. Its Christian message imparts the necessity for each human to become a saint militant, to journey on his own quest of the Living Land. Its Christian hero reveals a humility in his failure of memory and strange lassitude hardly characteristic of the proud king or knight of the medieval parody. Its paradise with the Christian symbols of Tree and

Star is, as Paul Kocher has suggested, equivalent to the Living Land of Elvenkind described in the mythology of Middle-earth.

But other elements suggest that the poem must be construed as a hybrid, a transitional work combining aspects of the medieval parody and the fairy-story. After all, the knight-errant in this parody is actually a saint. The elegiac ending focusing on Saint Brendan's death should mark it as "drama" in Tolkien's terms, like other medieval parodies; but the work also includes a consoling vision of a secondary world usually found in the fantasy of "literature" or the fairy-story. But most of all it contrasts a real place in the primary world (Ireland) of the past, usually described only in the parody, with the fantastic land of the other world in its eternal present, usually described only in the fairy-story. Note that this contrast is bolstered by the iconography of the landscapes: the "loud" waves near Ireland are juxtaposed with "silence like dew" falling "in that isle, / and holy it seemed to be"; the "tower tall and grey / the knell of Clúain-ferta's bell / was tolling in green Galway" is juxtaposed with the spire that is "lit with a living fire" and "tall as a column in High Heaven's hall, / its roots were deep as Hell" on the ancient land where "the kings of kings lie low"; finally, the "wood and mire" and "clouded moon" in the "rain-clad sky" of Ireland are juxtaposed with a paradisal white fair Tree with its white birds and surrounding fair flowers redolent of a smell "as sweet and keen as death / that was borne upon the breeze" ("Imram," p. 1561). As a hybrid synthesis of genres and Christian-Germanic themes "Imram" invites comparison with that greatest of Tolkienian works, Tolkien's epic, fusing together in complex orchestration all the motifs and ideas concerning kingship and lordship discussed in this study. In this sense the poem functions as an appropriate transition to *The Lord of the Rings*.

Chapter 5

THE LORD OF THE RINGS

Tolkien's Epic

But as the earliest Tales are seen through Elvish
eyes, as it were, this last great Tale, coming down
from myth and legend to the earth, is seen mainly
through the eyes of Hobbits: it thus becomes in
fact anthropocentric. But through Hobbits, not
Men so-called, because the last Tale is to exemplify
most clearly a recurrent theme: the place in "world
politics" of the unforeseen and unforeseeable acts
of will, and deeds of virtue of the apparently
small, ungreat, forgotten in the places of the Wise
and Great (good as well as evil). . . . [W]ithout the
high and noble the simple and vulgar is utterly
mean; and without the simple and ordinary the
noble and heroic is meaningless.

—J.R.R. Tolkien
Letter 131, to Milton Waldman of Collins (c. 1951)

The Lord of the Rings is of course a fundamentally
religious and Catholic work; unconsciously so at
first, but consciously in the revision.

—J.R.R. Tolkien
Letter 142, to Robert Murray, S.J. (1953)

The epic form has proven useful in reflecting the clash of value systems during periods of transition in literary history. In the Old English *Beowulf,* Germanic heroism conflicts with Christianity: the chivalric pride of the hero can become the excessive *superbia* condemned in Hrothgar's moralistic sermon. Similar conflicts occur in other epics or romance-epics: between the chivalric and the Christian in the twelfth-century German *Nibelungenlied* and in Sir Thomas Malory's fifteenth-century *Le Morte d'Arthur;* between the classical and the Christian in the sixteenth-century *Faerie Queene* of Edmund Spenser; and between chivalric idealism and modern realism in the late-sixteenth-century Spanish epic-novel of Cervantes, *Don Quixote.* Tolkien's *Lord of the Rings* delineates a clash of values during the passage from the Third Age of Middle-earth, dominated by the Elves, to the Fourth Age, dominated by Men. Such values mask very medieval tensions between Germanic heroism and Christianity evidenced earlier by Tolkien in his *Beowulf* article.

In this sense *The Lord of the Rings* resembles *The Hobbit,* which, as we have seen previously, must acknowledge a great thematic and narrative debt to the Old English epic, even though *The Hobbit*'s happy ending renders it closer to fantasy in Tolkien's definition than to the elegy with its tragic ending. The difference between the two most significant Tolkienian works stems from form: Randel Helms notes that the children's story narrated by the patronizing adult in *The Hobbit* has "grown up" sufficiently to require no fictionalized narrator in the text itself and to inhabit a more expansive and flexible genre like the epic: "[W]e have in *The Hobbit* and its sequel what is in fact the same story, told first very simply, and then again, very intricately. Both works have the same theme, a quest on which a most unheroic hobbit achieves heroic stature; they have the same structure, the 'there and back again' of the quest romance, and both extend the quest through the cycle of one year, *The Hobbit* from spring to spring, the *Rings* from fall to fall."[1] Although Helms does not mention their relationship with medieval ideas or even with the *Beowulf* article, still, given this reworking of a theme used earlier in *The Hobbit*, I would speculate that *The Lord of the Rings* must also duplicate many medieval ideas from *The Hobbit* and elsewhere in Tolkien.

As an epic novel *The Lord of the Rings* constitutes, then, a summa of Tolkien's full development of themes originally enunciated in the *Beowulf* article and fictionalized later in other works. It was, after all, begun in 1937—the same year *The Hobbit* was published and a year later than the *Beowulf* article—and completed in 1949, prior to the publication of many of the fairy-stories (1945–67) and the medieval parodies (1945–62). Its medial position in Tolkien's career indicates how he articulated his major ideas generally and comprehensively in this mammoth work before delving into their more specialized aspects in the later fairy-stories and parodies.

As a synthesis of Tolkienian ideas, both Germanic heroic or medieval and Christian, the *Lord of the Rings* reconciles value systems over which its critics have debated incessantly and single-mindedly. Some critics have explored its major medieval literary sources, influences, and parallels, particularly in relation to northern saga and Old and Middle English literature, language, and culture, chiefly *Beowulf* and *Sir Gawain and the Green Knight*.[2] Other critics have explored its direct and indirect religious, moral, or Christian (Roman Catholic) aspects.[3] No one seems to have understood fully how the dual levels of the *Beowulf* article might apply to *The Lord of the Rings*, although Patricia Meyer Spacks suggests provocatively that at least one level does apply: Tolkien's view of the "naked will and courage" necessary to combat chaos and death in the context of northern mythology (as opposed to Christianity) resembles the similar epic weapons of the Hobbit-heroes of his trilogy.[4] In addition, no critic has seemed to notice that even in genre and form this work combines an explicitly medieval bias (as epic, romance, or *chanson de geste*) with an implicitly Christian one (as fantasy or fairy-story).[5] The most interesting and most discussed genre has been that of medieval romance, with its tales of knights and lords battling with various adversaries. [6]

Its title, *The Lord of the Rings*, introduces the ambiguous role of the ruler as a leader ("The Lord") with power over but also responsibility for others ("the Rings"). Elsewhere in Tolkien's critical and creative works the lord has been depicted as an excessively proud Germanic warrior bent on the sacrifice of his men for his own ends (for example, "The Homecoming of Beorhtnoth Beorhthelm's Son"), or as a humble Elf-king modeled on Christ, intent on sacrificing himself for the sake of his followers (for example, "Smith of Wootton Major"). So in this epic Sauron typifies the Germanic lord in his monstrous use of his slaves as Gandalf typifies the Elf-king or Christ-figure in his self-sacrifice during the battle with the Balrog. But there are hierarchies of both monstrous and heroic lords in this epic, whose plenitude has frustrated critical attempts to discern *the* hero as either Aragorn, Frodo, or Sam—or, including Gollum, all four.[7] Aragorn may represent the Christian hero as Frodo and Sam represent the more Germanic hero—that is, the subordinate warrior—yet all three remain epic heroes. The complexity of Tolkien's system of heroic and monstrous "lords" in the trilogy becomes clearer through an examination of its structural unity.

In defining the parameters of the work's structure,[8] Tolkien declares that "[t]he only units of any structural significance are the books. These originally had each its title."[9] This original plan was followed in the publication in 1999 of the Millennium edition, with its seven slim volumes, one for each renamed book and the appendices: book 1 is "The Ring Sets Out"; book 2, "The Ring Goes South"; book 3, "The Treason of Isengard"; book 4, "The Ring Goes East"; book 5, "The War of the Ring"; book 6, "The End of the Third Age"; and book 7, "Appendices." Apparently Tolkien had initially substituted titles for each of the three parts at the instigation of his publisher, although he preferred to regard it as a "three-decker novel" instead of as a "trilogy" in order to establish it as a single, unified work, not three separate works.[10] But in either case, with six books or with three parts, the title of each thematically and symbolically supports the crowning title, "The Lord of the Rings," by revealing some aspect of the adversary or the hero through a related but subordinate title that fixes on the Ring's movements and the ambiguity of its "owner" or "bearer," and each of the three parts is itself supported thematically and symbolically by its two-book division.

In *The Fellowship of the Ring* the focus falls upon the lord as what might be termed both a hero and a monster, a divided self discussed in chapter 1, "The Critic as Monster." Frodo as the "lord" or keeper of the Ring in the first part mistakes the chief threat to the Hobbit Fellowship (a symbol of community) as physical and external (for example, the Black Riders) but matures enough to learn by the end of the second book that the chief threat exists in a more dangerous spiritual and internal form, whether within him as microcosm (the hero as monster) or within the Fellowship as macrocosm (his friend Boromir). *The Fellowship* as bildungsroman echoes the development of the hero Bilbo in *The Hobbit* discussed in chapter 2, "The King under the Mountain."

The Two Towers shifts attention from the divided self

of the hero as monster to the more specifically Germanic but also Christian monster seen in Saruman (representing intellectual sin in book 3) and Shelob (representing physical sin in book 4), who occupy or guard the two towers of the title. This part duplicates material in *The Hobbit* outlining monstrosity in terms of the *Beowulf* article and the *Ancrene Wisse* discussed primarily in chapter 2, "The King under the Mountain."

The evil Germanic lord often has a good warrior to serve him; the figure of the good servant merges with the Christian king healer (Aragorn) who dominates *The Return of the King* in opposition to the Germanic destroyer (Denethor) in book 5, the consequences of whose reign lead to a "Return," or regeneration within the macrocosm, in book 6. Ideas in this last part mirror chapter 3's "Christian King" appearing in fairy-stories and chapter 4's "Germanic Lord" appearing in medieval parodies. The structure of the epic then reveals a hierarchy of heroes and monsters implied by its title but also summoned from Tolkien's other critical and creative works.

I. *The Fellowship of the Ring:*
The Hero as Monster

Because the title of *The Fellowship of the Ring* links the wandering "Fellowship" with the "Ring" of *The Lord of the Rings,* a subtitle for the first part of the epic might be "All that is gold does not glitter, / Not all those who wander are lost."[11] Thematically, the title and its "subtitle" suggest that appearance does not equal reality: the Ring appears valuable because it glitters; the wandering Fellowship appears lost. But in reality the gold Ring may not be as valuable as it appears and the Fellowship may not be lost; further, the wanderer to whom the lines refer, despite his swarthy exterior and wandering behavior as Strider the

Ranger, may be real gold and definitely not lost. As the king of light opposed to the Dark Lord, Strider returns as king after the Ring has been finally returned to Mount Doom, ending the aspirations of the Lord of the Rings. *The Fellowship of the Ring* as a title stresses the heroic mission of Aragorn's "followers" to advance the cause of the good king. The band of gold represents by synecdoche the power of the evil Lord of the Rings, to be countered by the "band" of the Fellowship, whether the four Hobbits in book 1 or the larger Fellowship of Hobbits, Wizard (Istar, most likely a Vala), Elf, Dwarf, and Man in book 2.

Because the Fellowship is burdened with the responsibility of bearing the Ring and because its presence attracts evil, the greatest threat to the Fellowship and its mission comes not from without but within. The hero must realize that he can become a monster. The two books of the *Fellowship* trace the process of this realization: the first book centers on the presentation of evil as external and physical, requiring physical heroism to combat it; and the second book centers on the presentation of evil as internal and spiritual, requiring a spiritual heroism to combat it. The hero matures by coming to understand the character of good and evil—specifically, by descending into an underworld and then ascending into an overworld, a natural one in the first book and a supernatural one in the second. The second book, then, functions as a mirror image of the first. These two levels correspond to the two levels—Germanic and Christian—of *Beowulf* and *The Hobbit*. For Frodo, as for Beowulf and Bilbo, the ultimate enemy is himself.

Tolkien immediately defines "the hero as monster" by introducing the divided self of Gollum-Sméagol and, then, to ensure the reader's understanding of the hero as monster, Bilbo-as-Gollum. The Cain-like Sméagol rationalizes the murder of his cousin Deagol for the gold Ring he holds because it is his birthday (*LR*, 1:84). Sméagol deserves a gift, something "precious" like the Ring, because the occasion celebrates the fact of his birth, his special being. The parable of Sméagol's fall illustrates the nature of evil as *cupiditas*, or avarice, in the classical and literal sense. But as the root of all evil (in the words of Chaucer's Pardoner, alluding to St. Paul's letter to Timothy), *cupiditas* more generally and medievally represents that Augustinian selfishness usually personified as strong desire in the figure of Cupid (=cupidity, concupiscence or desire). The two names, Gollum and Sméagol, dramatize the fragmenting and divisive consequences of his fall into vice, the "Gollum" the bestial sound of his swallowing as an expression of his gluttony and greed, the "Sméagol," in its homonymic similarity to "Deagol," linking him to a group of others like him (the Stoors, as a third family-type of Hobbit) to establish his common Hobbitness—and heroism.[12] That is, Gollum's psychological resemblance to the Hobbits is revealed when good overpowers the evil in him and, as he witnesses his master Frodo asleep in Sam's lap, he reaches out a hand to touch his knee in a caress. At that moment he seems "an old weary hobbit, shrunken by the years that had carried him far beyond his time, beyond friends and kin, and the fields and streams of youth, an old starved pitiable thing" (*LR*, 2:411).

But also, Tolkien takes care to present the good Hobbit and heroic Bilbo as a divided self, "stretched thin" into a Gollum-like being because of his years carrying the Ring. The scene opens after all with Bilbo's birthday party, to reenact the original fall of Gollum, on his birthday. The role of Deagol is played by Bilbo's nephew Frodo: on Bilbo's birthday, instead of receiving a gift, Bilbo, like Gollum, must give away a gift—to the other Hobbit relatives and friends and to Frodo, recipient of the Ring. But at the moment of bequest Bilbo retreats into a Gollum-like personality as illustrated by similar speech patterns: "It is mine, I tell you. My own. My precious. Yes, my precious" (*LR*, 1:59). Bilbo refuses to give away the Ring because he feels himself to be more deserving and Frodo less deserving of carrying it. Later the feeling is described as a realization of the Other as monstrous (presumably with the concomitant belief in the self as good). In the parallel scene at the beginning of book 2, Bilbo wishes to see the Ring, and so he reaches out a hand for Frodo to give it to him; Frodo reacts violently because "a shadow seemed to have fallen between them, and through it he found himself eyeing *a little wrinkled creature with a hungry face and bony groping hands*. He felt a desire to strike him" (*LR*, 1:306; my italics). The Ring, then, a sign of imperial or ecclesiastical power in medieval contexts and a sign of the conjugal bond in personal and familial contexts, appropriately symbolizes here the slavish obeisance of Sméagol to Gollum and a wedding of self to self, in lieu of a true wedding of self to Other.

That is, wedding the self to Other implies a giving up of selfishness out of love and concern for another being. An expression of such *caritas* is hinted at in Gollum's momentary return to Hobbitness, when he seems to show love for his master Frodo, and is symbolized by the "band" of the Fellowship to which each member belongs—another "Ring." Such *caritas* opposes the view of the Other as monstrous. Even Frodo at first sees monstrous Gollum as despicable: "What a pity that Bilbo did not stab that vile creature when he had a chance!" (*LR*, 1:92). But just as the hero can become monstrous, so also can the monster become heroic: it is Gollum who helps Frodo and Sam across the Dead Marshes and, more important, who inadvertently saves Frodo from himself; Gollum also saves Middle-earth by biting the Ring off Frodo's finger as they stand on the precipice of Mount Doom in the third part. Therefore,

Gandalf cautions Frodo to feel toward the despicable Gollum not wrath or hatred but love as pity, as Bilbo has manifested toward Gollum: "Pity? It was Pity that stayed his hand. Pity, and Mercy: not to strike without need" (*LR*, 1:92). Gandalf explains: "Many that live deserve death. And some that die deserve life. Can you give it to them? Then do not be too eager to deal out death in judgment. For even the very wise cannot see all ends. I have not much hope that Gollum can be cured before he dies, but there is a chance of it. And he is bound up with the fate of the Ring. My heart tells me that he has some part to play yet, for good or ill, before the end; and when that comes, the pity of Bilbo may rule the fate of many—yours not least" (*LR*, 1:93). This pity as charity, or love binding one individual to another, cements together the "fellowship" of the Hobbits in book 1 and later, in book 2, the differing species who form the enlarged Fellowship. The "chain of love" such fellowship creates contrasts with the chains of enslavement represented by Sauron's one Ring. Described as "fair" in the Middle Ages, the chain of love supposedly bound one individual to another and as well bound together the macrocosm of the heavens: Boethius in *The Consolation of Philosophy* terms it a "common bond of love by which all things seek to be held to the goal of the good."[13] After Boethius explains that "love binds together people joined by a sacred bond; love binds sacred marriages by chaste affections; love makes the laws which join true friends," he wistfully declares, "O how happy the human race would be, if that love which rules the heavens rules also your souls!" (*The Consolation of Philosophy*, book 2, poem 8, p. 41).

The chain of enslavement, in contrast, involves a hierarchy of power, beginning with the "One Ring to rule them all, One Ring to find them, / One Ring to bring them all and in the darkness bind them" (*LR*, 1:vii), and encompassing the seven Dwarf-rings (could they be found) and the nine rings of the "Mortal Men doomed to die," the Ringwraiths.[14] If love binds together the heavens and the hierarchy of species known in the Middle Ages as the Great Chain of Being—which includes angels, humankind, beasts, birds, fish, plants, and stones—then hate and envy and pride and avarice bind together the hierarchy of species under the aegis of the One Ring of Sauron the fallen Vala. Only the "Three Rings for the Elven-kings under the sky"—the loftiest and most noble species—were never made by Sauron because, says Elrond, the Elves "did not desire strength or domination or hoarded wealth, but understanding, making, and healing, to preserve all things sustained" (*LR*, 1:352).

Tolkien intentionally contrasts the hierarchy of good characters, linked by the symbolic value of fellowship into an invisible band or chain of love, with the hierarchy of evil characters and fallen characters linked by the literal rings of enslavement—a chain of sin.[15] It is for this reason that the miniature Fellowship of Hobbits in the first book draws together in love different representatives from the Hobbit "species" or families—Baggins, Took, Brandybuck, Gamgee—as the larger Fellowship in the second book draws together representatives from different species—the four Hobbit representatives, Gimli the Dwarf, Strider and Boromir the Men, Legolas the Elf, and Gandalf the Wizard (Istar, Vala). In both cases, however, these representatives are young—the heirs of the equivalents of the "old men" who must revitalize and renew Middle-earth because it too has become "old" and decrepit, governed by the spiritually old and corrupt influence of Sauron. Symbolically, then, these "heirs," as the young, represent vitality, life, newness: Frodo is Bilbo's nephew and heir, Gimli is Groin's, Legolas is Thranduil's, Strider is Isildur's, Boromir is Denethor's, and the remaining Hobbits are the still youthful heirs of their aged fathers. Only Gandalf as the good counterpart to Sauron is "old." In part Gandalf constitutes a spiritual guide for Frodo, especially in book 2, as Aragorn-Strider constitutes a physical (literally powerful) guide in book 1.

The necessity for the young figure to become the savior hero (like the *novus homo*) of the old is introduced by Tolkien in the first pages of *The Fellowship.* Note the spiritual oldness of the fathers of the miniature "Fellowship" of Hobbits: the old Hobbits view those who are different, or "queer," as alien, evil, monstrous, or dangerous because the fathers themselves lack charity, pity, and understanding. They condemn the Brandybucks of Buckland as a "queer breed" for engaging in unnatural (at least for Hobbits) activities on water (*LR*, 1:45).Yet these old Hobbits are not evil, merely "old." Even the Gaffer vindicates Bag End and its "queer folk" by admitting, "There's some not far away that wouldn't offer a pint a beer to a friend, if they lived in a hole with golden walls. But they do things proper at Bag End" (*LR*, 1:47). Gaffer's literalness—his "oldness"—is characteristic of the Old Law of justice (note Gaffer's term "proper") rather than the New Law of mercy. Such old Hobbits also lack imagination, an awareness of the spirit rather than the letter. Sam's father expresses a literalism and earthiness similar to Sauron's: "'*Elves and dragons*'! I says to him, '*Cabbages and potatoes are better for me and you*'" (*LR*, 1:47). This "Old Man" Tolkien casts in the role of what might be termed the "Old Adam," for whom Christ as the New Adam will function as a replacement and redeemer. A gardener like Adam at Bag End, Gaffer condemns that of which he cannot conceive and accepts that of which he can—cabbages and potatoes—and presents his condemnation in the appropriately named inn, the "Ivy Bush." Although his son Sam is different and will become in effect the New Adam of the

Shire by the trilogy's end, generally, however, earthbound Hobbits (inhabiting holes underground) display a similar lack of imagination, symbolized by their delight in the pyrotechnic dragon created by Gandalf. They may not be able to imagine Elves and dragons, but they love what they can *see*, a "terribly lifelike" dragon leaving nothing to the imagination (*LR*, 1:52). This dragon, however, unlike that in *Beowulf*, poses no threat to their lives. In fact, it represents the "signal for supper."

The "New Man" represented by the Hobbits Frodo, Sam, Merry, and Pippin then must overcome a natural inclination toward "oldness," toward the life of the senses inherent in the Hobbit love of food, comfort, warm shelter, entertainment, and good tobacco. All of the Hobbits do so by the trilogy's end, but Frodo as Ring-bearer changes the most dramatically and centrally by the end of *The Fellowship*. His education, both oral lessons from guides and moral and life-threatening experiences, begins with the gift of the Ring after Bilbo's birthday party.

Designated as Bilbo's heir and recipient of the Ring at the birthday party (chapters 1–5) in the first book, Frodo is also designated as the official Ring-bearer after the Council of Elrond (chapters 1–3) in the second book, to which it is parallel. In the first book Gandalf relates the history of Gollum's discovery of the Ring and Bilbo's winning of it, and he explains its nature and properties. In the second book, at this similar gathering, the history of the Ring, from its creation by Sauron to the present, and the involvement therein of various species are related. The birthday party that allows Bilbo to "disappear" as if by magic from the Shire is like the council that allows Frodo and other members of the Fellowship to "disappear" as if by magic from Middle-earth—and from the searching Eye of Sauron, for the Dark Lord will never imagine them carrying the Ring *back* to Mordor. Further, the distribution of gifts to friends and relatives after the party resembles the council's decision to give back the "gift" of the Ring to its "relative," the mother lode of Mount Doom. The gifts in each episode make explicit the flaws of the recipient: Adelard Took, for example, receives an umbrella because he has stolen so many from Bilbo. In a sense Sauron too will indirectly receive exactly what he has always wanted and has continually tried to usurp or steal—the Ring. The point of these parallels should be clear: the concept of the divided self or the hero as monster was revealed in the symbolic birthday party through the figures of Gollum-Sméagol, Bilbo-Gollum, Frodo-Gollum—the hero as monster suggested by the notion of the "birthday." For the reader, Tolkien warns that the most dangerous evil really springs from inside, not from outside.

This message introduced at the beginning of the *Fellowship of the Ring* is what Frodo must learn by its end. The "Council of Elrond," its very title suggesting egalitarian debate among members of a community rather than group celebration of an individual, symbolically poses the converse message, that the most beneficial good similarly springs from the inside but must be directed to the community rather than to oneself. The humble member of the council—the insignificant Hobbit Frodo—is ultimately chosen to pursue the mission of the Ring because he *is* insignificant.[16] Frodo's insignificance in the community there contrasts with Bilbo's significance as a member of the Shire community. However, as the chapter of "A Long-Expected Party" (or what might be called "The Birthday Party") had dramatized the presence of evil among inheritance-seeking relatives (specifically the greedy and self-aggrandizing Sackville-Bagginses), so the "Council of Elrond" indicates the potential of evil threatening the Fellowship from within through the greed and self-aggrandizement of some of its members—Men like Boromir.

In the first book Frodo comes to understand evil as external and physical through the descent into the Old Forest, a parallel underworld to the supernatural underworld of Moria[17] in the second book. Both Old Man Willow and the barrow-wights represent the natural process of death caused, in Christian terms, by the Fall of Man.[18] Originally the Old Forest consisted of the "fathers of the fathers of trees," whose "countless years had filled them with pride and rooted wisdom, and with malice" (LR, 1:181), as if they had sprung from the one Tree of Knowledge of Good and Evil in Eden. The ensuing history of human civilization after the Fall of Adam and Eve resulted in similar falls and deaths: "There was victory and defeat; and towers fell, fortresses were burned, and flames went up into the sky. Gold was piled on the biers of dead kings and queens; and mounds covered them and the stone doors were shut and the grass grew over all" (LR, 1:181). As Old Man Willow and his malice represent the living embodiment of the parent Tree of Death, so the barrow-wights represent the ghostly embodiment of the dead parent civilizations of Men: "Barrow-wights walked in the hollow places with a clink of rings on cold fingers, and gold chains in the wind" (LR, 1:181). The Hobbits' first clue to the character of the Old Forest (note again Tolkien's emphasis on oldness) resides in the falling of the Hobbits' spirits—a "dying" of merriment—when they first enter. Their fear, depression, and gloom are followed by the deathlike sleep (again, a result of the Fall) as the chief weapon of Old Man Willow (LR, 1:165). All growth in Nature is abetted by sleep and ends in death, usually after oldness (again, the Old Man Willow figure). The barrow-wights who attack the Hobbits later in the Old Forest are also linked to the earth, like the roots of Old Man Willow, but here through the barrow, a Man-made grave which they inhabit as ghosts. The song of the barrow-wights invokes coldness and death, literally, the "bed" of the human grave, where "Cold be hand and heart and bone, / and cold be sleep under stone" (*LR*, 1:195).

The attacks of the Old Man Willow and the barrow-wights on the Hobbits are stopped by Tom Bombadil and his mate Goldberry, who personify their complementary and positive counterparts in Nature. [19] The principle of growth and revivification of all living things balances the process of mutability and death: what Goldberry lauds as "spring-time and summer-time, and spring again after!" (*LR*, 1:173), omitting autumn and winter as antithetical seasons. Tom Bombadil as master of trees, grasses, and the living things of the land (*LR*, 1:174) complements the "fair river-daughter" dressed in a gown "green as young reeds, shot with silver like beads of dew," her feet surrounded by water-lilies (*LR*, 1:172). Because their role in Nature involves the maintenance of the existing order, their songs often praise the Middle-earth equivalent of the medieval Chain of Being:

> Let us sing together
> Of sun, stars, moon and mist, rain and cloudy
>   weather,
> Light on the budding leaf, dew on the feather,
> Wind on the open hill, bells on the heather,
> Reeds by the shady pool, lilies on the water:
> Old Tom Bombadil and the River-daughter!
> (*LR*, 1:171)

As the Old Forest depresses the Hobbits, Tom Bombadil cheers them up so much that, by the time they reach his house, "half their weariness and all their fears had fallen from them" (*LR*, 1:171). It is no accident that Tom Bombadil always seems to be laughing and singing joyously.

Frodo learns from the descent into this underworld

of the Old Forest that the presence of mutability, change, and death in the world is natural and continually repaired by growth and new life. In the second book he learns through a parallel descent into the Mines of Moria that the spiritual form of death represented by sin stems from within the individual but is redeemed by the "new life" of wisdom and virtue counseled by Galadriel, the supernatural equivalent of Tom Bombadil, who resides in the paradisal Lothlórien. The descent also involves a return to the tragic past of the Dwarves, who fell because of the "oldness" of their kings, their avarice; the ascent involves an encounter with the eternal presence of Lothlórien, where all remains new and young, and filled with the healing spirit of Elven mercy and *caritas*.

The Dwarves led by both Durin and later Balin fell because of their greed for the jewels mined in Moria[20]— its depths a metaphorical equivalent of Old Man Willow's buried roots and the deep barrows inhabited by the wights. But unlike the sense of material death pervading the Old Forest, the death associated with the Mines of Moria is voluntary because it is spiritual in nature and one chooses it or at least fails to resist its temptation: this spiritual death exists in the form of avarice. Gandalf declares that "even as *mithril* was the foundation of their wealth, so also was their destruction: they delved too greedily and too deep, and disturbed that from which they fled, Durin's Bane" (*LR*, 1:413). Durin's Bane, the Balrog, monstrously projects the Dwarves' internal vice, which resurfaces later to overpower other Dwarves, including Balin. It is no accident that Balin dies at Mirrormere, a very dark mirror in which he is blind to himself. His mistaken goal of *mithril* and jewels contrasts with that of the Elves of Lórien, whose Galadriel possesses a clear mirror wisdom.

Lórien of the Blossom boasts an Eternal Spring where "ever bloom the winter flowers in the unfading grass" (*LR*,

1:454), a "vanished world" where the shapes and colors are pristine and new, for "[n]o blemish or sickness or deformity could be seen in anything, that grew upon the earth. On the land of Lórien there was no stain" (*LR*, 1:454–55). [21] In this paradise of restoration, like that of Niggle in "Leaf by Niggle," time almost ceases to pass and seems even to reverse, so that "the grim years were removed from the face of Aragorn, and he seemed clothed in white, a young lord tall and fair" (*LR*, 1:456). Evil does not exist in this land nor in Galadriel unless brought in from the outside (*LR*, 1:464). The physical and spiritual regeneration, or "life," characteristic of these Elves is embodied in their *lembas,* a food that restores spirits and lasts exceedingly long—a type of communion offered to the weary travelers. Other gifts of the Lady Galadriel—the rope, magic cloaks, golden hairs, phial of light, seeds of *elanor*—later aid them either physically or spiritually at times of crisis in their quest, almost as a type of Christian grace in material form. [22] Like Adam and Eve forced to leave paradise for the wilderness, although taking with them its memory as a paradise within, "happier far," in Miltonic terms, the travelers leave Lórien knowing "the danger of light and joy" (*LR*, 1:490). Legolas reminds Gimli the Dwarf that "the least reward that you shall have is that the memory of Lothlórien shall remain ever clear and unstained in your heart, and shall neither fade nor grow stale" (*LR*, 1:490). Gimli's Dwarfish and earthbound nature compels him to deny the therapeutic value of memory: "Memory is not what the heart desires. That is only a mirror, be it clear as Kheled-zâram" (*LR*, 1:490). The mirror to which he refers in Westron is called "Mirrormere" and, instead of reflecting back the faces of gazers, portrays only the reflection of a crown of stars representing Durin's own destructive desire. In contrast, the Mirror of Galadriel with its vision of the Eternal Present, connoting supernatural wisdom, invites the gazer to "see" or understand himself, however unpleasant. Gimli is wrong; memory *is* a mirror and reflects back the consolation of truth, at least for those wise and steadfast beings like the Elves, whose "memory is more like to the waking world than to a dream. Not so for Dwarves" (*LR,* 1:490).

This lesson in natural and supernatural evil and good also functions as a mirror for Frodo to see himself. He must learn there is both Dwarf and Elf in his heart, a Mines of Moria and Lothlórien buried in his psyche. Having learned, he must then exercise free will in choosing either good or evil, usually experienced in terms of putting on or taking off the Ring at times of external or internal danger. While his initial exercises are fraught with mistakes in judgment, the inability to distinguish impulse from deliberation or an external summons from an internal decision, eventually he does learn to control his own desires and resist the will of others. Told by Gandalf to fling the Ring into the fire after just receiving it, "with an effort of will he made a movement, as if to cast it away—but he found that he had put it back in his pocket" (*LR,* 1:94). As Frodo practices he grows more adept but still slips: at the Inn of the Prancing Pony, his attempt at singing and dancing to divert the attention of Pippin's audience from the tale of Bilbo's birthday party allows him to become so "pleased with himself" that he puts on the Ring by mistake and becomes embarrassingly invisible. The physical dangers Frodo faces in these encounters culminate in the attack of the Black Riders one night and later at the Ford. The Ring in the first instance so controls his will that "his terror swallowed up in a sudden temptation to put on the Ring, desire to do this laid hold of him, and he could think of nothing else. . . . [A]t last he slowly drew out the chain, and slipped the Ring on the forefinger of his left hand" (*LR,* 1:262–63). As a consequence, Frodo can see the Ringwraiths as they really are, but, unfortunately, they can also see him, enough to wound him in the shoulder. The worst test in the first book involves the encounter at the Ford. Counseled first by Gandalf to "Ride" from the Black Rider attacking them, Frodo is then counseled silently by the Riders to wait. When his strength to refuse diminishes, he is saved first by Glorfindel, who addressed his horse in Elvish to flee, and again by Gandalf, who drowns the horses of the Black Riders when they prevent Frodo's horse from crossing the Ford.

While Frodo fails these major tests in the first book and must rely on various manifestations of a deus ex machina to save himself, his established valor and courage represent the first steps to attaining the higher form of heroism expressed by wisdom and self-control in the second book, a heroism very like that Germanic form exhibited by Beowulf in the epic of the same name.[23] Frodo's physical heroism evolves in the combat with physical dangers in book 1: his cry for help when Merry is caught by Old Man Willow; his stabbing of the barrow-wight's hand as it nears the bound Sam; his dancing and singing to protect Pippin and their mission from discovery; his stabbing of the foot of one Rider during the night-attack; and his valor (brandishing his sword) and courage (refusing to put on the Ring, telling the Riders to return to Mordor) at the edge of the Ford. But this last incident reveals Frodo's spiritual naïveté: he believes physical gestures of heroism will ward off the Black Riders.

Only after Frodo's education in the second book, which details supernatural death and regeneration instead of its more natural and physical forms, as in the first book, does he begin to understand the necessity of *sapientia*, in addition to that heroism expressed by the concept of *fortitudo*. In the last chapter, "The Breaking of the Fellowship," he faces a threat from the proud and avaricious

Boromir *within* the macrocosm of the Fellowship. Fleeing from him, Frodo puts on the Ring to render himself invisible and safe. But this unwise move allows him to see clearly (too clearly) as he sits, symbolically, upon the Seat of Seeing atop Amon Hen ("Hill of the Eye"), built by the kings of Gondor, the searching of Sauron's own Eye.[24] What results is a second internal danger—the threat from *within* Frodo, the microcosm. A battle is staged within his psyche, and he is pulled first one way, then another, until, as a fully developed moral hero, he exercises the faculty of free will with complete self-control: "He heard himself crying out: *Never, never!* Or was it: *Verily I come, I come to you?* He could not tell. Then as a flash from some other point of power there came to his mind another thought: *Take it off! Take it off! Fool, take it off! Take off the Ring!*" He feels the struggle of the "two powers" within him: "For a moment, perfectly balanced between their piercing points, he writhed, tormented. Suddenly he was aware of himself again. Frodo, neither the Voice nor the Eye: free to choose, and with one remaining instant in which to do so. He took the Ring off his finger" (*LR*, 1:519). In this incident, parallel to the encounter of the Riders at the Ford in the last chapter of the first book, Frodo rescues *himself* instead of being rescued by Glorfindel or Gandalf. Further, in proving his moral education by the realization that he must wage his own quest alone to protect both their mission and the other members of the Fellowship, he displays *fortitudo et sapientia* (fortitude and wisdom) and *caritas* (charity)—hence, he acts as that savior of the Fellowship earlier witnessed in the figures of Tom Bombadil and Strider in the first book and Gandalf and Galadriel in the second. His education complete, Frodo can now function as a hero for he understands he may, at any time, become a "monster."

The turning point in the narrative allows a shift in

Tolkien's theme and the beginning of the second part of the epic novel in *The Two Towers*. The remaining members of the Fellowship are divided into two separate groups in this next book, a division symbolizing thematically not only the nature of conflict in battle in the macrocosm but also the psychic fragmentation resulting from evil. It is no mistake that the title is "The Two Towers"—the double, again, symptomatic of the divided self. There are not only two towers but two monsters.

II. *THE TWO TOWERS:* THE GERMANIC KING

The two towers of the title belong to Saruman and in a sense to Shelob because the quest of the remainder of the Fellowship in book 3 culminates in an attack on Orthanc and because the quest of Frodo and Sam in book 4 leads to their "attack" on Cirith Ungol, the sentry tower at the border of Mordor guarded by the giant spider.[25] Both Orthanc and Cirith Ungol copy the greatest tower of all, the Dark Tower of Sauron described as a "fortress, armory, prison, furnace . . . secure in its pride and its immeasurable strength" (*LR,* 2:204). Through these two monsters represented by their towers, this second part of *The Lord of the Rings* defines the nature of evil in greater detail than the first part. Thus, it also introduces the notion of the Christian deadly sins embodied in the monsters (found in the *Ancrene Wisse*), which must be combated by very Germanic heroes.[26]

The tower image is informed by the Tower of Babel in Genesis 11. In this biblical passage, at first, "[t]hroughout the earth men spoke the same language, with the same vocabulary," but then the sons of Noah built a town and "a tower with its top reaching heaven." They decided, "Let us make a name for ourselves, so that we may not be scattered about the whole earth."[27] Their desire to reach heaven and "make a name" for themselves represents the same desire of Adam and Eve for godhead. Because these men believe "[t]here will be nothing too hard for them to do" (11:6–7), the Lord frustrates their desire by "confusing" their language and scattering them over the earth. Their overweening ambition and self-aggrandizement result in division of and chaos within the nation.

Selfishness, or *cupiditas,* symbolized by the Tower of Babel, shows how a preoccupation with self at the expense of the Other or of God can lead to confusion, alienation, division. The recurring symbolism of *The Two Towers* in Tolkien's work helps to break down this idea of *cupiditas,* or perversion of self. The Tower of Saruman, or Orthanc, means "Mount Fang" in Elvish but "Cunning Mind" in the language of the Mark, to suggest perversion of the mind; the Tower of Shelob, or Cirith Ungol, means "Pass of the Spider" to suggest perversion of the body. While the creation of the Tower of Babel results in differing languages to divide the peoples, the two towers in Tolkien express division in a more microcosmic sense, in terms of the separation and perversion of the two parts of the self. Saruman's intellectual perversion has shaped his tower (formerly inhabited by the wardens of Gondor) to "his shifting purposes, and made it better, as he thought, being deceived—for all those arts and subtle devices, for which he forsook his former wisdom, and which fondly he imagined were his own, came but from Mordor" (*LR,* 2:204). Specifically, the pride and envy of Sauron impel him to achieve ever more power as his avarice impels him to seek the Ring and conquer more lands and forests through wrathful wars. Like Saruman, Shelob "served none but herself" but in a very different, more bestial way, by "drinking the blood of Elves and Men, bloated and grown fat with endless brooding on her feasts, weaving webs of shadow; for all living things were her food, and her vomit darkness" (*LR*, 2:422). Her gluttony is revealed in her insatiable appetite, her sloth in her demands that others bring her food, and her lechery in her many bastards (perhaps appropriately and symbolically quelled by Sam's penetration of her belly with his sword). Never can Shelob achieve the higher forms of perversion manifested by Saruman: "Little she knew of or cared for towers, or rings, or anything devised by mind or hand, who only desired death for all others, mind and body, and for herself a glut of life, alone, swollen till the mountains could no longer hold her up" (*LR*, 2:423). Guarding the gateway to Mordor at Cirith Ungol, Shelob suggests another guardian—of the gateway to Hell. In Milton's *Paradise Lost*, Satan's daughter Sin mated with her father to beget Death, the latter of whom pursued her lecherous charms relentlessly and incessantly.[28] In this case, Shelob is depicted not as Satan's daughter but as Sauron's cat (*LR*, 2:424).

Tolkien shows the analogy between the two monsters and their towers by structuring their books similarly. The perversion of mind embodied in Saruman is expressed by the difficulty in communication through or understanding of words or gestures in book 3, and the perversion of body personified in Shelob is expressed by the difficulty in finding food and shelter, or hospitality, in book 4. Specifically, Wormtongue, Grishnákh, and Saruman all display aspects of the higher sins of pride, avarice, envy, and wrath through their incomprehension or manipulation of language. Gollum and Shelob both illustrate the lower sins of gluttony, sloth, and lechery. Each book centers on the adventures of only part of the Fellowship, the nobler members in book 3 (Legolas, Gimli, Aragorn, and Merry and Pippin) and the more humble members in book 4 (Sam and Frodo). In each book, too, the adventures progressively become more dangerous, the enemies encountered more vicious.

The Uruk-hai in book 3 illustrate the disorder and contention caused by the literal failure to understand languages. When Pippin first awakens after being captured, he can understand only some of the Orcs' language: "Apparently the members of two or three quite different tribes were present, and they could not understand one another's orc-speech. There was an angry debate concerning what they were to do now: which way they were to take and what should be done with the prisoners" (*LR*, 2:60); debate advances to quarrel and then to murder when Saruman's Uglúk of the Uruk-hai kills two of Sauron's Orcs led by Grishnákh. The parable suggests that the tongues of different species of peoples create misunderstanding and hence conflict, disorder, and death, because of the inability to transcend selfish interests. Because they do not adhere to a common purpose, their enmity allows the Hobbits their freedom when Grishnákh's desire for the Ring overcomes his judgment and he unties the Hobbits just before his death.

This literal failure to communicate is followed in book 3 by the description of a deliberate manipulation of language so that misunderstanding will occur. Wormtongue's ill counsel renders the king impotent and his people leaderless. As a good counselor, Gandalf begs Théoden to "come out before your doors and look abroad. Too long have you sat in shadows and trusted to twisted tales and crooked promptings" (*LR*, 2:151). When Théoden spurns the "forked tongue" of the "witless worm" (the Satanic parallels are surely intentional) in exchange for wise counsel, the king of Rohan leaves the darkness: he stands erect, and drops his staff to act as "one new awakened." Gandalf—unlike Wormtongue, who has manipulated others by means of belittling words into death and despair—wisely counsels life and hope. Such good words unite the Rohirrim and the Fellowship in a common purpose—fighting Saruman—rather than one that divides, like that of the quarrelsome Uruk-hai and Orcs.

If Gandalf awakens Théoden from a sleep caused by evil counsel, then Merry and Pippin awaken Treebeard from no counsel at all, given his sleepy neglect of his charge as Shepherd of the Trees. [29] While Treebeard has been used as a source of information by Saruman, the latter has not reciprocated, even evilly: "[H]is face, as I remember it . . . became like windows in a stone wall: window with shutters inside" (*LR*, 2:96). But Treebeard must realize the threat to Fangorn posed by Saruman, who "has a mind of metal and wheels; and he does not care for growing things, except as far they serve him for the moment" (*LR*, 2:96). Saruman has abused Nature's growing things by destroying the trees and twisted human nature by creating mutants and enslaving the will of Men like Théoden to obtain his own will. In the Entmoot, an orderly civilized debate in contrast to the quarrels of the Orcs and the one-sided insinuation of Wormtongue, language serves properly to unite the Ents by awakening them to Saruman's threat. These talking trees—signifying the principle of reason and order inherent in Nature as the higher complement to the principle of life and growth signified by Tom Bombadil—join with the Men of Rohan (as Riders complementary to the Rangers we met in the figure of Strider in the first book) to combat the evil represented by "Cunning Mind."

These episodes that delineate the problem of language and communication in the attempt to join with or separate from the Other culminate in the most important epoisode of all in the chapter entitled "The Voice of Saruman." Here, in the final debate between the fallen and the reborn Wizards, Saruman fails to use language cunningly enough to obtain his end and hence he loses, literally and symbolically, that chief weapon of the "cunning mind," the *palantír* ("far-seer"). Unctuous Saruman almost convinces the group that he is a gentle Man much put upon who only desires to meet the mighty Théoden. But Gimli wisely perceives that "[t]he words of this wizard stand on their heads. . . . In the language of Orthanc help means ruin, and saving means slaying, that is plain" (*LR*, 2:235). In addition, Eomer and Théoden resist the temptation to believe the wily ex-Wizard, so that his truly corrupt nature[30] is then revealed through the demeaning imprecations he directs toward the house of Eorl.

The emphasis upon language in this book shows that human speech can reflect man's highest and lowest aspirations: good words can express the love for another as cunning words can seek to subvert another for the speaker's own selfish ends. The archetypal Word is Christ as the Incarnation of God's love;[31] but words or speech in general, according to Saint Thomas Aquinas in his essay "On Kingship," naturally distinguishes human from beast because they express a rational nature. However, the misuse of reason to acquire knowledge forbidden by God leads to human spiritual degeneration and the dehumanization of the Other. On the one hand, such behavior marks Saruman as a perverted Wizard accompanied by his equally perverted servant, Wormtongue—their perversion makes them monstrous. On the other hand, to underscore the extent of Saruman's perversion this book is filled with examples of the heroes' difficulty in communicating with others and understanding the signs and signals of another's language.

Thus, for example, when Aragorn, Legolas, and Gimli find the Hobbits missing but their whereabouts unknown, they face an "evil choice" because of this lack of communication, just as Merry and Pippin, once captured, almost succumb to despair because they do not know where they are or where they are going (*LR*, 2:59). In the attempt to pursue the Hobbits, the remainder of the Fellowship must learn to "read" a puzzling sign language: the letter *S* emblazoned on a dead Orc's shield (killed in Boromir's defense of the Hobbits), the footprints of Sam leading *into* the water but not back again (*LR*, 2:25), the heap of dead Orcs without any clue to the Hobbit presence (*LR*, 2:53), the appearance of a strange old man bearing away their horses (*LR*, 2:116), and the mystery of the bound Hobbits' apparent escape (*LR*, 2:116). All of these signs or riddles can be explained, and indeed, as Aragorn suggests, "we must guess the riddles, if we are to choose our course rightly" (*LR*, 2:21). Man's quest symbolically depends on his correct use of his reason; the temptation is to know more than one should by consulting a magical device like the *palantír.*

If book 3 demonstrates the intellectual nature of sin, then book 4 demonstrates its physical, or material, nature. Although the structure of Shelob's tower of Cirith Ungol ends this book as Orthanc ends the third, the tower is never described in this part. Instead, another tower—Minas Morgul—introduces the weary group to the land they approach at the book's end. In appearance Minas Morgul resembles a human corpse: "Paler indeed than the moon ailing in some slow eclipse was the light of it now, wavering and blowing like a noisome exhalation of decay, a *corpse-light,* a light that illuminated nothing. In the walls and tower windows showed, like countless black holes *looking inward* into emptiness; but the topmost course of the tower revolved slowly, first one way and then another, *a huge ghostly head* leering into the night" (*LR*, 2:396–97; my italics). The holes might be a skull's. As a type of corpse it focuses attention on the human body, whose perverse desires preoccupy Tolkien in this book.

So Gollum's obsession with fish and dark things of the earth disgusts Frodo and Sam: his name as the sound of swallowing aptly characterizes his monstrously glutton-

ous nature. Again, when Gollum guides the two Hobbits
across the Dead Marshes, it is dead bodies from the battle
between Sauron and the Alliance in the Third Age, or at
least their appearance, that float beneath the surface and
tempt Gollum's appetite (*LR*, 2:297). But the Hobbits'
appetites result in trouble too: they are captured by
Faramir when the smoke of the fire for the rabbit stew
cooked by Sam and generously intended for Frodo is de-
tected (just as Gollum is captured by Frodo at Faramir's
when he hunts fish in the Forbidden Pool). Faramir's chief
gift to the weary Hobbits is a most welcome hospitality,
including food and shelter as a respite from the barren
wasteland they traverse. Finally, the Hobbits are themselves
intended as food by Gollum for the insatiable spider
Shelob. Truly the monster (whether Gollum or Shelob) is
depicted as a glutton just as the hero—past, present, or
future (the corpse, the Hobbits, Faramir)—is depicted as
food or life throughout this book. Physical life can end
without food to sustain the body; it can also end, as the
previous book indicated, because of an inaccurate interpretation of language to guide rational judgment.

These monsters representing sin are opposed by heroes constructed as Germanic lords and warriors. As we
have seen, Théoden the weak leader of Rohan is transformed by Gandalf's encouragement into a very heroic
Germanic king in book 3, unlike the proud Beorhtnoth
of "The Battle of Maldon." In book 4 the Germanic warrior or subordinate (chiefly Sam) vows to lend his aid to his
master out of love and loyalty like the old retainer
Beorhtwold in "The Battle of Maldon." The bond between
the king as head of a nation and the reason as "lord" of the
individual corresponds to that between the subordinate
warrior as servant of the king and the subordinate body.

To enhance these Germanic correspondences Tolkien
describes Rohan as an Old English warrior nation complete

with appropriate names[32] and including a suspicious hall
guardian named Hama, very similar to the hall guardian in
Beowulf, and an *ubi sunt* poem modeled on a passage from
the Old English "Wanderer," as the following pair of passages from *Two Towers* and that Old English poem attest:

> Where now the horse and rider? Where is the horn
>   that was blowing?
> Where is the helm and the hauberk, and the bright
>   hair flowing?
> (*LR,* 2:142)

> Where went the horse, where went the man? Where
>   went the treasure-giver?
> Where went the seats of banquets? Where are the hall-
>   joys?[33]

In addition, throughout book 3 Tolkien stresses the physical heroism of the Rohirrim and the Fellowship in the
battle at Helm's Deep, which resembles those described in
"The Battle of Maldon," "Brunnanburh," and "The Fight
at Finnsburg."

But in book 4 the heroism of the "warrior" depends
more on love and loyalty than on expressions of valor in
battle. Four major subordinates emerge: Gollum, Sam,
Frodo, and Faramir. Each offers a very Germanic oath of
allegiance to his master or lord: Gollum, in pledging not
to run away if he is untied, swears by the Ring, "I will serve
the master of the Precious" (*LR,* 2:285). So Frodo becomes
a lord, "a tall stern shadow, a mighty lord who hid his
brightness in grey cloud, and at his feet a whining dog"
(*LR,* 2:285). Gollum must also swear an oath to Faramir
never to return to the Forbidden Pool or lead others there
(*LR,* 2:379). Sam similarly serves his master Frodo but, like
Gollum, betrays him, not to Shelob but to Faramir, by

cooking the rabbit stew. Likewise, Frodo the master seems to betray his servant Gollum by capturing him at the Forbidden Pool even though Gollum has actually saved him from death at the hands of Faramir's men—"betray," because the "servant has a claim on the master for service; even service in fear" (*LR*, 2:375). Finally, because Faramir has granted Frodo his protection, Frodo offers him his service while simultaneously requesting a similar protection for his servant, Gollum: "[T]ake this creature, this Sméagol, under your protection" (*LR*, 2:380). Ultimately even Faramir has vowed to serve his father and lord, Denethor, by protecting this isolated post. In the next part of the epic Denethor will view Faramir's service as incomplete, a betrayal. Because Faramir has not died instead of his brother Boromir, he will seem to fail, just as the warriors lying in the Dead Marshes have apparently succeeded only too well, given the fact of their death in battle. While the exchange of valor or service for protection by a lord duplicates the Germanic contract between warrior and king, the exchange in *The Two Towers* seems fraught with difficulty because of either the apparent laxity of the lord or the apparent disloyalty of the subordinate.

The enemy, interestingly enough, functions primarily as a version of Christian rather than Germanic values, but still there is some correspondence between the *ofermod* of the Germanic lord and the *superbia* of the Christian, both leading to other, lesser sins. The Germanic emphasis in this volume does continue in the next part of the epic but ultimately merges with a more Christian definition of both servant and king.

III. *THE RETURN OF THE KING:* THE CHRISTIAN KING

This part of *The Lord of the Rings* sees the climax of the struggle between good and evil through battle between the

Satan-like Dark Lord and the Christ-like true king, Aragorn. Because Aragorn "returns" to his people to accept the mantle of responsibility, the third volume is entitled *The Return of the King,* with emphasis upon "kingship" in book 5 and "return" in book 6. Dramatic foils for the Christian king as the good steward are provided in book 5 by the good and bad Germanic lords Théoden and Denethor, whose names suggest anagrams of each other (Théo + den : Dene + thor). The good Germanic subordinates Pippin and Merry, whose notion of service echoes that of the good Christian, similarly act as foils for the archetypal Christian servant Sam, whose exemplary love for his master, Frodo, transcends all normal bounds in book 6. Finally, the concept of renewal attendant upon the return of the king pervades the latter part of the sixth book as a fitting coda to the story of the triumph of the true king over the false one.

The contrast between the two Germanic lords is highlighted early in book 5 by the offers of service presented respectively by Pippin to Denethor in chapter 1 and by Merry to Théoden in chapter 2. As the Old Man, the Germanic king more interested in glory and honor than in his men's welfare, Denethor belittles Pippin because he assumes smallness of size equals smallness of service. This literalistic mistake has been made earlier by other "Old Men," especially *Beowulf* critics, the narrator of *The Hobbit,* and Nokes in "Smith of Wootton Major." Why, Denethor muses, did the "halfling" escape the Orcs when his much larger son Boromir did not? In return for the loss of Denethor's son, Pippin feels moved—by pride—to offer in exchange himself, but as an eye-for-an-eye, justly rendered payment of a debt: "Then Pippin looked the old man in the eye, for pride stirred strangely within him, still stung by the scorn and suspicion in that cold voice. 'Little service, no doubt, will so great a lord of Men think to find in a hobbit, a halfling from the northern Shire; yet such as it is, I will offer it, in payment of my debt'" (*LR*, 3:30). Pippin's offer is legalized by a contractual vow binding him both to Gondor and the Steward of the realm either until death takes him or his lord releases him. The specific details of the contract invoke the usual terms of the bond between lord and warrior: according to the Germanic *comitatus* ethic, Pippin must not "fail to reward that which is given: fealty with love, valor with honor, oath-breaking with vengeance" (*LR*, 3:31).

Merry's vow to Théoden, in contrast, expresses a voluntary love for, rather than involuntary duty to, his king, characteristic of the ideal Germanic subordinate in Tolkien's "Ofermod" commentary. And Théoden, unlike Denethor, represents the ideal Germanic lord who truly loves instead of uses his Men. Viewing Merry as an equal, he invites him to eat, drink, talk, and ride with him, later suggesting that as his esquire he ride on a hill-pony especially found for him. Merry responds to this loving gesture with one equally loving and spontaneous: "Filled suddenly with love for this old man, he knelt on one knee, and took his hand and kissed it. 'May I lay the sword of Meriadoc of the Shire on your lap, Théoden King?' he cried. 'Receive my service, if you will!'" (*LR*, 3:59). In lieu of the legal contract of the lord Denethor and the servant Pippin there is Merry's oral promise of familial love: "'As a father you shall be to me,' said Merry" (*LR*, 3:59).

These private vows of individual service to the governors of Gondor and Rohan are followed in chapters 2 and 3 by more public demonstrations of national or racial service. In the first incident the previous Oathbreakers of the past—that is, the Dead of the Gray Company—redeem their past negligence by bringing aid to Aragorn in response to his summons. This contractual obligation fulfilled according to the letter of prophecy, Théoden and his

Rohirrim can fulfill their enthusiastic and loving pledge of aid by journeying to Gondor. They themselves are accompanied by the Wild Men in chapter 5 as a symbolic corollary to their spontaneity, love, and enthusiasm—the new law of the spirit.

In addition, two oath*makers* of Rohan—Eowyn and Merry—in contrast to the Oathbreakers mentioned above, literally appear to violate their private vows of individual service but actually render far greater service than any outlined in a verbal contract. When Eowyn relinquishes her duty to her father and king, Théoden, of taking charge of the people until his return, by disguising herself as the warrior Dernhelm so that she may fight in battle, she also allows Merry to relinquish his vow to Théoden when he secretly rides behind her into battle. But when Théoden is felled by the Nazgûl Lord, it is she who avenges him— Dernhelm "wept, for he had loved his lord as a father" (*LR,* 3:141)—as well as Merry: "'King's man? King's man!' his heart cried within him. 'You must stay by him. As a father you shall be to me, you said'" (*LR,* 3:141). Dernhelm slays the winged creature ridden by the Lord of the Nazgûl; Merry helps her slay the Lord. The service they render, a vengeance impelled by pity and love for their lord, is directed not only to the dead king and father Théoden, or to Rohan and Gondor, but to all of Middle-earth. Interestingly, her bravery in battle arouses Merry's: "Pity filled his heart and great wonder, and suddenly the slow-kindled courage of his race awoke. He clenched his hand. She should not die, so fair, so desperate! At least she should not die alone, unaided" (*LR,* 3:142). Simple love for another results in Merry's most charitable and heroic act. These subordinates have completely fulfilled the spirit, if not the letter, of their pledges of allegiance to their lords.

Tolkien also compares and contrasts the lords of book 5. The evil Germanic lord Denethor is matched by the good Germanic lord Théoden; both contrast with the Christian lord Aragorn. Denethor fails as a father, a master, a steward, and a man (if the characteristic of Man is rationality). In "The Siege of Gondor" (chapter 4) and later in "The Pyre of Denethor" (chapter 7), Denethor reveals his inability to love his son Faramir when, Lear-like, he measures the quality and quantity of his worth. The Gondor steward to the king prefers the dead Boromir to Faramir because of the former's great courage and loyalty to him: "Boromir was loyal to me and no wizard's pupil. He would have remembered his father's need, and would not have squandered what fortune gave. He would have brought me a mighty gift" (*LR*, 3:104). So he chastises Faramir for his betrayal: "[H]ave I not seen your eye fixed on Mithrandir, seeking whether you said well or too much? He has long had your heart in his keeping" (*LR*, 3:103). Even in the early chapters Denethor has revealed his failure as a master: he has assumed that the service of a small individual like Pippin must be domestic and menial in character, involving waiting on Denethor, running errands, and entertaining him (*LR*, 3:96). As a steward of Gondor Denethor fails most egregiously by usurping the role of lord in his misguided zeal for power and glory and by using his men to further his own ends. He views this act in monetary terms: the Dark Lord "uses others as his weapons. So do all great lords, if they are wise, Master Halfling. Or why should I sit here in my tower and think, and watch, and wait, spending even my sons?" (*LR*, 3:111). Unlike Théoden, who heads his troops on the battlefield, Denethor remains secure in his tower while his warriors die in the siege of Gondor. Most significantly, he fails to exhibit that rational self-control often described in the Middle Ages through the metaphor of kingship. Such unnatural behavior results in despair and irrationality and he loses his head. When he nurses his madness to suicide and adds even his son Faramir to the pyre, he is termed by Gandalf a "heathen," like those kings dominated by the Dark Power, "slaying themselves in pride and despair, murdering their kin to ease their own death" (*LR,* 3:157). As Denethor succumbs to his pride he refuses to "be the dotard chamberlain of an upstart. . . . I will not bow to such a one, last of a ragged house long bereft of lordship and dignity" (*LR,* 3:158). Symbolically, the enemy hurls back the heads of dead soldiers branded with the "token of the Lidless Eye" to signal the loss of reason and hope— the loss of the "head"—and the assault of despair on this city and its steward (*LR,* 3:117).

Théoden and Aragorn epitomize in contrast the good king. As a Germanic king Théoden serves primarily heroically after his contest with Wormtongue, giving leadership in battle and loving and paternal treatment of his warriors outside it, as we have seen with Merry. So he rides at the head of his troop of warriors as they near the city and provides a noble and inspiring example for them to follow:

Arise, arise . . .
Fell deeds awake fire and slaughter!
spear shall be shaken, shield be splintered,
a sword-day, a red day, ere the sun rises!
Ride now, ride now! Ride to Gondor!
(*LR,* 3:137)

The alliterative verse echoes the Old English heroic lines of "The Battle of Maldon" in both its form and content.

Aragorn differs from Théoden in his role as Christian king because of his moral heroism as a healer rather than his valor as a destroyer.[34] Ioreth, the Gondors' wise woman, declares, "*The hands of the king are the hands of a healer, and so shall the rightful king be known*" (*LR,* 3:169).

In "The Houses of Healing" (chapter 8), Aragorn carries the herb kingsfoil to the wounded Faramir, Eowyn, and Merry to revive and awaken each of them in highly symbolic acts. Also known as *athelas,* kingsfoil brings "Life to the dying": its restorative powers, of course, transcend the merely physical. It represents life itself juxtaposed with death, similar to the restorative powers of the paradisal Niggle in "Leaf by Niggle." Indeed, when Aragorn places the leaves in hot water, "all hearts were lightened. For the fragrance that came to each was like a memory of dewy mornings of unshadowed sun in some land of which the fair world in Spring is itself but a fleeting memory" (*LR,* 3:173). In awakening Faramir, Aragorn awakens as well knowledge and love so that the new steward to the king responds in words similar to those of a Christian disciple: "My lord, you called me. I come. What does the king command?" (*LR,* 3:173). In contrast, instead of responding rationally to the king, Eowyn awakens from her deathlike sleep to enjoy her brother's presence and to mourn her father's death. Merry awakens hungry for supper. The revival of self witnessed in these three incidents symbolizes what might be called the renewal of the three human faculties: rational, appetitive, and sensitive.

Structurally, Tolkien supports his thematic contrasts and parallels. The House of Healing presented in chapter 8 is positioned back-to-back with chapter 7's House of the Dead, in which Denethor commits fiery suicide. More than physical, Denethor's death is chiefly spiritual. Both a spiritual and physical rebirth follow Aragorn's laying on of kingsfoil in the House of Healing. This ritualistic and epiphanic act also readies the narrative for the final symbolic Christian gesture of all the free peoples in the last two chapters of book 5. In "The Last Debate" (chapter 9) they decide to sacrifice themselves, if necessary, out of love for their world in the hope that their action will distract

Sauron long enough for Sam and Frodo to reach Mount Doom. As an entire community of "servants," they each alone act as freely, spontaneously, and charitably as did Merry or Eowyn toward Théoden earlier. Aragorn declares, "As I have begun, so I will go on. . . . Nonetheless I do not yet claim to command any man. Let others choose as they will" (*LR*, 3:192). Even the title of "The Last Debate" portrays the egalitarian spirit of the group.

In contrast, in the last chapter (10), "The Black Gate Opens," only one view—that of the Dark Lord, voiced by his "Mouth," the Lieutenant—predominates. Sauron too demands not voluntary service but servitude: the Lieutenant "would be their tyrant and they his slaves" (*LR*, 3:205). Finally, the arrogance of Sauron's "Steward" functions antithetically to the humility and love of the good "servants" and stewards. Mocking and demeaning them, Sauron's Lieutenant asks if "any one in this rout" has the "authority to treat with me? . . . Or indeed with wit to understand me?" (*LR*, 3:202). The Lieutenant's stentorian voice grows louder and more defensive when met with the silence of Aragorn, whom he has described as brigandlike.

Although this "attack" of the free peoples on the Black Gate of Mordor seems to parallel that of Sauron's Orcs on the Gate of Gondor in chapter 4, it differs in that this attack on the Black Gate, from Tolkien's point of view, is not so much a physical attack as it is a spiritual defense by Gondor. In this present instance, when the peoples realize that the Lieutenant holds Sam's short sword, the gray cloak with its Elven brooch, and Frodo's mithril-mail, they almost succumb to despair—Sauron's greatest weapon, as witnessed in the siege of Gondor. But Gandalf's steely self-discipline and wisdom so steady their nerves that they are buoyed by his refusal to submit to the Mouth's insolent terms. Well that he does, for Sauron then surrounds them on all sides, betraying his embassy of peace. They are saved from physical destruction by the eagles as deus ex machina and from spiritual destruction by Frodo, Sam, and Gollum as they near Mount Doom in book 6.

The Ring finally reaches its point of origin in the first three chapters of book 6. Initiating the romance idea of "Return,"[35] this event introduces tripartite division of the book in narrative and theme. In chapters 4 to 7 Aragorn returns as king of his people, after which his marriage to Arwen, in addition to Faramir's to Eowyn, symbolizes the renewal of society through the joining of different species, Man and Elf, and of different nations, Rohan and Gondor. A later marriage will represent a more natural form of rejuvenation, when Sam the gardener marries an appropriately named Rosie Cotton, as if to illustrate further the imminent fertility that will emblazon the reborn Shire, and they conceive Elanor, whose Elven name sums up the equivalent of grace. Finally, in the third part (chapter 8), Frodo and his Hobbits return to the Shire, where the false "mayor" Sharkey is ousted and a new one, Sam, elected. In the last chapter Tolkien hints at more supernatural forms of return and rebirth. On one level, those chosen few "return" to the Gray Havens, where they seem to acquire an immortality reminiscent of Christianity. But on another level, others of a less spiritual cast must return to the duties of the natural world. So Sam returns at the very end, a "king" who must continue to serve his "people," his family, and his "kingdom," the Shire, by remaining in this world: "'Well, I'm back,' he said" (*LR*, 3:385).

Throughout the first part of book 6, before the Ring has been returned and Sauron similarly "returns" as gray smoke (in contrast to the Gray Havens reached by Frodo and Gandalf at the end), Sam exemplifies the ideal Christian servant to his master, Frodo, in continuation of the Christian-king-as-servant theme enunciated in the last part. Physically Sam provides food for Frodo as he weakens, offers him his share of the remaining water, carries him bodily over rough terrain, and lifts his spirits. But spiritually Sam serves Frodo through the moral character that reveals him to be, as the most insignificant Hobbit and character in the epic, the most heroic.[36] Sam will become an artist by the work's end, but even during the trek across Mordor his sensitivity to spiritual reality is expressed by his understanding of the beauty beneath the appearance of waste, of light beyond darkness, of hope beyond despair.

This insight is triggered by the appearance of a star above, an instance of divine grace that illumines understanding and bolsters hope: "The beauty of it smote his heart, as he looked up out of the forsaken land, and hope returned to him. For like a shaft, clear and cold, the thought pierced him that in the end the Shadow was only a small and passing thing: there was light and high beauty for ever beyond its reach. . . . Now, for a moment, his own fate, and even his master's ceased to trouble him" (*LR*, 3:244). Strangely, Sam remains the only character who has worn the Ring but who is never tempted to acquire it by overpowering his master. Yet like Frodo earlier, Sam refuses to kill the detested Gollum when an opportunity arises because of his empathy for this "thing lying in the dust, forlorn, ruinous, utterly wretched" (*LR*, 3:273). Having borne the Ring himself, Sam finally understands the reason for Gollum's wretchedness. This charitable refusal permits Gollum, as a foil for the good servant, to serve his master and Middle-earth in the most ironic way imaginable. When Frodo betrays himself enough to keep the Ring at the last moment, Gollum bites off both Ring and finger only to fall into the furnace of Mount Doom, the most ignominious "servant" finally achieving the coveted role of "Lord of the Rings." The least dangerous adversary finally fells the most dangerous—Sauron.

In the last two parts, the reunion of the entire Fellowship and all the species, the coronation of the king, and the double weddings mark the restoration of harmony and peace to Middle-earth. Symbolically the Eldest of Trees blooms again to replace the barren and withered Tree in the Court of the Fountain (*LR*, 3:308–9). A new age—the Age of Man, the Fourth Age—begins. Even in the Shire rejuvenation occurs: note the domestic and quotidian image implied by the title of chapter 8, "The *Scouring* of the Shire" (my emphasis).

In a social sense the Shire must be washed and purified of the reptilian monsters occupying it. Once Sharkey and Worm have disappeared, Sam the new Mayor as gardener can replenish its natural stores as well. After he plants the seed given him by Galadriel, new trees, including a mallorn with silver bark and gold flowers, burst into bloom in the spring. The lush growth introduces a season or rebirth in Shire year 1420 through sunshine, rain in moderation, "an air of richness and growth, and a gleam of beauty beyond that of mortal summers that flicker and pass upon this Middle-earth. All the children born or begotten in that year, and there were many, were fair to see and strong, and most of them had a rich golden hair that had before been rare among Hobbits. The fruit was so plentiful that young Hobbits very nearly bathed in strawberries and cream. . . . And no one was ill, and everyone was pleased, except those who had to mow the grass" (*LR*, 3:375). Sam as gardener becomes a natural artist who fuses together the Niggle and Parish of "Leaf by Niggle."

The ending of this epic may seem optimistic. But as the Second Age has passed into the Third, so now the Third passes into the Fourth, a lesser one because dominated by Man, a lesser species than the Elf. Also, as Sauron replaced Morgoth, perhaps an even Darker Lord will replace Sauron in the future. Yet Tolkien's major interest does not lie in predicting the future or in encouraging Man to hope for good fortune. He wishes to illustrate how best to conduct one's life, both privately and publicly, by being a good servant and a good king, despite the vagaries of fortune, the corruption of others, and the threat of natural and supernatural death.

So this epic constitutes a sampler of Tolkienian concepts and forms realized singly and separately in other works. The critic as monster depicted in the *Beowulf* article reappears as Tolkien the critic in the foreword to *The Lord of the Rings*, a "grown up" version of Tolkien the narrator in *The Hobbit.* The hero as monster finds expression, as it has earlier in Bilbo, in Frodo, who discovers the landscape of the self to be a harsher terrain than that of Mordor. The series of monsters typifying the deadly sins— Saruman, Shelob—ultimately converge with the evil Germanic king of the trilogy—Denethor—combining ideas of the "King under the Mountain" in *The Hobbit* with the idea of the Germanic lord presented in "The Homecoming" and other medieval parodies. The good Germanic lord, hero-as-subordinate, too, from *The Hobbit* and the medieval parodies, converges with the Christian concept of the king-as-servant from the fairy-stories, in the last two volumes of the trilogy.

In addition, the genres and formal constructs that Tolkien most loves reappear here. The preface, lecture, or prose nonfiction essay is transformed into the foreword; the "children's story" for adults is expanded into the adult story of the epic, also for children; the parody of medieval literature recurs not only in the epic or romance form used here but also in the presentation of the communities of Rohan and Gondor; the fairy-story with its secondary world of Faërie governed by a very Christian Elf-king is translated into Elven form here.

Thus, all of Tolkien's work manifests a unity, with understanding of its double and triple levels, in this respect like the distinct dual levels, Germanic and Christian, of *Beowulf* first perceived in Tolkien's own *Beowulf* article. So the Tolkien reader, like Bilbo in *The Hobbit* and Sam in *The Lord of the Rings*, must return to the beginning—not to the Shire, but to the origin of the artist Tolkien—in "Beowulf: The Monsters and the Critics."

Chapter 6

THE CREATOR OF THE SILMARILS

Tolkien's "Book of Lost Tales"

In the cosmogony there is a fall: a fall of Angels we
should say. . . . There cannot be any "story"
without a fall—all stories are ultimately about the
fall—at least not for human minds as we know
them and have them.

—J.R.R. Tolkien
Letter 131, to Milton Waldman
of Collins (c. 1951)

The Silmarillion may be considered a "lost book" in at least
six senses. Originally entitled "The Book of Lost Tales,"
The Silmarillion in its earliest incarnation contained only
the three stories written in 1917 (or earlier), "The Fall of
Gondolin," "Of Túrin Turambar," and "Of Beren and
Lúthien."[1] In a second sense, as if it had been lost and then
discovered as a "mythology *for England*," "The Book of
Lost Tales" represents yet another attempt by Tolkien to
pretend that he is the editor or translator of work belonging to a previous era, as he does in *Farmer Giles of Ham,*
The Adventures of Tom Bombadil, and *The Lord of the Rings*

(especially in the foreword and appendices), even though, in the case of "The Book of Lost Tales," the mock preface and editorial apparatus are missing. This fictional "loss" and recovery by its author mirrors an actual loss and recovery, of the Finnish *Kalevala*, a third "book of lost tales," which *The Silmarillion* mimics. According to Luigi de Anna (paraphrasing and translating E. Lodigliani), "[I]n fact the *Silmarillion* is conceived on a similar plan to that of the [Finnish] *Kalevala*, that is to say, in the shape of a collection, made a posteriori, of 'lost tales.'"[2] A model in many ways for Tolkien, especially in combining magic and humor, the *Kalevala* as a Finnish national collection of epic mythology was put together in the early twentieth century by a modern editor, E. Lönnrot. Its legends of "scandalous" and "low-brow" heroes deeply pleased Tolkien: beginning as early as 1910, Tolkien read the *Kalevala* and in 1911, in his final term at King Edward's School, when he became a prefect and secretary of the Debating Society, he also delivered a paper on Norse sagas illustrated with quotations from the original.[3] Tolkien himself noted several times that his legendarium had its beginning in the "tragic" tale of Kullervo in the *Kalevala:* "But the beginning of the legendarium, of which the Trilogy is part (the conclusion), was an attempt to reorganize some of the *Kalevala*, especially the tale of Kullervo the hapless, into a form of my own."[4] As the tale of a hapless hero (or tales of heroes, as many seem to be hapless *and* hopeless), "The Book of Lost Tales" suggests the use of "lost" in a fourth sense.

But *The Silmarillion* is a lost book in a fifth and literal sense, in that it was never completed, for a variety of reasons, in the sixty years between its inception in 1914 and Tolkien's death in 1973. By 1923 "The Book of Lost Tales" was nearly finished, but instead of ending it with the early tale of the voyage of Earendel the evening star as he had originally planned, Tolkien rewrote it.[5] During his busy career he continued to revise and rewrite it; even after his retirement from Oxford, its completion continued to be interrupted by proofs to be read, letters to be written, earlier publications to be revised, and translations he wished to publish. It had been submitted to his publishers as a possible successor to the popular *Hobbit* in 1937, although Stanley Unwin declined to publish it, for it "is a mine to be explored in writing further books like *The Hobbit* rather than a book in itself."[6] And when at the age of sixty Tolkien wanted to publish it together with the recently completed *Lord of the Rings,* Rayner Unwin, Stanley's son, objected: "[S]urely this is a case for an editor who would incorporate any *really* relevant material from *The Silmarillion* into *The Lord of the Rings* without increasing the already enormous bulk of the latter and, if feasible, even cutting it."[7] Some of those who knew Tolkien in the last years of his life imply that he never intended to complete the work—it was simply too vast in scope.[8] The title "The Book of Lost Tales" in fact came to be used by Christopher Tolkien for the first two volumes of *The History of Middle-earth,* divided into two parts (published 1983–1984).

Thus, any critical study of *The Silmarillion* must be prefaced by this important caveat: we do not know exactly what Tolkien's intentions were. The text available at present resulted from son Christopher Tolkien's posthumous revision and editing of a work complicated to begin with, but which, in addition, existed in multiple versions, and often in versions differing in detail from each other and from *The Lord of the Rings* (chapters on Galadriel and the Ents had to be added for this reason).[9] Although one scholar has attempted to reconstruct the plan according to Tolkien's comments about its shape,[10] it is not clear his version would be preferable to that we now have. "The

Silmarillion" proper, as Charles E. Noad reminds us, is only one part of *The Silmarillion,* which now consists of two introductory short narratives, the *Ainulindalë* and the *Valaquenta,* along with "The Silmarillion" proper (*Quenta Silmarillion*) and two "independent pieces," the *Akallabêth* and *Of the Rings of Power and the Third Age.*[11] What would have been *omitted,* according to Noad, had Tolkien followed up with its completion, were the *Annals, Ambarkanta,* and all references to Eriol/Ælfwine; what would have been *included* would be four major parts, first, the *Quenta Silmarillion;* second, Concerning the Powers (*Ainulindalë* and the *Valaquenta*); third, The Great Tales (*The Lays of Leithian, Narn I Hîn Húrin, The Fall of Gondolin, Eärendil the Wanderer*); and fourth, The Later Tales (*Akallabêth* and *Of the Rings of Power*); with appendices containing *The Tale of Years, Of the Laws and Customs among the Eldar, Dangweth Pengoleð, Athrabeth Finrod ah Andreth,* and *Quendi and Eldar.*[12]

The Silmarillion is a "lost book" in a sixth sense, in that as a work of fiction it remains so dominated by Tolkien's love of philology that it is nearly reduced to the state of a dictionary or encyclopedia of words and myths, although Christopher Tolkien has provided a major service to Tolkien readers and scholars by editing what he calls in his foreword this "compendious narrative." The "Index of Names" he supplies at the end lists a daunting eight to nine hundred, many of which are mentioned only once in this three hundred–page work. Tolkien's interest in philology nearly adumbrates the work as a fictional narrative. Like Morgoth and Fëanor in *The Silmarillion,* Tolkien seems to love what he has created as an end in itself, but the ensuing catalogue of names confuses, if not stifles, the reader, as one example will attest: "At length the Vanyar and the Noldor came over Ered Luin, the Blue Mountains, between Eriador and the westernmost land of Middle-earth, which the Elves after named Beleriand; and the fore-most companies passed over the Vale of Sirion and came down to the shores of the Great Sea between Drengist and the Bay of Balar. . . . And the host of the Teleri passed over the Misty Mountains, and crossed the wide lands of Eriador, being urged on by Elwë Singollo, for he was ea-ger to return to Valinor."[13] The love of private language is here almost too private for the general reader to share, despite the editor's helpful aids to readers included at the work's end—the genealogical tables, index of names, notes on pronunciation, an appendix entitled "Elements on Quenya and Sindarin Names," and two maps (not to mention the subsequent publication of volumes of *The Unfinished Tales* and *The History of Middle-earth*).[14] Even with its epic theme the collection still lacks continuity, if not unity, and is hard to follow. But the completeness of Tolkien's mythology as it exists now with their publication by Christopher Tolkien surely allows readers to use them either as a resource and encyclopedia or as a narrative.

As a mythological work constructed along the lines of a genealogy of created beings, it resembles other col-lections of mythological tales that often begin with Cre-ation—like the Bible, Ovid's *Metamorphoses,* Hyginus's *Fabulae,* the *Eddas,* the Welsh *Mabinogion,* and the Irish myths and legends of the hero Cuchulain. Its epic conflicts, themes, and symbols relate to those analyzed in the pre-ceding chapters on fictional and nonfiction works. Specifi-cally, Tolkien reworks religious concepts and symbols in his invented legends, as he has in previous works—the theme of pride and fall, related to the desire for power over others as symbolized in the role of the king or wise leader, and knowledge as an end in itself as symbolized in skill-fully worked material objects loved for themselves. Al-though Tolkien contrasts with this the regenerative powers of art, as he has in other works, in this collection there is no Christian king, healer, or artist as in the fairy-stories, *The Hobbit*, or *The Lord of the Rings*. Instead, a much more Old Testament emphasis predominates: it is the art of the Neoplatonic Creator, Eru the One, that is celebrated at beginning and end, and the promise of natural and spiritual renewal for all of creation upon the fulfillment of obedience to the will of the One. The difficulty for Tolkien (as for Neoplatonists Plotinus and pseudo-Dionysius) is that of using the "separable and limited vocabulary of human language to talk about inseparable, unlimited being"; so he begins by moving from Eru, the One, to Ilúvatar, as he is called in Arda, although he solves the problem differently from the Neoplatonists, not by a philosophical explanation but by his use of language in his sub-creation.[15] Nor is there the specifically medieval English emphasis on the chivalric concept of the lord or knight using his own men to establish his reputation or on the Old English concept of the loyal warrior as good servant. The development of strong fictional characters here gives way to the importance of theme, image, and idea in the cycle of myths, many of which are, however, indebted to medieval sources in myth and literature.

It is no mistake that this work begins with the words "There was Eru, the One," and concludes with the words "story and song." Because these tales celebrate the power of creation and goodness through the image of song, music, and its triumph over destruction and evil as represented by broken and inharmonious song, this very "Book of Lost Tales" might be viewed as itself a praise of creation—and creativity.

The best guide to Tolkien's intentions and to the unity of *The Silmarillion* is letter 131, to Milton Waldman, in which Tolkien carefully outlines his governing concept of time and its devolution in the legendarium. Each of *The Silmarillion*'s five parts by means of various tales relates the history and genealogy of one or more species in the order of their creation—the Ainur, Valar, Elves, Dwarves, and Men. *Ainulindalë* ("The Music of the Ainur") and *Valaquenta* ("Account of the Valar and Maiar") briefly outline the creation of the Ainur (or Valar to the Elves, gods to Men) by the One and summarize their individual characters. The third and longest part, *Quenta Silmarillion* ("The History of the Silmarils"), in its twenty-four chapters deals with the history of those beings created by the One (that is, the immortal Elves and mortal Men granted the gift of death) and the beings (that is, the Dwarves) created by the Vala Aulë, ruler of earth. The last two parts record the downfall of Man, the noblest tribe of Men in *Akallabêth* ("The Downfall of Númenor"), about the Second Age, and the lesser tribes in *Of the Rings of Power and the Third Age.*

Furthermore, the tragic fall of a Vala—equivalent to the fall of an angel in the Old Testament—initiates the whole trajectory of this history, or story, as Tolkien revealed most stories do, in this same letter to Waldman (cited at the opening of this chapter), and leads to the falls of the Elves, Men, and Hobbits.[16] Basically the mythology dramatizes the fall of the Vala Melkor, or Morgoth, followed by the rise to power of his Maia servant Sauron, after the former's initial, primary conflict with the One, Eru or Ilúvatar, "Father of All." At the beginning Melkor, conceived like the other Ainur as a "thought" of the One, rebels against him, like the angel Lucifer against God in Genesis. The most talented of the Ainur, Melkor refuses to sing his part in their cosmic music because "desire grew hot within him to bring into Being things of his own" (*Silmarillion*, p. 16). What he creates instead is his own loud, vain "clamorous unison as of many trumpets braying upon a few notes" instead of the slow, beautiful, sorrowful music of the One.

Yet both the clamorous and beautiful pieces are translated by Eru into a created world and its inhabitants so that even Melkor and his discord find a part. Among the children of the Ainur, Fëanor as the greatest of the Elven tribe of the Noldor also wishes like the Valar to create "things of his own" and he learns through the art of Melkor how to capture the blessed light of the Two Trees (made by the Vala Yavanna) in three jewels, the Silmarils. Like Melkor, Fëanor too succumbs to a "greedy love" of them that leads to his and his son's downfall. In the next-to-last section of *The Silmarillion*, Ar-Pharazôn, mightiest and proudest of the Númenóreans, themselves noblest of Men, calls himself "The Golden" and wishes to be king, for "his heart was filled with the desire of power unbounded and the sole dominion of his will. And he determined without counsel of the Valar, or any wisdom but his own, that the title of King of Men he would himself claim, and would compel Sauron to become his vassal and his servant; for in his pride he deemed that no king should ever arise so mighty as to vie with the Heir of Eärendil" (*Silmarillion*, p. 270). Ar-Pharazôn rebels against the Elves; Melkor earlier had rebelled against the One. In the last section even the Maia Sauron desires to control Middle-earth out of a similar pride and envy, and he fashions the One Ring to do so, itself a created thing misused by its creator like the three Elven "jewels of Fëanor."

Despite the ensuing fall of Elves and Men and the destruction of Middle-earth, "peace came again, and a new Spring opened on earth; and the Heir of Isildur was crowned King of Gondor and Arnor, and the might of the Dúnedain was lifted up and their glory renewed" (*Silmarillion*, p. 304), with the beginning of the Fourth Age, of Man. Evil stands revealed as only a part of the whole goodness of Creation perceived by the One Himself, and Himself alone. So the "secret thoughts" of

Melkor's mind—his pride, envy, greed, hatred—formed "but a part of the whole and tributary to its glory" (*Silmarillion*, p. 17), as Eru had explained to him even before Middle-earth was created.

The central message of *The Silmarillion* emerges from the ruin and sorrow as delivered by the prophetic Messenger sent by the Valar to warn Men: "Beware! The will of Eru may not be gainsaid; and the Valar bid you earnestly not to withhold the trust to which you are called, lest it become again a bond by which you are constrained. . . . The love of Arda [Middle-earth] was set in your hearts by Ilúvatar, and he does not plant to no purpose" (*Silmarillion*, p. 265). Love and trust, not pride and willfulness, are the key words.

The themes of *The Silmarillion* can be seen as clearly biblical and Old Testament,[17] prefiguring Christianity. The conflict between Melkor, or Morgoth (and his spiritual descendants), and the One, or the creation of the One, mirrors that between God and the fallen angel Satan; Melkor's corruption of the "third theme" of creation, of the Elves and men, mirrors that of Adam and Eve by Satan; the desire for power and godlike being is the same desire for knowledge of good and evil witnessed in the Garden of Eden. As symbols of such desire the Silmarils and One Ring show that pride as chief of the deadly sins leads to envy, covetousness, and, in the figure of the giant spider Ungoliant, companion of Morgoth, gluttony and lust.

The theme of good and evil that derives from the conflict between Melkor and the One is underscored by music and jewel symbolism. "The Silmarillion" entitles the whole collection and not just the long middle section describing the history of the three jewels, in part because it complements the companion epic-novels of *The Lord of the Rings* with their ring symbolism. In part, too, it helps to unify the entire mythology: the Silmarils, like the music of Melkor dominating the first part and the Ring of Sauron dominating the fifth, are created things misused by their creators and like them they symbolize the domination of will that springs from pride and greed, the chief elements of selfishness. After creating the jewels in order to preserve the light of the Two Trees, the glory of the Blessed Realm, Fëanor "began to love the Silmarils with a greedy love, and grudged the sight of them to all save his father and his seven sons; he seldom remembered now that the light within them was not his own" (*Silmarillion*, p. 69). Melkor, too, of course, burns with the desire to possess them; the greed of both leads to alienation from others, division among family and nation, and much destruction. The jewels are cursed with an oath of hatred, so that when the Dwarves later behold the Silmaril set in the necklace named Nauglamír, "they were filled with a great lust to possess them, and carry them off to their far homes in the mountains" (*Silmarillion*, p. 233). One should not imitate the Creator in order to aggrandize creation for selfish reasons, but instead to praise both Creator and creation, to reflect one's love for and trust in both and one's obedience to the will of Ilúvatar. Such purpose advances understanding and promotes healing, for the beauty created by the artist reflects only the beauty of the larger creation and not the greatness of its creator.

Indeed, if the powers that foster creation and cosmogony are classified, it will be clear that Tolkien is following an early Stoic hierarchy of natural philosophy in his arrangement and balance of Valar and Valier, male and female powers[18] of air, water, earth, and the underworld/ supernature, spirits of the dead and dreams, deeds, prowess. All of the seven Valar except Ulmo (water) have a matching mate that governs some equal realm or spirit: the highest in rank, Manwë (air), is coupled with female

Varda (stars); Aulë (earth) is coupled with female Yavanna (fruits); the two Fëanturi (masters of spirits) Námo (Mandos) (keeper of Houses of the Dead) is coupled with Vairë the Weaver (webs of time) and Irmo (Lórien) (master of visions, dreams) is coupled with Estë the gentle, healer (brother); Tulkas (Astaldo) the valiant (deeds, prowess) is coupled with Nessa the dancer (deer lover); and Oromë the hunter of monsters, lover of trees, is coupled with Vána the Ever-young (flowers) (sister of Yavanna). Only Nienna the quiet (lamentation), sister to the Fëanturi, is solo, like Ulmo, who controls water.

The Valar and Valier, Powers of Arda (*Silmarillion,* pp. 18–23)

Manwë (air)	Varda (stars)
Ulmo (water)	
Aulë (earth)	Yavanna (fruits)
Fëanturi (masters of spirits)	
Námo (Mandos)	Vairë the Weaver (webs of time)
(keeper of Houses of the Dead)	
Irmo (Lórien)	Estë the gentle, healer (brother)
(master of visions, dreams)	
	Nienna the quiet (lamentation)
Tulkas (Astaldo) the valiant	Nessa the dancer (deer lover)
(deeds, prowess)	
Oromë the hunter of monsters,	Vána the Ever-young (flowers)
lover of trees	(sister of Yavanna)

It is the Ainur Ulmo who is especially fond of the Teleri, that middle branch of the Elves associated with water and water journeys in *The Silmarillion* (just as the Fair-Elves, the Vanyar, are associated with air and the Ainur Manwë; and the Low-Elves, the Noldor, are associated with earth and the Ainur Aulë). And therefore the Teleri are also linked with Eärendil the Mariner, whose role at the end of *The Silmarillion* is so crucial, and so interesting to us because of his etymological parallel with the Old English Earendel in *Crist*, the seed for much of *The Silmarillion*. *Crist*, a poem divided into three parts, on the advent, crucifixion, and redemption of Christ, opens with Earendel, he who comes before, the equivalent of John the Baptist to Christ, and therefore highlights the analogous position of Eärendil the Mariner in *The Silmarillion* as a rescuer who comes before the true king, Aragorn, in *Return of the King*. The flight of the Elves into the West provides the denouement of the Fall of the Elves and makes their history into a tragedy, a dyscatastrophe, a Fall, mimicked by all other species of Middle-earth.

It is no accident that such flight plays a key role in *The Silmarillion;* one of Tolkien's posthumously published works, an edition and translation of the Old English translation of the biblical book of Exodus, dramatizes the flight of the Israelites from Egypt and the passage through the Red Sea.[19] The flight, according to the introduction to the translation in the commentary, signifies the exile of the soul from God's grace: Tolkien describes it as "at once an historical poem about events of extreme importance, an account of the preservation of the chosen people and the fulfilment of the promises made to Abraham; and it is an allegory of the soul, or of the Church of militant souls, marching under the hand of God, pursued by the powers of darkness, until it attains to the promised land of Heaven" (Tolkien, *Exodus*, p. 33).

Additionally, the scene in Tolkien's *Exodus* is imbued with Germanic heroic concepts: the "chieftain" Moses, to whom God gives the "lives of his kinsmen," is "prince of his people, a leader of the host, sage and wise of heart, valiant captain of his folk" (Tolkien, *Exodus*, p. 20). The "enemies of God," Pharaoh's race, receives plagues and the "fall of their princes," so that "mirth was hushed in the halls bereft of treasure" (Tolkien, *Exodus*, p. 20). A poem reminiscent of *Beowulf* and the deadly visitation of the hall Heorot by the monster Grendel, *Exodus* describes how "far and wide the Slayer ranged grievously afflicting the people" (Tolkien, *Exodus*, p. 21). For the chieftain Moses, "high the heart of him who led the kindred" (Tolkien, *Exodus*, p. 21); the war scene, with the "gallant men" led by Moses, is elaborated with Germanic touches like the brightness of the host (line 107) and the flashing of the shields (line 108). Abraham, son of Noah who follows as tenth in generations after Moses, is also described as in exile (Tolkien, *Exodus*, line 332, p. 28). And when Moses leads the Israelites in flight, they too are described as "Exiles from home, in mourning they possess this hall of passing guests, lamenting in their hearts" (Tolkien, *Exodus*, lines 457–59, p. 31).

The *Silmarillion,* which also bears the imprint of Old Norse and Germanic heroic elements,[20] has been described by Tolkien as a work about Death and the desire for Deathlessness. For this reason darkness becomes an appropriate image to associate with monstrosity, and light with good. Men see death, for example, as a curse because "coming under the shadow of Morgoth it seemed to them that they were surrounded by a great darkness, of which they were afraid; and some grew wilful and proud and would not yield, until life was reft from them" (*Silmarillion,* p. 256). History as the passage of time—divided into Ages marking hegemonic being—is for Tolkien the movement from light into dark and back again. Tolkien divides the history of Middle-earth into Ages, First, Second, Third, and the beginning of the Fourth, to unify this seemingly disunified work. In letter 131, in which (among other things) Tolkien reveals the anthropomorphic center of the epic to be the "Elves," it is the Elves—or their "most gifted kindred"—who fall, are exiled from Valinor ("a kind of

Paradise, the home of the gods"), in the West, re-enter Middle-earth (where they were born), and battle with the Enemy (*Letters*, pp. 147–48). The primeval jewels of the *Silmarilli* were made by the Elves, symbolic of beauty and the source of the Light of Valinor ("made visible in the Two Trees of Silver and Gold") (*Letters*, p. 148). When the Trees were killed, Valinor was darkened except for the Sun and the Moon; Fëanor had, however, "imprisoned" light in three of them, but then he and his kin jealously guard them, even after the *Silmarilli* are taken by the Enemy Morgoth for his Iron Crown. After Fëanor's sons take their oath of vengeance against the takers, a "hopeless war" is begun and Elves kill Elves. As Tolkien observes, "The Silmarillion is the history of the War of the Exiled Elves against the enemy" (*Letters*, p. 148).

The four Ages, then, include the First, of the Ancient World, with the creation and loss of the Jewels, one in the sea, one in the earth, one in the heavens as a star ("Elbereth Gilthoniel"), in which Tolkien holds the greatest interest. In the Second Age, Men and Elves interact, most noticeably in the tale of Beren and Lúthien, Man and Elf; but also in the tale of the Children of Húrin, about Túrin Turambar and his sister Níniel, the tale of the Fall of Gondolin (chief of the Elvish citadels), and the tale of Eärendil the Wanderer, which, in the words of Tolkien, not only brings *The Silmarillion* proper to an end but points to the future tales of Ages through Eärendil's progeny. The Second Age is a Dark Age of battles, when the Exiled Elves were told to stay in the West, at the Lonely Isle of Eressëa, but the Men of Three Houses might dwell in the "lost" ("Atlantis") isle of Númenor. During this Age, Sauron grows in power and the Shadow spreads over Men, while the Delaying Elves stay on in Middle-earth: this is dealt with in *The Rings of Power* and *Downfall of Númenor* (*Letters*, p. 151). The Downfall is the Second Fall of Man, and the end of the Old World and legend, and the beginning of the Third Age.

Although the collection dramatizes the history of Middle-earth ("Middle-earth," from the Old English phrase for "Earth" derived from Old Norse) from the beginning of Creation to the point at which *The Hobbit* and *The Lord of the Rings* end, it seems to lack a central epic hero (a Beowulf, Bilbo, or Frodo) who might pull together the various strands of the narrative. Possibly Tolkien himself realized its lack of focus, for he originally intended that these tales be framed by "the introductory device of the seafarer [Eärendil? Eriol? Ælfwine?] to whom the stories were told."[21] By "the seafarer" Tolkien may have meant Eärendil the Mariner, from *The Silmarillion,* or Ælfwine the Mariner and his double, Eriol the Mariner, from *The Book of Lost Tales.* There are other mariner figures elsewhere in Tolkien, but what he intended was apparently some kind of link between the Elven and human worlds who might transmit the tales of earlier Ages. Verlyn Flieger broadens the role to that of the "Elf-Friend" (which is what "Ælfwine" means) —"not an Elf but a friend of Elves"— who "is neither wholly outside nor completely inside but in between, and thus qualifies as a true mediator."[22] The epithet is a polite greeting in *The Lord of the Rings* but also a "sign of election to a special company" at the Council of Elrond. The name also refers to Ælfwine the Mariner in "The History of Eriol or Ælfwine," in *The Book of Lost Tales,* pt. 2, p. 278–334 (that is, the second volume of *The History of Middle-earth*), and to Smith and the first Master Cook in *Smith of Wootton Major.* Flieger adds to these Tolkien, as the "overarching" Elf-Friend (Flieger, "The Footsteps of Ælfwine," p. 197).

Of course Tolkien did not supply such a link, whatever his intentions. Of the three figures who might then serve as unifying heroes for "The Book of Lost Tales," aside from Eärendil the Mariner, whose name in Elvish means "Great Mariner" or "Sea-lover," there is Beren the Man, linked with the Elf Lúthien, together a couple in whom Tolkien recognized himself and his wife Edith; and Túrin Turambar, whose incestuous story is derived from those of "Sigurd the Volsung, Oedipus, and the Finnish Kullervo" (*Letters,* p. 150), a story that reappears in many of Tolkien's works.[23] About the unfinished story of Túrin, Richard West notes that this leader of Elves and Men who wanders seeks their good, but also suffers from the same sin of pride (*ofermod*) as the leader Beorhtnoth in the Old English poem *The Battle of Maldon* (whose death Torhthelm and Tídwald must deal with in Tolkien's *The Homecoming of Beorhthelm Beorhtnoth's Son*).[24] The problem with all these figures is that their stories are unfinished, and therefore their roles in the final "Book of Lost Tales" still and forever lost to recovery.

Tolkien's triumph in this last but first work, then, lies not only in its creation of a whole history (and in a sense morality) for Middle-earth, providing thereby a context for *The Hobbit* and *The Lord of the Rings.* For, when Christopher Tolkien in the foreword claims that this "compendious narrative" of mythological tales was "made long afterward from sources of great diversity (poems and annals, and oral tales) that had survived in agelong tradition," one is not sure whether he is describing the literary output of one man or of one nation. Perhaps he merely means to agree that, in Tolkien's fantasy mythology for Middle-earth, his father had indeed finally written that "mythology *for England.*"

NOTES

INTRODUCTION

1. Randel Helms, *Tolkien's World* (Boston: Houghton Mifflin, 1974), pp. 1–2.

2. Humphrey Carpenter, *J.R.R. Tolkien: A Biography* (London, Boston, and Sydney: Allen and Unwin, 1977), p. 75.

3. Carpenter, pp. 59, 71, 89, 94. For Finnish and Quenya, see especially Helena Rautala, "Familiarity and Distance: Quenya's Relation to Finnish," in *Scholarship and Fantasy: Proceedings of the Tolkien Phenomenon, May 1992, Turku, Finland* (special issue), ed. K.J. Battarbee, Anglicana Turkuensia, no. 12 (Turku: University of Turku, 1993), pp. 21–31.

4. Carpenter, pp. 64, 71. See also the discussion on the relationship between this Old English line from *Crist* and Tolkien's *Silmarillion* in Clive Tolley, "Tolkien and the Unfinished," in Battarbee, pp. 151–52; in Tom Shippey, *The Road to Middle-earth*, 1982, rev. ed. (London: Allen and Unwin, 1992), pp. 173–77; and in Verlyn Flieger, "The Footsteps of Ælfwine," in *Tolkien's Legendarium: Essays on "The History of Middle-earth,"* ed. Verlyn Flieger and Carl F. Hostetter, Contributions to the Study of Science Fiction and Fantasy, no. 86 (Westport, Conn., and London: Greenwood Press, 2000), pp. 183–98.

5. See Clyde S. Kilby, *Tolkien and "The Silmarillion"* (Wheaton, Ill.: Harold Shaw Publishers, 1976), p. 53.

6. See *The Annotated Hobbit,* annotated by Douglas A. Anderson (Boston: Houghton Mifflin, 1988), p. 1, for the very early date of 1928 proposed by Tolkien's son Michael for the writing of the first sentence, with the continuation of its writing in 1929. The date of 1930 exists in penciled notes by Tolkien on a letter of 18 January 1938 from G.H. White of the Examination Schools that was exhibited in the "Oxford Writers" exhibit at Oxford University in March, 1978.

7. Christopher Tolkien, foreword to J.R.R. Tolkien, *The Silmarillion*, ed. Christopher Tolkien (London: Allen and Unwin; Boston: Houghton Mifflin, 1977), p. 7.

8. The lecture was published in *Proceedings of the British Academy*, 22 (1936): 245–95, and reprinted in *An Anthology of Beowulf Criticism*, ed. Lewis E. Nicholson (Notre Dame, Ind.: University of Notre Dame Press, 1963), pp. 51–103; in *The Beowulf Poet*, ed. Donald K. Fry (Englewood Cliffs, N.J. : Prentice-Hall, 1968), pp. 8–56; in *Interpretations of Beowulf: A Critical Anthology*, ed. R. Fulk (Bloomington and Indianapolis: Indiana University Press, 1991), pp. 14–44; and, in truncated form, in *Readings on Beowulf*, ed. Katie de Koster, The Greenhaven Press Literary Companion to British Literature (San Diego, Calif.: Greenhaven Press, 1998), pp. 24–30. All references derive from the Nicholson anthology.

9. For an example of the influence of Tolkien's *Beowulf*-essay on Old English studies, see Bruce Mitchell, "J.R.R. Tolkien and Old English Studies: An Appreciation," in *Proceedings of the J.R.R. Tolkien Centenary Conference, Keble College, Oxford, 1992*, ed. Patricia Reynolds and Glen H. Goodknight, *Mythlore* 80 and *Mallorn* 30 in one volume (Milton Keynes, England: Tolkien Society; Altadena, Calif.: Mythopoeic Press, 1995), pp. 206–12.

10. For discussions of Tolkien's claim to canonicity, see the recent studies by Patrick Curry, *Defending Middle-earth: Tolkien, Myth and Modernity* (Edinburgh: Floris Books, 1997); Joseph Pearce, *Tolkien: Man and Myth* (London: HarperCollins Publishers, 1998); and Tom Shippey, *J.R.R. Tolkien: Author of the Century* (London: HarperCollins Publishers, 2000). See also Harold Bloom's recent Chelsea House collection on *The Lord of the Rings*, important in itself as an indicator of Tolkien's stature, despite Bloom's disclaimer in the preface: *Modern Critical Interpretations: J.R.R. Tolkien's "Lord of the Rings"* (Philadelphia: Chelsea House Publishers, 2000).

For the work of Anglo-Saxonists on Tolkien—specifically, on Tolkien's *Beowulf* essay and its importance for an understanding of Tolkien's fiction—see the following recent essays: on the influence of the *Liber monstrorum* on both Tolkien and the *Beowulf* poet, see Andy Orchard, "Tolkien, the Monsters, and the Critics," in Battarbee, pp. 73–84; on Anglo-Saxon language and literature in relation to Tolkien, see Paul Bibire, "Sægde se þe cuþe: J.R.R. Tolkien as Anglo-Saxonist," in Battarbee, pp. 111–31; on the role of the *Beowulf* essay and specifically the dragon/dragon-slayer legend (the Sigemund digression) in forming Tolkien's mythological conception of the dragon, see Jonathan

Evans, "The Dragon-Lore of Middle-earth: Tolkien and Old English and Old Norse Tradition," in *J.R.R. Tolkien and His Literary Resonances: Views of Middle-earth*, ed. George Clark and Daniel Timmons (Westport, Conn., and London: Greenwood Press, 2000), pp. 25–26; and, on the role of the Old English hero in *Beowulf* and the *Battle of Maldon*, as understood by Tolkien in the *Beowulf* essay and "The Homecoming of Beorhtnoth Beorhthelm's Son," in the formation of Tolkien's own concept of heroism (essentially the idea of this volume), see George Clark, "J.R.R. Tolkien and the True Hero," in Clark and Timmons, pp. 39–51, who writes, "in them, as in his fictions, Tolkien conducted his own quest" (p. 39).

11. See the collection of essays on *Beowulf* that develops this tension in the history of twentieth-century scholarship on the poem, edited by Nicholson, in which Tolkien's essay on *Beowulf* is also reprinted.

12. On Tolkien's concept of the hero as derived from the hero in *Beowulf* and the *Battle of Maldon*, see also Clark, "J.R.R. Tolkien and the True Hero," in Clark and Timmons, pp. 39–51.

13. For the medieval and Renaissance antecedents of the healing king employed by Tolkien, see Gisbert Krantz, "Der Heilende Aragorn," *Inklings-Jahrbuch* 2 (1984): 11–24.

14. See Evans, "The Dragon-Lore of Middle-earth: Tolkien and Old English and Old Norse Tradition," in Clark and Timmons, pp. 21–38; see also other, similar, creatures' link with evil, in Tom Shippey, "Orcs, Wraiths, Wights: Tolkien's Images of Evil," in Clark and Timmons, pp. 183–98.

15. On Milton and Tolkien, see also Colin Duriez, "Sub-creation and Tolkien's Theology of Story," in Battarbee, pp. 133–50; and Debbie Sly, "Weaving Nets of Gloom: 'Darkness Profound,'" in Clark and Timmons, pp. 109–19.

Chapter 1. The Critic as Monster

1. Randel Helms, *Tolkien's World* (Boston: Houghton Mifflin, 1974), pp. 2–7, does discuss briefly the impact of the article on Tolkien's development of a theory of fantasy, pointing to Tolkien's strategic identification with the *Beowulf* poet and the poem: "In the lecture we see him, perhaps almost without realizing it, identify himself with the *Beowulf* poet and in his own defense, as it were, provide telling critical justifications for ancient poetic strategies he was even then reviving in his own work" (p. 2). However, Helms does not perceive the critic as a monster, proceed further in analyzing the article, or trace

Notes to Page 13

its impact on Tolkien's fiction. In addition, although she ignores the *Beowulf* article per se, Bonniejean Christensen does compare the poem *Beowulf* to *The Hobbit:* see *"Beowulf* and *The Hobbit:* Elegy into Fantasy in J.R.R. Tolkien's Creative Technique," *Dissertation Abstracts International* 30 (1970): 4401A-4402A (University of Southern California); see also the article derived from her dissertation, "Tolkien's Creative Technique: *Beowulf* and *The Hobbit,"* *Orcrist* 7 (1972–73): 16–20; and finally, see her "Gollum's Character Transformation in *The Hobbit,"* in *A Tolkien Compass,* ed. Jared Lobdell (La Salle, Ill.: Open Court Press, 1975), pp. 9–28, which mentions, in passing, the parallel between *Beowulf* and *The Hobbit.* See also note 9 in the introduction and the discussion of criticism that was published after the first edition of *Tolkien's Art: A "Mythology for England."*

  2. J.R.R. Tolkien, "Beowulf: The Monsters and the Critics," *Proceedings of the British Academy* 22 (1936): 245–95, reprinted in *An Anthology of Beowulf Criticism,* ed. Lewis E. Nicholson (Notre Dame, Ind.: University of Notre Dame Press, 1963), pp. 51–104. All citations refer to the Nicholson reprint (this reference, p. 51).

  3. For discussions of the battle between "Lang." and "Lit.," see Tom Shippey, *The Road to Middle-earth,* 1982, rev. ed. (London: Allen and Unwin, 1992), chap. 1, "Lit. and Lang.," pp. 1–25, who makes the point that Tolkien attacked teachers of "Lit." in two poems published in his and E.V. Gordon's privately printed collection "Songs for Philologists" in 1936 (p. 5). Shippey explains that teachers of "Lang." and "Lit." competed for students, funds, and time (p. 5) and offers "philology" as a third term, the one that Tolkien espoused (p. 7). Unfortunately, Shippey never really relates this political battle to the metaphorical battles of the *Beowulf* essay, the latter a work that he does discuss on pp. 42–49. See also the related discussion of Anglo-Saxon scholarship in Tolkien's day by Paul Bibire, "Sægde se þe cuþe: J.R.R. Tolkien as Anglo-Saxonist," in *Scholarship and Fantasy: Proceedings of the Tolkien Phenomenon, May 1992, Turku, Finland* (special issue), edited by K.J. Battarbee, Anglicana Turkuensia, no. 12 (Turku: University of Turku, 1993), esp. pp. 111–14. Bibire notes that Tolkien "complained, as others have done, of the strange Anglo-Latinism with which the English disown their ancestors, just as the English schools of most British universities have now chosen, to differing degrees, to disown the language and writings of those ancestors. In a period which, unhappily, Tolkien lived to see, 'Anglo-Saxon' (used almost exclusively as a term of contempt) and 'language' (similarly) were largely eliminated or exiled from the academic study of English in Britain" (p. 111).

4. See Shippey, *Road to Middle-earth,* pp. 9–20.

5. See, for this concept discussed throughout the book, Clyde S. Kilby, *Tolkien and the "Silmarillion"* (Wheaton, Ill.: Harold Shaw Publishers, 1976), but especially p. 6.

6. J.R.R. Tolkien, "On Fairy-Stories," in *Tree and Leaf* (London: Allen and Unwin, 1964; Boston: Houghton Mifflin, 1965), p. 3. Note that the pagination of *Tree and Leaf* is identical to the reprint of the book in *The Tolkien Reader* (New York: Ballantine, 1966).

7. See J.R.R. Tolkien, "Mythopoeia," in *Tree and Leaf, Including the Poem "Mythopoeia,"* introduced by Christopher Tolkien, rev. ed. (London: Allen and Unwin, 1988; Boston: Houghton Mifflin, 1989), pp. 97–101, here, p. 97. See Christopher Tolkien's discussion of his father's annotation of the two types, Philomythus and Misomythus, in his introduction, p. 7. See also Humphrey Carpenter, *J.R.R. Tolkien: A Biography* (London, Boston, and Sydney: Allen and Unwin, 1977), pp. 146–48, about the night of 19 September 1931 when the discussion among the two men and Hugo Dyson took place; it led to Tolkien's writing of "Mythopoeia" during an Examination Schools invigilation. C.S. Lewis apparently argued for what Tolkien called the "true myth" of Jesus Christ, as opposed to the "false myths."

8. J.R.R. Tolkien, *Farmer Giles of Ham* (London: Allen and Unwin, 1949; Boston: Houghton Mifflin, 1950), p. 7.

9. J.R.R. Tolkien, foreword to *The Lord of the Rings,* 3 vols., rev. ed. (London: Allen and Unwin; Boston: Houghton Mifflin, 1965), 1:ix.

10. J.R.R. Tolkien and E.V. Gordon, eds., *Sir Gawain and the Green Knight,* 2d ed., rev. Norman Davis (Oxford: Clarendon Press, 1967), p. vii.

11. J.R.R. Tolkien, prefatory note, *The English Text of the Ancrene Riwle: Ancrene Wisse,* Early English Text Society, n.s., no. 249 (London, New York, and Toronto: Oxford University Press, 1962), pp. vi–viii.

12. P. vii. Note the similarity to the comments in J.R.R. Tolkien's introduction to *Sir Gawain and the Green Knight, Pearl, and Sir Orfeo,* trans. J.R.R. Tolkien (London: Allen and Unwin; Boston: Houghton Mifflin, 1975), p. 17. Ignoring discussions of the sources of *Sir Gawain* largely because there are no direct ones, Tolkien declares, "For that reason, since I am speaking of this poem and this author, and not of ancient rituals, nor of pagan divinities of the Sun, nor of Fertility, nor of the Dark and the Underworld, in the almost wholly lost antiquity of the North and of these Western Isles—as remote from Sir Gawain of Camelot as the gods of the Aegean are from Troilus and Pandarus in Chaucer—for that reason I have not said anything about the story,

or stories, that the author used." Of course, in this very long *occupatio* (a rhetorical figure used frequently in the Middle Ages) he has said quite a lot.

13. J.R.R. Tolkien, preface to *The Ancrene Riwle,* trans. M[ary]. B. Salu (London: Burns and Oates, 1955), p. v.

14. J.R.R. Tolkien, prefatory remarks, *Beowulf and the Finnesburg Fragment,* trans. John R. Clark Hall (1940; rev. ed. 1950; reprinted London: Allen and Unwin, 1972), p. x.

15. J.R.R. Tolkien, "*Ancrene Wisse* and *Hali Meiðhad,*" *Essays and Studies by Members of the English Association* 14 (1929): 104. For similar expressions of his interest in Old and Middle English philology and linguistics, see Tolkien's *A Middle English Vocabulary* (Oxford: Clarendon Press, 1922), designed to be used with Kenneth Sisam, *Fourteenth-Century Verse and Prose* (Oxford: Clarendon Press, 1921); "Some Contributions to Middle-English Lexicography," *Review of English Studies* 1 (1925): 210–15; "The Devil's Coach-Horses," *Review of English Studies* 1 (1925): 331–36; foreword to *A New Glossary of the Dialect of the Huddersfield District,* by Walter E. Haigh (London: Oxford University Press, 1928), pp. xiii–xviii; "Sigelwara Land," pt. 1, *Medium Aevum* 1 (1932): 183–96, and pt. 2, *Medium Aevum* 3 (1934): 95–111; "Chaucer as Philologist: The Reeve's Tale," *Transactions of the Philological Society* (1934): 1–70; and "Middle English 'Losenger': Sketch of an Etymological and Semantic Enquiry," in *Essais de Philologie Moderne* (Paris: Société d'édition "Les Belles Lettres," 1953), pp. 63–76. Tom Shippey's *Road to Middle-earth* analyzes the relationship between Tolkien's interest in philology and etymology and the development of his languages, mythology, and fictional writings.

16. S.T.R.O. d'Ardenne, "The Man and the Scholar," in *J.R.R. Tolkien, Scholar and Storyteller: Essays in Memoriam,* ed. Mary Salu and Robert T. Farrell (Ithaca and London: Cornell University Press, 1979), p. 32.

17. J.R.R. Tolkien, *The Adventures of Tom Bombadil* (London: Allen and Unwin; Boston: Houghton Mifflin, 1962), p. 7.

18. For a discussion of the enormous time and energy Tolkien devoted to his teaching, research, and other professional responsibilities, see Carpenter, pp. 131–42.

19. Kilby, pp. 22–23.

20. Kilby, p. 23.

21. Kilby, p. 20.

22. Kilby, p. 33.

23. Kilby, pp. 17, 31, and 32.

24. J.R.R. Tolkien, *The Two Towers; Being the Second Part of "The Lord of the Rings,"* rev. ed. (London: Allen and Unwin; Boston: Houghton Mifflin, 1965), p. 204.

25. See, for example, *Cursor Mundi,* ed. Richard Morris, Early English Text Society, o.s., nos. 57, 59, 62, 66, 68, 99, 101 (London: K. Paul, Trench, Trübner, 1874–93), pp. 84–86. For other medieval descriptions of the Tree, see Morton W. Bloomfield, *The Seven Deadly Sins: An Introduction to the History of a Religious Concept* (East Lansing: Michigan State College, 1952).

26. Saint Augustine, *On Christian Doctrine,* trans. D.W. Robertson Jr. (Indianapolis, Ind., and New York: Bobbs-Merrill, 1958), p. 14 (1.13).

27. On the idea of the "flesh" of parable, Macrobius in his fourth-century commentary on the *Somnium Scipionis,* an extremely influential work in the Middle Ages, described fabulous narrative as the truth "treated in a fictitious style," or "a decent and dignified conception of holy truths, with respectable events and characters, . . . presented beneath a modest veil of allegory." Such a style must be employed because "a frank, open exposition of herself is distasteful to Nature, who, just as she has withheld an understanding of herself from the uncouth senses of men by enveloping herself in variegated garments, has also desired to have her secrets handled by more prudent individuals through fabulous narratives." See Macrobius, *Commentary on the Dream of Scipio,* trans. William Harris Stahl (1952; reprint, New York and London: Columbia University Press, 1966), pp. 85–86 (1.2.10–11 and 17). "Allegory" was also regarded by poets as a kind of "cover" or "cloak" for bare truth in the twelfth century: see the discussion of *integumentum* in Jane Chance, *Medieval Mythography,* vol. 1, *From Roman North Africa to the School of Chartres, 433–1177* (Gainesville and London: University Press of Florida, 1994), pp. 412ff.

28. See, for example, John Conley, ed., *The Middle English Pearl: Critical Essays* (Notre Dame, Ind., and London: University of Notre Dame Press, 1970).

29. C.S. Lewis to Fr. Peter Milward, 10 December 1956, in *Letters of C.S. Lewis,* ed. W.H. Lewis (1966; reprint, New York and London: Harcourt Brace Jovanovich, 1975), p. 273.

30. d'Ardenne, p. 35.

31. For example, Lionel S. Lewis, *Scaling the Ivory Tower: Merit and Its Limits in Academic Careers* (Baltimore, Md., and London: Johns Hopkins University Press, 1975), pp. 1–2, 4–6, traces back the history of the American university split between the Germanic research uni-

versity and the English teaching college to the mid-nineteenth century, when the Teutonic presence first asserted itself in the institution.

32. Carpenter, p. 131. For the two sides of his personality, one public and cheerful, one private and pessimistic, which apparently developed after the death of his mother, see p. 31.

CHAPTER 2. THE KING UNDER THE MOUNTAIN

1. See, for example, Mary R. Lucas, review of *The Hobbit*, *Library Journal* 63 (1 May 1938): 385: "It will have a limited appeal unless properly introduced and even then will be best liked by those children whose imagination is alert." More recently Randel Helms viewed it as intended "for children and filled with a whimsy few adults can accept," in *Tolkien's World* (Boston: Houghton Mifflin, 1974), p. 19.

2. For a discussion of the children's story elements, primarily the narrative intrusions, plus those episodes that foreshadow incidents in *The Lord of the Rings* (a work that, in contrast, "stretches the adult imagination") (p. 19), see Paul H. Kocher, *Master of Middle-earth: The Fiction of J.R.R. Tolkien* (Boston: Houghton Mifflin, 1972), pp. 19–33.

3. See *The Annotated Hobbit*, annotated by Douglas A. Anderson (Boston: Houghton Mifflin, 1988), p. 321; also the excellent and careful cataloguing of differences among editions by Wayne G. Hammond, with Douglas A. Anderson, in *J.R.R. Tolkien: A Descriptive Bibliography* (Winchester: St. Paul's Bibliographies; New Castle, Delaware: Oak Knoll Books, 1993), esp. pp. 4–71 (just on *The Hobbit*); and Bonniejean Christensen's excellent analysis of the various changes in Gollum as a result of Tolkien's revisions, but with awareness of the awkward mixture of the two levels, children's and adult, in Bonniejean Christensen, "Gollum's Character Transformation in *The Hobbit*," in *A Tolkien Compass*, ed. Jared Lobdell (La Salle, Ill.: Open Court Press, 1975), pp. 9–28.

4. Christensen, "Gollum's Character Transformation," p. 27.

5. Dorothy Matthews, "The Psychological Journey of Bilbo Baggins," in Lobdell, pp. 29–42, views Bilbo's maturation in Jungian terms; Helms, *Tolkien's World*, pp. 41–55, interprets it in Freudian terms and the whole work, in addition, as a microcosm of *The Lord of the Rings* (pp. 19–40); and William H. Green provides an incisive psychoanalytic study of this bildungsroman in *"The Hobbit": A Journey into Maturity* (New York: Twayne Publishers, 1994).

6. The narrator seems to have the voice of Tolkien, according to Paul Edmund Thomas, who draws on Wayne Booth's *The Rhetoric of*

Fiction for his critical terms, in "Some of Tolkien's Narrators," in *Tolkien's Legendarium: Essays on "The History of Middle-earth,"* edited by Verlyn Flieger and Carl F. Hostetter, Contributions to the Study of Science Fiction and Fantasy, no. 86 (Westport, Conn., and London: Greenwood Press, 2000), p. 163. Tolkien's role as narrator in *The Hobbit* is discussed in terms of "teasers," glosses on the action, shifter of viewpoints, and describer of events (pp. 161–81).

7. J.R.R. Tolkien, quoted by Philip Norman in "The Prevalence of Hobbits," *New York Times Magazine,* 15 January 1967, p. 100.

8. Thomas, pp. 161–81.The early drafts of "A Long-expected Party" have been published by Christopher Tolkien in *The Return of the Shadow,* vol. 6 of *The History of Middle-Earth,* ed. Christopher Tolkien, 12 vols (London: Allen and Unwin, 1983–95; Boston: Houghton Mifflin, 1984–96).

9. According to penciled notes by Tolkien on a letter of 18 January 1938 from G.H. White of the Examination Schools, Tolkien began writing *The Hobbit* after he moved to 20 Northmoor Road in 1931, although his children had heard some episodes from it before 1930. Michael Tolkien, according to Anderson, *The Annotated Hobbit,* p. 1, recalls that the first sentence was written in 1928 and portions of the remainder in 1929. The typescript (except the last chapters) was shown to Lewis in 1932 and the work was retyped for Allen and Unwin in 1936.

10. Tolkien, letter to *The Observer,* 20 February 1938, p. 9.

11. Tolkien critics have, curiously, ignored his own *Beowulf* article as a possible parallel to *The Hobbit,* although they have adduced parallels between the novel and other medieval works, including *Beowulf* itself. For the names of the Dwarves derived in part from the *Eddas,* see Patrick J. Callahan, "Tolkien's Dwarfs and the Eddas," *Tolkien Journal* 15 (1972): 20; for the antecedents of Gandalf, the Dwarves, the Elves, the Ring, and other elements in Norse mythology, see Mitzi M. Brunsdale, "Norse Mythological Elements in The Hobbit," *Mythlore* 9 (1983): 49–50; and Lynn Bryce, "The Influence of Scandinavian Mythology in the Works of J.R.R. Tolkien," *Edda* 7 (1983): 113–19. See also Richard Schindler's fine analysis of the medieval sources informing some of Tolkien's artistry in *The Hobbit's* illustrations, especially in relation to Beorn's hall and the town of Dale, in "The Expectant Landscape: J.R.R. Tolkien's Illustrations for *The Hobbit,*" in *J.R.R. Tolkien: The Hobbit Drawings, Watercolors, and Manuscript* (Milwaukee, Wis.: Marquette University Press, 1987), pp. 14–27.

12. Christensen, "Tolkien's Creative Technique: *Beowulf* and *The Hobbit,*" *Orcrist* 7 (1972–73): 16.

13. For the influence of *Beowulf* on *The Hobbit,* see also Bonniejean Christensen, *"Beowulf* and *The Hobbit:* Elegy into Fantasy in J.R.R. Tolkien's Creative Technique," *Dissertation Abstracts International* 30 (1970): 4401A-4402A (University of Southern California) (the dissertation from which her essay, "Tolkien's Creative Technique," was derived).

14. J.R.R. Tolkien, "Beowulf: The Monsters and the Critics," *Proceedings of the British Academy* 22 (1936): 245–95, reprinted in *An Anthology of Beowulf Criticism,* ed. Lewis E. Nicholson (Notre Dame, Ind.: University of Notre Dame Press, 1963), pp. 51–103. All citations refer to the Nicholson reprint (here, p. 81).

15. See Green, *"The Hobbit": A Journey to Maturity.*

16. For another view of *The Hobbit* as four-part in structure, see also William Howard Green, "*The Hobbit* and Other Fiction by J.R.R. Tolkien: Their Roots in Medieval Heroic Literature and Language," *Dissertation Abstracts International* 30 (1970): 4944A (Louisiana State University). Green catalogues medieval analogues for *The Hobbit*'s characters, events, and symbols; his work, like Christensen's, is important because it reveals Tolkien's indebtedness to medieval literature in *The Hobbit* and other works.

17. On eucatastrophe and fantasy, see J.R.R. Tolkien, "On Fairy-Stories," in *Tree and Leaf* (London: Allen and Unwin, 1964; Boston: Houghton Mifflin, 1965), pp. 68–73, reprinted in *The Tolkien Reader* (1966; reprinted New York: Ballantine, 1975). On *Beowulf* as an elegy, see Tolkien, "Beowulf: The Monsters and the Critics," p. 85. See also Christensen, "Tolkien's Creative Technique," p. 16.

18. Levin L. Schücking, "Das Königsideal im *Beowulf," MHRA Bulletin* 3 (1929): 143–54, reprinted and translated as "The Ideal of Kingship in *Beowulf,*" in Nicholson, pp. 35–49.

19. J.R.R. Tolkien discusses the dialectical features of this work in "*Ancrene Wisse* and *Hali Meiðhad," Essays and Studies by Members of the English Association* 14 (1929): 104–26; applauds the translation of *The Ancrene Riwle* by M[ary]. B. Salu (London: Burns & Oates, 1955), in his preface to it (p. v); and himself edits *The English Text of the Ancrene Riwle: Ancrene Wisse* for the Early English Text Society, no. 249 (London, New York, and Toronto: Oxford University Press, 1962).

20. For a rather confusing six-part structure based on the two monsters, Gollum and the dragon, in *The Hobbit,* see Paul Bibire, "By Stock or Stone: Recurrent Imagery and Narrative Pattern in *The Hobbit,*" in *Scholarship and Fantasy: Proceedings of the Tolkien Phenomenon, May 1992, Turku, Finland* (special issue), ed. K.J. Battarbee,

Anglicana Turkuensia, no. 12 (Turku: University of Turku, 1993), esp. pp. 203–16. Bibire says, "The Matter of the Mountain thus consists of a large three-fold structure (Bilbo's descents into the dwarf-mines), and a large binary structure (potential and actual war), framing a central unitary episode (the death of Smaug). It sums up the narrative structure and motifs, imagery and characters of the whole of the rest of the text" (p. 214). See also the diagram provided by Green, *"The Hobbit": A Journey to Maturity.*

21. For a more recent discussion of the deadly sins in *The Hobbit, Lord of the Rings,* and *Silmarillion,* see Charles W. Nelson, "The Sins of Middle-earth: Tolkien's Use of Medieval Allegory," in *J.R.R. Tolkien and His Literary Resonances: Views of Middle-earth,* ed. George Clark and Daniel Timmons (Westport, Conn., and London: Greenwood Press, 2000), pp. 83–94.

22. J.R.R. Tolkien, *The Hobbit; or, There and Back Again* (1937, 1938; rev. ed. London: Allen and Unwin; Boston: Houghton Mifflin, 1965), p. 83.

23. For the stone-giants in *The Hobbit* and an analysis of their etymological origin, from Greek *gigas* (rebellious giants who assaulted Mount Olympus), from *eoten* in Old English, and even, in Middle English, from *ent*; and for the appearance elsewhere in Tolkien of the word giant (especially in relation to the Númenóreans of Gondor, the Ents, and the Giant in *Farmer Giles of Ham*), see the fine analysis by Anders Stenström, "Some Notes on Giants in Tolkien's Writings," in Battarbee, pp. 53–71.

24. On the Wargs, see J.S. Ryan, "Warg, Wearg, Earg and Werewolf," *Mallorn* 23 (1986): 25–29.

25. Kocher, *Master of Middle-earth,* pp. 19–23.

CHAPTER 3. THE CHRISTIAN KING

1. Mrs. [Mary Martha] Sherwood, ed., *The Governess, or The Little Female Academy* (1820), cited in Gillian Avery, *Nineteenth-Century Children: Heroes and Heroines in English Children's Stories, 1780–1900* (London: Hodder and Stoughton, 1965), p. 41.

2. According to the editorial in *Redbook,* December 1967, p. 6, wherein "Smith" was first published (pp. 58–61, 101, 103–7). Also reprinted in *The Tolkien Reader* (New York: Ballantine, 1966); and in *Smith of Wootton Major and Farmer Giles of Ham* (London: Allen and Unwin; Boston: Houghton Mifflin, 1967).

3. Randel Helms, *Tolkien's World* (London: Allen and Unwin;

Boston: Houghton Mifflin, 1974), p. 118.

4. Paul Kocher, *Master of Middle-earth: The Fiction of J.R.R. Tolkien* (London: Allen and Unwin; Boston: Houghton Mifflin, 1972), pp. 161–69.

5. For "Leaf," see Helms, *Tolkien's World*, pp. 110–18; and Kocher, *Master of Middle-earth*, pp. 144–51; for "Smith," see Kocher, *Master of Middle-earth*, pp. 173–81.

6. Helms, *Tolkien's World*, pp. 119–25: Smith is Tolkien; the Master Cook resembles Bilbo. As Tolkien in 1949 would have been fifty-seven, on completing *The Lord of the Rings* in that same year he might have felt ready to relinquish his artistic "gift."

7. J.R.R. Tolkien, cited by Philip Norman, "The Prevalence of Hobbits," *The New York Times Magazine* (15 January 1967), p. 100.

8. J.R.R. Tolkien, "Beowulf: The Monsters and the Critics," *Proceedings of the British Academy* 22 (1936): 245–95; reprinted in *An Anthology of Beowulf Criticism*, ed. Lewis E. Nicholson (Notre Dame, Ind.: University of Notre Dame Press, 1963), pp. 51–103. All references derive from the Nicholson anthology.

9. J.R.R. Tolkien, "On Fairy-Stories," *Essays Presented to Charles Williams*, ed. C.S. Lewis (London: Oxford University Press, 1947; Grand Rapids, Mich.: William B. Eerdmans, 1966); rev. and reprinted in *Tree and Leaf* (London: Allen and Unwin, 1964; Boston: Houghton Mifflin, 1965), p. 66; reprinted in *The Tolkien Reader* (New York: Ballantine, 1966; reprinted 1975). All references derive from *The Tolkien Reader* (p. 67 for this citation), but pagination is the same as that in *Tree and Leaf.*

10. See Peter M. Gilliver, "At the Wordface: J.R.R. Tolkien's Work on the Oxford English Dictionary," in *Proceedings of the J.R.R. Tolkien Centenary Conference, Keble College, Oxford, 1992*, ed. Patricia Reynolds and Glen H. Goodknight. *Mythlore* 80 and *Mallorn* 30 in one volume (Milton Keynes, England: Tolkien Society; Altadena, Calif.: Mythopoeic Press, 1995), pp. 173–86.

11. See *The Ancrene Riwle*, trans. M.B. Salu (London: Burns and Oates, 1955), p. 173.

12. See Etienne Gilson, *Reason and Revelation in the Middle Ages* (1938; reprint, New York: Charles Scribner's Sons, 1966).

13. See Colin Duriez, "Sub-creation and Tolkien's Theology of Story," in *Scholarship and Fantasy: Proceedings of the Tolkien Phenomenon, May 1992, Turku, Finland* (special issue), ed. K.J. Battarbee, Anglicana Turkuensia, no. 12 (Turku: University of Turku, 1993), esp. pp. 133–49 (here, p. 137).

14. See Bonniejean Christensen, "*Beowulf* and *The Hobbit:* Elegy into Fantasy in J.R.R. Tolkien's Creative Technique," *Dissertation Abstracts International* 30 (1970): 4401A-4402A (University of Southern California); and the article derived from the dissertation, "Tolkien's Creative Technique: *Beowulf* and *The Hobbit*," *Orcrist* 7 (1972–73): 16–20. For Friedrich Klaeber's edition of *Beowulf*, see *Beowulf and the Fight at Finnsburg*, 3d ed. (Boston: D.C. Heath, 1950).

15. Anthony J. Ugolnik, "*Wordhord Onleac:* The Medieval Sources of J.R.R. Tolkien's Linguistic Aesthetic," *Mosaic* 10 (winter 1977): 21.

16. J.R.R. Tolkien, "Leaf by Niggle," *Dublin Review*, 216 (1945): 461, reprinted in *Tree and Leaf*; and in *The Tolkien Reader* (p. 104). Pagination is the same in both *Tree and Leaf* and *The Tolkien Reader*.

17. See especially D.W. Robertson Jr., "The Doctrine of Charity in Mediaeval Literary Gardens: A Topical Approach through Symbolism and Allegory," *Speculum* 26 (1951), reprinted in Nicholson, pp. 165–88; see esp. pp. 168–73.

18. Macrobius, *Commentary on the Dream of Scipio*, trans. William Harris Stahl (1952; reprint, New York and London: Columbia University Press, 1966), p. 131. But see also pp. 128ff.

19. In his twelfth-century commentary on the first six books of the *Aeneid*, Bernardus Silvestris describes this Neoplatonic version of the over- and underworld. See Jane Chance (Nitzsche), *The Genius Figure in Antiquity and the Middle Ages* (New York and London: Columbia University Press, 1975), pp. 43–45.

20. Reprinted in J.R.R. Tolkien, *Smith of Wootton Major and Farmer Giles of Ham* (New York: Ballantine, 1969), p. 21.

CHAPTER 4. THE GERMANIC LORD

1. This anthology of *Songs for the Philologists* was printed at the Department of English of University College in London on its private press at the request of A.H. Smith. The anthology was compiled (according to its title page) as a "printing exercise" by other well-known scholars in addition to J.R.R. Tolkien, E.V. Gordon, and A.H. Smith, including G. Tillotson, B. Pattison, and other members of the English department of University College in London. Of the original copies known to have been privately printed in 1936, only thirteen were believed to have survived a fire where the press was located and may still exist, according to Rulon-Miller Books of St. Paul, Minnesota, who listed a copy for sale for $10,000 on the Internet in early 2001 and indicated there were only two other copies listed on the OCLC, at the

State University of New York at Buffalo and at Oxford University. See the description by Humphrey Carpenter, *J.R.R. Tolkien: A Biography* (London, Boston, and Sydney: Allen and Unwin, 1977), p. 105; and Tom Shippey, *Road to Middle-earth*, 1982, rev. ed. (London: Allen and Unwin, 1992), pp. 5, 24, 244–45, 285, 303–9. Shippey notes that Tolkien's "Bagme Bloma," contained in the collection, is the only extant poem in Gothic (p. 24). Excerpts of four of the more autobiographical poems and their translations by Shippey, including "Bagme Bloma" and three others in Old English, are presented in an appendix in Shippey, *Road to Middle-earth*, pp. 303–9.

2. Shippey labels two of these Tolkien poems, "Two Little Schemes" and "Lit. and Lang.," which attacked teachers who sided with "Lit." rather than "Lang." in the curriculum and turf battles of the era, "the worst he ever wrote." See *Road to Middle-earth*, p. 5.

3. For Friedrich Klaeber's edition of *Beowulf*, see *Beowulf and the Fight at Finnsburg*, 3d ed. (Boston: D.C. Heath, 1950).

4. J.R.R. Tolkien, "The Lay of Aotrou and Itroun," *Welsh Review* 4 (1945): 254–66. See Paul Kocher's discussion of the work in *Master of Middle-earth: The Fiction of J.R.R. Tolkien* (Boston: Houghton Mifflin, 1972), pp. 169–78. Curiously, Kocher terms it a "fairy-tale tragedy," ignoring both its medieval genre and Tolkien's own definition of "fairy-story" and "tragedy." See also, for this poem and others, George Burke Johnston, "The Poetry of J.R.R. Tolkien," in "The Tolkien Papers" (special issue), *Mankato Studies in English* 2 (1967): 63–75; and Shippey, *Road to Middle-earth*, who relates "The Lay" to a Breton lay in *Unfinished Tales*, the story of "Aldarion and Erendis: The Mariner's Wife" about a wife, Erendis, left by her husband, to a Breton lay by Marie de France, and more indirectly, to a Breton song, "Le Seigneur Nann et la Fée," pp. 217, 246–47, 300. (See J.R.R. Tolkien, *Unfinished Tales of Númenor and Middle-earth*, edited by Christopher Tolkien [London: Allen & Unwin, 1979; Boston: Houghton Mifflin, 1980], pp. 181–227.) For the story of Erendis, Shippey traces its origin to the story of Skathi, daughter of the mountain-giant, who married the sea-god Njǫrthr, in Snorri Sturluson's *Prose Edda* (Shippey, p. 217).

5. J.R.R. Tolkien, *Farmer Giles of Ham* (London: Allen and Unwin, 1949; Boston: Houghton Mifflin, 1950); reprinted in *The Tolkien Reader* (New York: Ballantine, 1966); and in *Smith of Wootton Major and Farmer Giles of Ham* (New York: Ballantine, 1969). All references to *Farmer Giles* derive from *The Tolkien Reader* reprint. For a discussion of its genre, see J.A. Johnson, "*Farmer Giles of Ham*: What Is It?" *Orcrist* 7 (1972–73): 21–24. Johnson adds epic to fabliau and

romance and also sees in *Farmer Giles* echoes of the Icelandic saga, the chronicle, and the fable. See also Shippey, *The Road to Middle-earth*, who discusses its source in the nursery rhyme, esp. pp. 88–91, and (like this earlier incarnation), its use of the philologist as a figure, pp. 241– 42.

    6. J.R.R. Tolkien, "The Homecoming of Beorhtnoth Beorhthelm's Son," *Essays and Studies by Members of the English Association*, n.s., 6 (1953): 1–18; reprinted in *The Tolkien Reader*. See Tolkien's prefatory comments on its verse form (p. 5), and his concluding gloss on its genre (p. 19). See also Shippey, *Road to Middle-earth*, pp. 140–41, 187, 270.

    7. J.R.R. Tolkien, "Imram," *Time and Tide* 36 (1955): 1561. For a fine analysis of the poem and a comparison with its source, see Kocher, *Master of Middle-earth*, pp. 204–12. For a brief history of this source in the Middle Ages, see George Boas, *Essays on Primitivism and Related Ideas in the Middle Ages* (Baltimore, Md.: Johns Hopkins University Press, 1948), pp. 158–59. See also, for an analysis of its relation to the *imram*, the ending of "Akallabêth" in *The Silmarillion*, and a paradise drawn from the life of St. Brendan in the *South English Legendary*, Shippey, *Road to Middle-earth*, pp. 252–53.

    8. J.R.R. Tolkien, *The Adventures of Tom Bombadil* (London: Allen and Unwin, 1962; Boston: Houghton Mifflin, 1962); reprinted in *The Tolkien Reader*. For a discussion of "scholarly parody" in this work, see Randel Helms, *Tolkien's World* (Boston: Houghton Mifflin, 1974), pp. 126–47; and Shippey, *Road to Middle-earth*, pp. 247–50.

    9. In addition to the introduction and chapter 2 of this study, on medieval ideas in *The Hobbit*, see, for example, Bonniejean Christensen's "*Beowulf* and *The Hobbit*: Elegy into Fantasy in J.R.R. Tolkien's Creative Technique," *Dissertation Abstracts International* 30 (1970): 4401A-4402A (University of Southern California); the epitome of that dissertation in Christensen, "Tolkien's Creative Technique: *Beowulf* and *The Hobbit*," *Orcrist* 7 (1972–73): 16–20; William Howard Green, "*The Hobbit* and Other Fiction by J.R.R. Tolkien: Their Roots in Medieval Heroic Literature and Language," *Dissertation Abstracts International* 30 (1970): 4944A (Louisiana State University); and, for a philological analysis of its sources, Shippey, *Road to Middle-earth*, pp. 61–94.

    On medieval ideas in *The Lord of the Rings*, see, in addition to the introduction and chapter 5 of this study, for example, John Tinkler, "Old English in Rohan," in *Tolkien and the Critics*, ed. Neil D. Isaacs and Rose A. Zimbardo (Notre Dame, Ind., and London: University of Notre Dame Press, 1968), pp. 164–69; Sandra L. Miesel, "Some Motifs and Sources for *Lord of the Rings,*" *Riverside Quarterly* 3 (1968): 125–28; E.L. Epstein, "The Novels of J.R.R. Tolkien and the Ethnology of Medieval Christendom," *Philological Quarterly* 48 (1969): 517–25; Lin Carter, *Tolkien: A Look Behind "The Lord of the Rings"* (New York: Ballantine, 1969); and, for a philological analysis of its sources, Shippey, *Road to Middle-earth,* passim.

10. J.R.R. Tolkien, "Beowulf: The Monsters and the Critics," *Proceedings of the British Academy* 22 (1936): 245–95, reprinted in *An Anthology of Beowulf Criticism,* ed. Lewis E. Nicholson (Notre Dame, Ind.: University of Notre Dame Press, 1963). All references derive from the Nicholson anthology (here, p. 85).

11. J.R.R. Tolkien, "On Fairy-Stories," *Essays Presented to Charles Williams,* ed. C.S. Lewis (London: Oxford University Press, 1947; Grand Rapids, Mich.: William B. Eerdmans, 1966), pp. 38–89; revised and reprinted in *Tree and Leaf* (London: Allen and Unwin, 1964; Boston: Houghton Mifflin, 1965); reprinted in *The Tolkien Reader*; here, pp. 68–70.

12. For a Boethian definition of medieval tragedy and its Chaucerian application, see D.W. Robertson Jr., "Chaucerian Tragedy," *ELH* 19 (1952): 1–37; reprinted in *Chaucer Criticism,* vol. 2, *"Troilus and Criseyde" and the Minor Poems,* ed. Richard J. Schoeck and Jerome Taylor (Notre Dame, Ind.: University of Notre Dame Press, 1961), pp. 86–121.

13. When Clyde S. Kilby met Tolkien in 1964, Tolkien relayed this plan of complementary writing to him. See Clyde S. Kilby, *Tolkien and the "Silmarillion"* (Wheaton, Ill.: Harold Shaw Publishers, 1976), p. 11. See also C.S. Lewis, *Perelandra, Out of the Silent Planet,* and *That Hideous Strength* [*the Perelandra trilogy*] (London: John Lane/Bodley Head, 1938–45; New York: Macmillan, 1942–46).

14. Kocher, *Master of Middle-earth,* p. 170.

15. See the influence of Chaucer's tale of Sir Thopas from the *Canterbury Tales* on Tolkien, in parts of "Errantry" and "The Lady of Eärendil," in John D. Rateliff, "J.R.R. Tolkien: 'Sir Topas' Revisited." *Notes and Queries,* n.s., 227 (1982): 348. For the influence of the *Gawain* poet on Tolkien's scholarship, see the clever study by Tom Shippey of the importance of certain Middle English words that appear in the glossary in Tolkien's and E.V. Gordon's critical edition of *Sir Gawain* (for example, *etayneȝ, dreped, wodwos*) and compared with his translation, in "Tolkien and the *Gawain* poet," in *Proceedings of the J.R.R. Tolkien Centenary Conference, Keble College, Oxford, 1992,* ed. Patricia Reynolds and Glen H. Goodknight, *Mythlore* 80 and *Mallorn*

30 in one volume (Milton Keynes, England: Tolkien Society; Altadena, Calif.: Mythopoeic Press, 1995), pp. 213–19. See also, for the influence of the *Gawain* poet on Tolkien's fiction, principally *The Lord of the Rings*, Miriam Youngerman Miller's treatment of imagery derived from the *Gawain* poet, in "'Of sum mayn meruayle, þat he myȝt trawe': *The Lord of the Rings* and *Sir Gawain and the Green Knight*," in *Medievalism: Inklings and Others* (special issue), ed. Jane Chance, *Studies in Medievalism* 3, no. 3 (1991): 345–65. On Tolkien's indebtedness to the Green Knight in *The Lord of the Rings* in relation to the Ents, Treebeard, and Old Man Willow, see Verlyn Flieger, "The Green Man, the Green Knight, and Treebeard: Scholarship and Invention in Tolkien's Fiction," in *Scholarship and Fantasy: Proceedings of the Tolkien Phenomenon, May 1992, Turku, Finland* (special issue), ed. K.J. Battarbee, Anglicana Turkuensia, no. 12 (Turku: University of Turku, 1993), esp. pp. 85–98. See also Roger C. Schlobin, who looks for parallels between the characters of *Sir Gawain* and those of *The Lord of the Rings*, in "The Monsters Are Talismans and Transgressions: Tolkien and *Sir Gawain and the Green Knight*," in *J.R.R. Tolkien and His Literary Resonances: Views of Middle-earth*, ed. George Clark and Daniel Timmons (Westport, Conn., and London: Greenwood Press, 2000), pp. 71–81.

16. For these works, see J.R.R. Tolkien and E.V. Gordon, eds., *Sir Gawain and the Green Knight*, 2d ed., rev. Norman Davis (Oxford: Clarendon Press, l967), p. vii; "Ofermod," in "The Homecoming of Beorhtnoth Beorhthelm's Son," pp. 13–18; and J.R.R. Tolkien, trans., *Sir Gawain and the Green Knight, Pearl, and Sir Orfeo*, ed. Christopher Tolkien (London: Allen and Unwin, 1975; Boston: Houghton Mifflin, 1975).

17. Tolkien's argument in "The Devil's Coach-Horses" is that *aver* (West Midland *eaver*, from Old English *afor* and *eafor*) in the twelfth-century *Hali Meiðhad* (a work on which he would publish in 1929, in "*Ancrene Wisse* and *Hali Meiðhad*," *Essays and Studies by Members of the English Association* 14 [1929]: 104–26) does not refer to a rotting boar—which the Devil appears to be riding—but instead, and almost equally irregularly, a large cart horse; see *Review of English Studies* 1 (1925): 331–36. Tolkien relates his philological analysis, in his humorous conclusion, to Chaucer: "The devil appears to have ridden his coach-horses like a postilion, but he was in worse case than Chaucer's shipman who 'rood upon a rouncy as he couthe,' his steeds seem indeed to have been heavy old dobbins that needed all his spurring" (p. 336). See also his 1934 study of the dialectical differences between the clerks of northern medieval England and a miller and his family of

southern England, in "Chaucer as Philologist: The Reeve's Tale," *Transactions of the Philological Society* (1934): 1–70.

18. Kocher, *Master of Middle-earth,* p. 186. Kocher's excellent discussion (pp. 178–95) stresses the work as a scholarly parody rather than as a literary parody of fourteenth-century works or of Tolkien's own creative works, especially *The Hobbit.*

19. See Charles Muscatine, *Chaucer and the French Tradition: A Study in Style and Meaning* (Berkeley and Los Angeles: University of California Press, 1957).

20. In the recording of "The Homecoming" taped in Tolkien's home, Tolkien's marvelous sound effects include the banging of file cabinet drawers to simulate the bumping of cartwheels over an uneven field of corpses. Occasionally, however, street sounds intrude. The tape is available on a souvenir cassette offered to conference participants in 1992 at Keble College Oxford, for "Tolkien: The Centenary, 1892–1992," to commemorate the hundredth birthday of Tolkien and the 1001st anniversary of the actual battle of Maldon. It contains, in addition to the reading by Tolkien, the portion of *The Battle of Maldon* described as "Beorhtnoth's Death" and Tolkien's "Ofermod" read by Christopher Tolkien (London: Grafton, 1992).

21. Canute has been revealed as especially well disposed toward the house at Ely, in a study published prior to "The Homecoming" that Tolkien may have read. David Knowles, in *The Monastic Order in England: A History of Its Development from the Times of Saint Dunstan to the Fourth Lateran Council, 943–1216* (Cambridge, Eng.: Cambridge University Press, 1949), declares that "Cnut, once in power, showed himself not only a strong and able ruler, but a patron of the monastic order and the friend of Aethelnoth of Canterbury and other monk-bishops. His reign shows no change in the policy of appointing monks to vacant sees, and Cnut and his chief magnates appear as benefactors to a number of important houses. In East Anglia, hitherto bare of monasteries, two great foundations owed their origin to the Danish king, Saint Benet's of Holme, near the coast not far from Norwich, and Bury Saint Edmunds. Both of these received colonists from Ely, a house for which Cnut always entertained a particular affection" (p. 70).

CHAPTER 5. THE LORD OF THE RINGS

1. Randel Helms, *Tolkien's World* (Boston: Houghton Mifflin, 1974), p. 21. For the entire analysis of the parallels, see chapter 2, "Tolkien's Leaf."

2. For its medieval (and classical) linguistic, literary, and mythological sources, influences, and parallels in general, see, for example, Caroline Whitman Everett, "The Imaginative Fiction of J.R.R. Tolkien" (master's thesis, Florida State University, 1957), chap. 4; Alexis Levitin, "J.R.R. Tolkien's *The Lord of the Rings*" (master's thesis, Columbia University, 1964), chap. 2; John Tinkler, "Old English in Rohan," in *Tolkien and the Critics,* ed. Neil D. Isaacs and Rose A. Zimbardo (Notre Dame, Ind., and London: University of Notre Dame Press, 1968), pp. 164–69; Sandra L. Miesel, "Some Motifs and Sources for *Lord of the Rings,*" *Riverside Quarterly* 3 (1968): 125; E.L. Epstein, "The Novels of J.R.R. Tolkien·and the Ethnology of Medieval Christendom," *Philological Quarterly* 48 (1969): 517–25; Lin Carter, *Tolkien: A Look Behind the Lord of the Rings* (New York: Ballantine, 1969), passim; Kenneth J. Reckford, "Some Trees in Virgil and Tolkien," in *Perspectives of Roman Poetry: A Classics Symposium,* ed. G. Karl Galinsky (Austin, Tex., and London: University of Texas Press, 1974), pp. 57–92; Charles A. Huttar, "Hell and the City: Tolkien and the Traditions of Western Literature," in *A Tolkien Compass,* ed. Jared Lobdell (La Salle, Ill.: Open Court Press, 1975), pp. 117–42; and Ruth S. Noel, *The Mythology of Middle-earth* (London: Thames and Hudson, 1977).

For the source and genre of *LR* as northern saga, see especially Gloria Ann Strange Slaughter St. Clair, "*The Lord of the Rings* as Saga," *Mythlore* 6 (1979): 11–16; St. Clair's earlier "Studies in the Sources of J.R.R. Tolkien's *The Lord of the Rings,*" *Dissertation Abstracts International* 30 (1970): 5001A (University of Oklahoma); and more recently, St. Clair, "An Overview of the Northern Influences on Tolkien's Works" and "Volsunga Saga and Narn: Some Analogies," in *Proceedings of the J.R.R. Tolkien Centenary Conference, Keble College,* Oxford, 1992, ed. Patricia Reynolds and Glen H. Goodknight, *Mythlore* 80 and *Mallorn* 30 in one volume (Milton Keynes, England: Tolkien Society; Altadena, Calif.: Mythopoeic Press, 1995), pp. 63–67 and 68–72.

On the conflict in *The Lord of the Rings* between the Germanic pessimism that *lif is læne* (life is loaned) (from Old English literature) and the medieval Christian idea that submission to God's will provides hope in a transitory world without meaning, see Ronald Christopher Sarti, "Man in a Mortal World: J.R.R. Tolkien and *The Lord of the Rings,*" *Dissertation Abstracts International* 45 (1984): 1410A (Indiana University). On the similarity between Unferth (in *Beowulf*) and Wormtongue, see Clive Tolley, "Tolkien and the Unfinished," in *Scholarship and Fantasy: Proceedings of the Tolkien Phenomenon, May 1992, Turku, Finland* (special issue), ed. K.J. Battarbee, Anglicana Turkuensia, no. 12 (Turku: University of Turku, 1992), pp. 154–56; on the influence of *Beowulf* and *The Battle of Maldon* on Tolkien's epic, see George Clark, "J.R.R. Tolkien and the True Hero," in *J.R.R. Tolkien and His Literary Resonances: Views of Middle-earth*, ed. George Clark and Daniel Timmons (Westport, Conn., and London: Greenwood Press, 2000), pp. 39–51.

Tom Shippey analyzes the indebtedness of "Orcs," "Ents," and "Hobbits" to Old Norse and Old English etymologies in "Creation from Philology in *The Lord of the Rings*," in *J.R.R. Tolkien, Scholar and Story-Teller: Essays in Memoriam*, ed. Mary Salu and Robert T. Farrell (Ithaca and London: Cornell University Press, 1979), 286–316. For analyses of the Greek, Latin, and Hebrew antecedents of Tolkienian names, see Dale W. Simpson, "Names and Moral Character in J.R.R. Tolkien's Middle-earth Books," *Publications of the Missouri Philological Association* 6 (1981): 1–5. Note that Shippey also traces the influence of Old Norse and Old English on detail used by Tolkien in the trilogy, such as the word "fallow" as an epithet for an Elven cloak, names of characters, and place names. See also Tom Shippey, *Road to Middle-earth*, 1982, rev. ed. (London: Allen and Unwin, 1992).

On Frodo compared to Gawain in *Sir Gawain and the Green Knight*, particularly in relation to the loss of innocence and understanding of self, see Christine Barkley and Muriel B. Ingham, "There But Not Back Again: The Road from Innocence to Maturity," *Riverside Quarterly* 7 (1982): 101–4; see also Roger C. Schlobin, who looks for parallels between the characters of *Sir Gawain* and *The Lord of the Rings*, in "The Monsters Are Talismans and Transgressions: Tolkien and *Sir Gawain and the Green Knight*," in Clark and Timmons, pp. 71–81.

3. For religious, moral, Christian, or Roman Catholic aspects of the trilogy, see Edmund Fuller, "The Lord of the Hobbits: J.R.R. Tolkien," *Books with Men behind Them* (New York: Random House, 1959), pp. 169–96; Patricia Meyer Sparks, "Ethical Patterns in *The Lord of the Rings*," *Critique* 3 (1959): 30–42, reprinted as "Power and Meaning in *The Lord of the Rings*," in *Tolkien and the Critics*, ed. Isaacs and Zimbardo, pp. 81–99; Levitin, "Inherent Morality and Its Concomitants," chap. 5 of "J.R.R. Tolkien's *The Lord of the Rings*," pp. 87–106); Sandra Miesel, "Some Religious Aspects of *Lord of the Rings*," *Riverside Quarterly* 3 (1968): 209–13; Gunnar Urang, "Tolkien's Fantasy: The Phenomenology of Hope," in *Shadows of Imagination: The Fantasies of C.S. Lewis, J.R.R. Tolkien, and Charles Williams*, ed. Mark R. Hillegas (Carbondale and Edwardsville: Southern Illinois University Press, 1969), pp. 97–110; Paul Kocher, "Cosmic Order," chap. 3 of *Master of*

Middle-earth: The Fiction of J.R.R. Tolkien (Boston: Houghton Mifflin, 1972); and Richard Purtill, *Lord of the Elves and Eldils: Fantasy and Philosophy in C.S. Lewis and J.R.R. Tolkien* (Grand Rapids, Mich.: Zondervan, 1974). Other references will be cited where relevant.

4. Sparks, pp. 83–84.

5. For *The Lord of the Rings* as traditional epic, see Bruce A. Beatie, "Folk Tale, Fiction, and Saga in J.R.R. Tolkien's *The Lord of the Rings,*" in "The Tolkien Papers" (special issue), *Mankato Studies in English* 2 (1967): 1–17; as fantasy drawing upon epic, *chanson de geste,* and medieval romance, see Carter, pp. 96–133; as fantasy, see Douglass Parker, "Hwæt We Holbytla . . ." (Review of *Lord of the Rings*), *Hudson Review* 9 (1956–57): 598–609; as fairy-story, see R.J. Reilly, "Tolkien and the Fairy Story," *Thought* 38 (1963): 89–106, reprinted in *Tolkien and the Critics,* pp. 128–50; as a genreless work, see Charles Moorman, "The Shire, Mordor, and Minas Tirith," in Isaacs and Zimbardo, *Tolkien and the Critics,* pp. 201–2.

6. The most satisfying genre may be that of the romance, drawn from medieval or Arthurian antecedents. Characteristic of romance are its symbolism, quest themes of search and transition, the sense of death or disaster, and the maturation of the young. But Tolkien inverts the romance structure so that Frodo relinquishes his quest at the end and the heroes peacefully overcome death. See George H. Thomson, "*The Lord of the Rings:* The Novel as Traditional Romance," *Wisconsin Studies in Contemporary Literature* 8 (1967): 43–59; Richard C. West, "The Interlace Structure of *The Lord of the Rings,*" in Lobdell, *A Tolkien Compass,* pp. 77–94; Derek S. Brewer, "The Lord of the Rings as Romance," in Salu and Farrell, pp. 249–64; and David M. Miller, "Narrative Pattern in *The Fellowship of the Ring,*" in Lobdell, *A Tolkien Compass,* pp. 95–106. See also, for the influence of French and German Arthurian romance (and the Perceval story) on Tolkien in *LR,* J.S. Ryan, "Uncouth Innocence: Some Links Between Chrétien de Troyes, Wolfram von Eschenbach and J.R.R. Tolkien," *Inklings-Jahrbuch* 2 (1984): 25–41; and *Mythlore* 11 (1984): 8–13. For a tracing of the Fellowship's journeys through various kinds of landscape in *LR,* see the fifty-one maps in Barbara Strachey, *Journeys of Frodo: An Atlas of J.R.R. Tolkien's "The Lord of the Rings"* (London: HarperCollins, 1998; Boston: Houghton Mifflin, 1999).

7. For Aragorn as hero, see Kocher, *Master of Middle-earth,* chap. 6; for Frodo, see Roger Sale, *Modern Heroism: Essays on D.H. Lawrence, William Empson, and J.R.R. Tolkien.* (Berkeley, Los Angeles, and London: University of California Press, 1973); and for Aragorn as the epic

hero and Frodo as the fairy tale hero, see Levitin, pp. 60–76. Because heroism and *ofermod* are incompatible, it is difficult to choose "the Hero" of the work; see Miesel's brief mention of this idea in "Some Religious Aspects of *Lord of the Rings*," p. 212; further, real heroism depends more on service than mastery, making Sam, who resembles Niggle in "Leaf by Niggle," the best choice for hero: see Jack C. Rang, "Two Servants," in "The Tolkien Papers," pp. 84–94. See also Flieger's concept of the split hero, in four individuals, which she identifies with the multigenre form of *The Lord of the Rings:* for Frodo as the fairy-tale hero, Aragorn as the epic hero, Gollum as the *Beowulf* monster (who combines Grendel and the Dragon), and Sam Gamgee as the loyal servant Wiglaf in *Beowulf* and Bedivere in *Morte d'Arthur,* see Verlyn Flieger, "Medieval Epic and Romance Motifs in J.R.R. Tolkien's *The Lord of the Rings*," *Dissertation Abstracts International* 38 (1978): 4157A (Catholic University of America); and the article that epitomizes her argument in "Frodo and Aragorn: The Concept of the Hero," in *Tolkien and the Critics,* ed. Isaacs and Zimbardo, pp. 40–62.

    8. For other views of structure in the trilogy see, for example, Helms, "Tolkien's World: The Structure and Aesthetic of *The Lord of the Rings*," chap. 5 of *Tolkien's World.*

    9. Quoted from a letter by J.R.R. Tolkien appended to Everett, p. 87.

    10. In addition to the innovative millennium edition (London: HarperCollins, 1999), *The Lord of the Rings* has also been published in a single-volume, "India paper" deluxe edition, with slipcase, by Allen and Unwin (London, 1968); again, without a slipcase and on regular paper, in 1991 (London: HarperCollins); and in quarter-leather with a slipcase and in limited numbers (London: HarperCollins, 1997). That these formats change the way the reader understands *The Lord of the Rings* is important in grasping Tolkien's intentions.

    11. J.R.R. Tolkien, *The Lord of the Rings,* 3 vols., 2d ed. (London: Allen and Unwin, 1966; Boston: Houghton Mifflin, 1967), 1:231.

    12. See David Callaway, "Gollum: A Misunderstood Hero," *Mythlore* 37 (1984): 14–17, 22.

    13. Boethius, *The Consolation of Philosophy,* trans. Richard Green (Indianapolis, Ind., New York, and Kansas City: Bobbs-Merrill, 1962), p. 97 (book 4, poem 6). On the Great Chain of Being, the "fair chain of love," and the Renaissance concept of *discordia concors* (also found in Hugh of Saint Victor) and its influence on order in the trilogy, see Rose A. Zimbardo, "The Medieval-Renaissance Vision of The Lord of the Rings," in *Tolkien: New Critical Perspectives,* ed. Neil D. Isaacs and

Rose A. Zimbardo (Lexington: University Press of Kentucky, 1981), 63–71: there is a place for all beings and things in Middle-earth, so that evil arises when one being or thing seeks its own desires without regard for the whole. For the Boethian reconciliation of Providence, Fate, and free will, as a source for the conflicting statements Tolkien makes in the trilogy about chance and intentionality in the universe, see Kathleen Dubs, "Providence, Fate and Chance: Boethian Philosophy in *The Lord of the Rings," Twentieth-Century Literature* 27 (1981): 34–42.

14. For an incisive discussion of the origins, kinds, and natures of the rings, see Melanie Rawls, "The Rings of Power," *Mythlore* 40 (1984): 29–32.

15. For a classification and discussion of good and/or evil species, see Rose A. Zimbardo, "Moral Vision in *The Lord of the Rings,"* in *Tolkien and the Critics,* ed. Isaac and Zimbardo, pp. 100–108; Thomas J. Gasque, "Tolkien: The Monsters and the Critics," in *Tolkien and the Critics,* ed. Isaac and Zimbardo, pp. 151–63; Robley Evans, *J.R.R. Tolkien* (New York: Warner Paperback Library, 1972), chaps. 3 to 5; and Kocher, *Master of Middle-earth,* chaps. 4 to 5.

16. The insignificance and ordinariness of Tolkien's heroic Hobbits are glossed in several of his letters, particularly 180, 181, and 246: see J.R.R. Tolkien, *Letters,* selected and edited by Humphrey Carpenter, with the assistance of Christopher Tolkien (London: Allen and Unwin, 1980; Boston: Houghton Mifflin, 1981), pp. 230–32, 232–37, and 325–33.

17. For a discussion of the descent into Hell in the second book and its traditional implications, see Huttar, "Hell and the City," in *A Tolkien Compass,* ed. Lobdell, pp. 117–42.

18. On Old Man Willow and Tolkien's empathy with trees, see Verlyn Flieger, "Taking the Part of Trees: Eco-Conflict in Middle-earth," in Clark and Timmons, pp. 147–58.

19. On Tom Bombadil as an embodiment of the classical and medieval god of nature (or human nature), drawn in part from John Gower's *Confessio Amantis,* see Gordon E. Slethaug, "Tolkien, Tom Bombadil, and the Creative Imagination," *English Studies in Canada* 4 (1978): 341–50. On Tolkien's theology of nature and grace, see also Colin Duriez, "Sub-creation and Tolkien's Theology of Story," in Battarbee, pp. 133–49.

20. On the names of the Dwarves, see Patrick J. Callahan, "Tolkien's Dwarfs and the Eddas," *Tolkien Journal* 15 (1972): 20; and for their connection with Norse mythology, see Brunsdale, "Norse

Mythological Elements in The Hobbit," *Mythlore* 9 (1983): 49–50; and Lynn Bryce, "The Influence of Scandinavian Mythology in the Works of J.R.R. Tolkien," *Edda* 7 (1983): 113–19.

21. See also, for Tolkien's Paradise, U. Milo Kaufmann, "Aspects of the Paradisiacal in Tolkien's Work," in *Tolkien Compass*, ed. Lobdell, pp. 143–52; and for Valinor as based on the Earthly Paradise, Gwenyth Hood, "The Earthly Paradise in Tolkien's *The Lord of the Rings*," in Reynolds and Goodknight, pp. 139–56.

22. On the Roman Catholic and religious features of *The Lord of the Rings*, see Miesel, "Some Religious Aspects of *Lord of the Rings*," pp. 209–13; Catherine Madsen, "Light from an Invisible Lamp: Natural Religion in *The Lord of the Rings*," *Mythlore* 53 (spring 1988): 43–47; and Carl F. Hostetter, "Over Middle-earth Sent unto Men: On the Philological Origins of the Earendel Myth," *Mythlore* 65 (spring 1991): 5–8.

23. On the Anglo-Saxon and Germanic heroism of Frodo, see George Clark, "J.R.R. Tolkien and the Hero," in Clark and Timmons, pp. 39–51.

24. The emphasis on sight and seeing is often linked in the trilogy with the *palantíri*, one of which Saruman has and that Sauron uses to control him, so that Frodo's "sight" here atop the Hill opens up new vistas and visions beyond his capability: see J.R.R. Tolkien, *Unfinished Tales of Númenor and Middle-earth*, ed. Christopher Tolkien (London: Allen and Unwin, 1979; Boston: Houghton Mifflin, 1980), pp. 421–33.

25. For the two towers of this volume as central symbols, see also Tolkien's own unused designs for the cover, in Wayne G. Hammond and Christina Scull, *J.R.R. Tolkien: Artist and Illustrator* (New York: Houghton Mifflin, 1995), pp. 179–83. The two towers were used recently on the cover of a HarperCollins reissue, for the second of the three volumes (London, 2000).

26. *Ancrene Wisse* treats the deadly sins as animals, as we have seen previously. Tolkien himself links propensities to different sins among different species—sloth and stupidity, with the Hobbits; pride, with the Elves; envy and greed, with the Dwarves; a type of pride ("folly and wickedness"), with Men; and a more dangerous form of pride ("treachery and power-lust"), with Wizards, in letter 203 (Tolkien, *Letters*, p. 262). On deadly sin in *The Lord of the Rings*, as well as *The Hobbit* and *The Silmarillion*, see Charles W. Nelson's recent discussion, "The Sins of Middle-earth: Tolkien's Use of Medieval Allegory," in Clark and Timmons, pp. 83–94. See also, for a comparison of the battle between Sam and Frodo and Shelob and the battle between the Vices

and Virtues in Prudentius's *Psychomachia,* J.S. Ryan, "Death by Self-Impalement: The Prudentius Example," *Minas Tirith Evening Star* 15 (1986): 6–9.

27. Genesis 11:1–4, *The Jerusalem Bible,* ed. Alexander Jones (Garden City, N.Y.: Doubleday, 1966), p. 26. Tolkien participated as a principal collaborator (one of twenty-seven) in the translation and literary revision of this Bible.

28. For parallels between *The Lord of the Rings* and *The Silmarillion* and Milton's *Paradise Lost,* see Debbie Sly, "Weaving Nets of Gloom: 'Darkness Profound' in Tolkien and Milton," in Clark and Timmons, pp. 109–19.

29. On the Ents, Treebeard, and Old Man Willow, and Tolkien's indebtedness to the Green Knight, see Verlyn Flieger, "The Green Man, the Green Knight, and Treebeard: Scholarship and Invention in Tolkien's Fiction," in Battarbee, pp. 85–98.

30. For information about the Wizards, see Tolkien, *Unfinished Tales,* pp. 405–20.

31. For the theological concept of the Word of God (=Jesus Christ, his Son, or the incarnation of God's love), as the basis for Tolkien's literary aesthetic, see S.T.R.O. d'Ardenne, "The Man and the Scholar," in Salu and Farrell, p. 35. Just as the combination of adjective and noun in the Anglo-Saxon kenning gave the Anglo-Saxon *scop* with his *wordhord* control over the thing described, so kennings allow Tolkien to create his own world, through the compounds and epithets for the One Ring, the Ring of Power, the Ring of Doom, Gollum's Precious, etc. Tolkien's constructed languages also give insight into the peoples who use them: Dwarvish is Old Norse; Quenya and Sindarin, High-Elvish and Common Elvish, as languages of song mirror Faërie's desire for good; Black Speech is suited to a race whose dentals consist of fangs and is therefore not a good language for song. See Anthony J. Ugolnik, "*Wordhord Onleac:* The Medieval Sources of J.R.R. Tolkien's Linguistic Aesthetic," *Mosaic* 10 (winter 1977): 15–31. In this case, "Sauron," as a name that describes his being, derives from the Greek for "lizard." See Gwyneth E. Hood, "Sauron as Gorgon and Basilisk," *Seven* 8 (1987): 59–71.

32. For Rohan as Old English, see Tinkler, "Old English in Rohan," in *Tolkien and the Critics,* ed. Isaac and Zimbardo, pp. 164–69.

33. My translation of lines 92–93. See the original in *The Exeter Book, The Anglo-Saxon Poetic Records,* in vol. 3, ed. George Philip Krapp and Elliott Van Kirk Dobbie (Morningside Heights, N.Y.: Columbia University Press, 1936).

34. For Aragorn as a healing king, and the medieval and Renaissance antecedents of the concept, see Gisbert Krantz, "Der Heilende Aragorn," *Inklings-Jahrbuch* 2 (1984): 11–24.

35. For a related discussion of the implications of return and renewal in the last book see Evans, *J.R.R. Tolkien*, pp. 190–93.

36. See also Jack C. Rang, "Two Servants," in "The Tolkien Papers," pp. 84–94.

CHAPTER 6. THE CREATOR OF THE SILMARILS

1. Humphrey Carpenter, *J.R.R. Tolkien: A Biography* (London, Boston, and Sydney: Allen and Unwin, 1977), p. 89. See also Randel Helms, *Tolkien and the Silmarils* (Boston: Houghton Mifflin, 1981), chap. 2. Tolkien himself joked that it might have begun at birth; other dates for the composition of "The Fall of Gondolin" mentioned by Tolkien were 1914–18, especially when he was in the hospital on leave, and for the composition of "Beren and Lúthien," during a leave in 1913, according to *Diplomat* (October 1966), p. 39. Tolkien indicated to Clyde S. Kilby he had had the mythic whole in mind as early as 1906. See Clyde S. Kilby, *Tolkien and the "Silmarillion"* (Wheaton, Ill.: Harold Shaw Publishers, 1976), p. 47.

2. Luigi de Anna, "The Magic of Words: J.R.R. Tolkien and Finland," in *Scholarship and Fantasy: Proceedings of the Tolkien Phenomenon, May 1992, Turku, Finland* (special issue), ed. K.J. Battarbee, Anglicana Turkuensia, no. 12 (Turku: University of Turku, 1993), pp. 7–19, here, p. 18, citing E. Lodigliani, *Invito alla lettura di Tolkien* (Milan: 1982), p. 113.

3. What Tolkien liked best about these "low-brow" heroes was their lack of hypocrisy and their "low-brow" nature—they were "scandalous heroes" (from the placard about the Debating Society at the 1992 exhibit at King Edwards). The edition he read was *Kalevala: The Land of Heroes*, compiled by Elias Lönnrot (1849), translated by W. F. Kirby (London: J.M. Dent and Sons, 1907).

4. See Tolkien's letter to Auden, *J.R.R. Tolkien, Letters*, selected and edited by Humphrey Carpenter, with the assistance of Christopher Tolkien (London: Allen and Unwin, 1980; Boston: Houghton Mifflin, 1981), p. 214. In his letter to Christopher Bretherton of 16 July 1964, Tolkien also notes: "The germ of my attempt to write legends of my own to fit my private languages was the tragic tale of the hapless Kullervo in the Finnish *Kalevala*" (*Letters*, p. 345). In addition to these other telling statements about the connection between the legendarium

and Finnish literature and language, Ruth S. Noel sees Lemminkäinen as a Finnish character who influenced Tolkien, in *The Mythology of Middle-earth: A Study of Tolkien's Mythology and Its Relationship to the Myths of the Ancient World* (London: Thames and Hudson, 1977), p. 97. On Finnish literature and language, or at least its sound, and their importance to Tolkien, see de Anna, "The Magic of Words," in Battarbee, pp. 7–19; and on language itself, or its sound, see Helena Rautala, "Familiarity and Distance: Quenya's Relation to Finnish," in Battarbee, pp. 21–32.

    5. Carpenter, p. 107.

    6. Carpenter, p. 184.

    7. Carpenter, p. 210.

    8. See, for example, Kilby, *Tolkien and "The Silmarillion,"* chap. 3.

    9. Carpenter, pp. 251–52.

    10. On the construction of *The Silmarillion* from the earliest parts to the final version, with a description of what Tolkien might have intended, see Charles E. Noad, "On the Construction of 'The Silmarillion,'" in *Tolkien's Legendarium: Essays on "The History of Middle-earth,"* ed. Verlyn Flieger and Carl F. Hostetter, Contributions to the Study of Science Fiction and Fantasy, no. 86 (Westport, Conn., and London: Greenwood Press, 2000), pp. 31–68, esp. pp. 66–67, for a diagram.

    11. Noad, p. 31.

    12. Noad, pp. 66–67.

    13. J.R.R. Tolkien, *The Silmarillion,* ed. Christopher Tolkien (London: Allen and Unwin; Boston: Houghton Mifflin, 1977), p. 54. Subsequent references will be indicated within the text.

    14. See J.R.R. Tolkien, *Unfinished Tales of Númenor and Middle-earth,* ed. Christopher Tolkien (London: Allen and Unwin, 1979; Boston: Houghton Mifflin, 1980); and *The History of Middle-Earth,* ed. Christopher Tolkien, 12 vols. (London: Allen and Unwin, 1983–95; Boston: Houghton Mifflin, 1984–96). On *The History of Middle-Earth* and *Unfinished Tales,* see the convenient diagram of books and the main dates of composition, matched with their parts and their principal subjects, in David Bratman, "The Literary Value of *The History of Middle-earth,"* in Flieger and Hostetter, pp. 69–91. Bratman reads the twelve-volume work as a narrative, for pleasure; he prefaces his discussion by balancing some readers' reactions to *The Silmarillion, Unfinished Tales,* and *The History of Middle-earth,* including those who argue that Tolkien did not in fact live to complete any one of them.

    15. For Eru as the Neoplatonic One, see especially Verlyn Flieger, "Naming the Unnamable: The Neoplatonic 'One' in Tolkien's

Silmarillion," in *Diakonia: Studies in Honor of Robert T. Meyer,* ed. Thomas Halton and Joseph P. Williman (Washington, D.C.: Catholic University of America Press, 1986), pp. 127–33. Flieger also focuses on the language of *The Silmarillion,* in *Splintered Light: Logos and Language in Tolkien's World* (Grand Rapids, Mich.: William B. Eerdmans, 1983).

16. See Eric Schweicher, who analyzes aspects of the Fall in Valar, Elves, Dwarves, and Men, in "Aspects of the Fall in *The Silmarillion,*" in *Proceedings of the J.R.R. Tolkien Centenary Conference, Keble College, Oxford, 1992,* ed. Patricia Reynolds and Glen H. Goodknight, *Mythlore* 80 and *Mallorn* 30 in one volume (Milton Keynes, England: Tolkien Society; Altadena, Calif.: Mythopoeic Press, 1995), pp. 167–71.

17. Among the first Tolkien critics to trace a correspondence between *The Silmarillion* and the Old Testament was Kilby, *Tolkien and "The Silmarillion,"* pp. 59–65; for the legendarium's "prefiguration" of Christianity, see also Colin Duriez, "Tolkien's Sub-creation and Tolkien's Theology of Story," in Battarbee, p. 146. Duriez notes: "In sub-creating, Tolkien's theme is to reveal the essential meaning behind human history" (p. 146). Tolkien himself declares (in letter 211, to Rhona Beare) that the "Númenórean" might best be imagined as the "Egyptian," although in "theology" the Númenóreans are "Hebraic and even more puritanic" (*Letters,* p. 281).

18. See the excellent analysis of female characters and cosmology in Melanie Rawls, "The Feminine Principle in Tolkien," *Mythlore* 38 (spring 1984): 5–13.

19. J.R.R. Tolkien, *The Old English Exodus: Text, Translation, and Commentary by J.R.R. Tolkien,* ed. Joan Turville-Petre (Oxford: Oxford University Press, 1981). Subsequent references will be indicated by parentheses and page or line number(s) in the text.

20. On the Old Norse elements in *The Silmarillion:* after a succinct comparison of the creation mythology of *The Silmarillion* with that of the *Eddas,* Paul Kocher notes that Tolkien was not attracted to the "complex and all too physical account of Creation" in Norse-Icelandic mythology (p. 5), then provides a kind of paraphrase of *The Silmarillion* in *A Reader's Guide to the "Silmarillion"* (Boston: Houghton Mifflin, 1980). Kocher suggests Tolkien borrowed Melkor's character from Loki (p. 7), and his Elves and Dwarves from the light and dark Elves and the Dwarves of the *Eddas* (pp. 7–11). See also Marjorie Burns, "Gandalf and Odin," in Flieger and Hostetter, pp. 219–31, who sees a resemblance between Manwe and the Norse god Odin; in addition, from the *History* books compiled by Christopher, along with *Unfinished Tales* and *The Silmarillion,* it is clear that Gandalf in many

ways resembles Odin (his eagles, for example; his floppy hat; his gray beard and his cloak), reinforcing the idea that he may be a Vala, even Manwë himself. Burns traces the evolution of scholarly thinking about these connections to develop William Green's hint that Sauron and Gandalf may represent the "Promethean and Plutonic faces of Odin" (Burns, p. 221), adding Saruman, who, like Gandalf in *The Lord of the Rings*, is also dressed in a wide-brimmed hat and cloak. In *The Silmarillion*, Morgoth assumes some of the malevolence of Odin. For the Old English parallel between Túrin and Beorhtnoth, see Richard West, "Túrin's *Ofermod*," in Flieger and Hostetter, pp. 233–45.

21. Carpenter, p. 251.

22. See Verlyn Flieger, "The Footsteps of Ælfwine," in Flieger and Hostetter, pp. 183–98, here, p. 186.

23. About Kullervo, Tolkien notes that the "tragic tale" about him (or the *Kalevala* in general) inspired him to write legends for his private language, mentioned in his letters, to Edith Bratt in 1914 (*Letters*, p. 7), to W.H. Auden in 1955 (*Letters*, p. 214); and to Christopher Bretherton on 16 July 1964 (*Letters*, p. 345). See also Annika Holmberg's review of Humphrey Carpenter's biography of Tolkien for passages from the tale, "J.R.R. Tolkien, Kalevala och det finska språket," *Horisont* 5 (1986): 73–74. In his *Biography* Carpenter mentions Tolkien's interest in the *Kalevala* beginning in 1910 and acknowledges elements of incest, found in the hero Kullervo's tale, also in *The Tale of the Children of Húrin*, written in 1917 in a military hospital (pp. 49, 96). For *The Tale of the Children of Húrin*, see *Unfinished Tales*, pp. 97–146. See also the convenient itemization of all of Túrin's manifold appearances in Tolkien, in Richard West, "Túrin's *Ofermod*: An Old English Theme in the Development of the Story of Túrin," in Flieger and Hostetter, pp. 240–41, the fullest of which is in *The Silmarillion*, but which also encompasses "Turambar and the Foalókë" (1919), published in *The Book of Lost Tales*, pt. 2; *The Lay of the Children of Húrin* (1920–25), published in *The Lays of Beleriand; Narn I Hîn Húrin*, subtitled "The Tale of the Children of Húrin" (1920s–1930s?), published in *Unfinished Tales;* other volumes of *The History of Middle-earth* touching on the First Age (published as *The Shaping of Middle-earth, The Lost Road, Morgoth's Ring,* and *The War of the Jewels*); and chapter 21 of *The Silmarillion*, "Of Túrin Turambar" (1977). See also, for the parallel between the hero Kullervo in the *Kalevala* and Túrin in *The Silmarillion*, Marie Barnfield, "Túrin Turambar and the Tale of the Fosterling," *Mallorn* 31 (1994): 29–36.

24. West, "Túrin's *Ofermod*," pp. 233–45.

SELECT BIBLIOGRAPHY

PRINCIPAL WORKS OF J.R.R. TOLKIEN
(IN CHRONOLOGICAL ORDER)

A Middle English Vocabulary. Oxford: Clarendon Press, 1922.

"Some Contributions to Middle-English Lexicography." *Review of English Studies* 1 (1925): 210–15.

"The Devil's Coach-Horses." *Review of English Studies* 1 (1925): 331–36.

Sir Gawain and the Green Knight. Ed. Tolkien and E.V. Gordon. 1925. Rev. Norman Davis, 1960. 2nd ed. Reprint, Oxford: Clarendon Press, 1967.

Foreword to *A New Glossary of the Dialect of the Huddersfield District,* by Walter E. Haigh. London: Oxford University Press, 1928.

"*Ancrene Wisse* and *Hali Meiðhad.*" *Essays and Studies by Members of the English Association* 14 (1929): 104–26.

"Sigelwara Land." Part 1 in *Medium Aevum* 1 (1932): 183–96; part 2 in *Medium Aevum* 3 (1934): 1–70.

"Beowulf: The Monsters and the Critics." *Proceedings of the British Academy* 22 (1936): 245–95. Reprinted in *An Anthology of Beowulf Criticism,* ed. Lewis E. Nicholson. Notre Dame, Ind.: University of Notre Dame Press, 1963; reprinted in *The Beowulf Poet,* ed. Donald K. Fry. Englewood Cliffs, N.J. : Prentice Hall, 1968; reprinted in *Interpretations of Beowulf: A Critical Anthology,* ed. R. Fulk, pp. 14–44. Bloomington and Indianapolis: Indiana University Press, 1991; and reprinted in abbreviated form, in *Read-*

229

ings on Beowulf, ed. Katie de Koster, pp. 24–30. The Greenhaven Press Literary Companion to British Literature. San Diego, Calif.: Greenhaven Press, 1998.

Poems. In *Songs for the Philologists*. Compiled by members of the English Department, University College London. London: Department of English, University College London, 1936.

The Hobbit; or There and Back Again. 2d ed. London: Allen and Unwin, 1937, 1951; Boston: Houghton Mifflin, 1938, 1958; New York: Ballantine, 1965, reprinted 1974.

Letter to the editor. *The Observer*, 20 February 1938, p. 9.

Preface to *Beowulf and the Finnesburg Fragment: A Translation into Modern English Prose*, by John R. Clark Hall. 1940. Rev. ed. 1950. Reprint, London: Allen and Unwin, 1972.

"Leaf by Niggle." *Dublin Review* 216 (1945): 46–61. Reprinted with "On Fairy-Stories" in *Tree and Leaf*. London: Allen and Unwin, 1964; Boston: Houghton Mifflin, 1965; and in *The Tolkien Reader*. New York: Ballantine, 1966.

"The Lay of Aotrou and Itroun." *Welsh Review* 4 (1945): 254–66.

"On Fairy-Stories." In *Essays Presented to Charles Williams*, ed. C.S. Lewis, pp. 38–89. London: Oxford University Press, 1947. Reprint, Grand Rapids, Mich.: William B. Eerdmans, 1966. Rev. and reprinted in *Tree and Leaf* with "Leaf by Niggle" and again together in *The Tolkien Reader*.

Farmer Giles of Ham. London: Allen and Unwin, 1949; Boston: Houghton Mifflin, 1950. Reprinted in *The Tolkien Reader* and *Smith of Wootton Major and Farmer Giles of Ham*. New York: Ballantine, 1969.

"Middle English 'Losenger': Sketch of an Etymological and Semantic Enquiry." *Essais de Philologie Moderne*. Paris: Société d'édition "Les Belles Lettres," 1953.

"The Homecoming of Beorhtnoth Beorhthelm's Son." *Essays and Studies by Members of the English Association*, n.s., 6 (1953):1–18. Reprinted in *The Tolkien Reader*.

The Lord of the Rings. 3 vols. 2d ed. London: Allen and Unwin, 1966; Boston: Houghton Mifflin, 1967. Reprinted in a single-volume, "India paper" deluxe edition. London: Allen and Unwin, 1968. Reprinted on regular paper. London: Harper Collins, 1991. Reprinted in quarter-leather. London: Harper Collins, 1997. Reprinted in Millennium Edition. 7 vols. London: Harper Collins, 1999. Reprinted with Tolkien's designs for original jackets. London: Harper Collins, 2000.

"Imram." *Time and Tide* 36 (1955): 1561.

Preface to *The Ancrene Riwle*. Trans. M.B. Salu. London: Burns and Oates, 1955; Notre Dame, Ind.: University of Notre Dame Press, 1956.

The English Text of the Ancrene Riwle: Ancrene Wisse. Early English Text Society, no. 249. London, New York, and Toronto: Oxford University Press, 1962.

The Adventures of Tom Bombadil. London: Allen and Unwin, 1961; Boston: Houghton Mifflin, 1962. Reprinted in *The Tolkien Reader*.

"English and Welsh." In *Angles and Britons: The O'Donnell Lectures*. Cardiff: University of Wales Press, 1963.

The Tolkien Reader. New York: Ballantine, 1966.

The Road Goes Ever On: A Song Cycle. London: Allen and Unwin, 1966; Boston: Houghton Mifflin, 1967.

Smith of Wootton Major. London: Allen and Unwin; Boston: Houghton Mifflin, 1967; *Redbook* 130 (1967): 58–61, 101, 103–7. Reprinted in *The Tolkien Reader* and in *Smith of Wootton Major and Farmer Giles of Ham*.

"For W.H.A." *Shenandoah* 18 (1967): 96–97.

Smith of Wootton Major and Farmer Giles of Ham. New York: Ballantine, 1969.

"A Letter from J.R.R. Tolkien." In William Luther White, *The Image of Man in C.S. Lewis*. Nashville, Tenn.: Abingdon Press, 1969.

"Once Upon a Time" and "The Dragon's Visit." In *The Young Magicians*, ed. Lin Carter. New York: Ballantine, 1969.

Sir Gawain and the Green Knight, Pearl, and Sir Orfeo. Trans. Tolkien. Ed. Christopher Tolkien. London: Allen and Unwin, 1974; Boston: Houghton Mifflin, 1975.

The Father Christmas Letters. Ed. Baillie Tolkien. London: Allen and Unwin, 1975; Boston: Houghton Mifflin, 1976.

The Silmarillion. Ed. Christopher Tolkien. London: Allen and Unwin, 1976; Boston: Houghton Mifflin, 1977.

Pictures. Foreword and notes by Christopher Tolkien. London: Allen and Unwin, 1978; Boston: Houghton Mifflin, 1979.

Unfinished Tales of Númenor and Middle-earth. Ed. Christopher Tolkien. London: Allen and Unwin, 1979; Boston: Houghton Mifflin, 1980.

Letters. Selected and edited by Humphrey Carpenter, with the assistance of Christopher Tolkien. London: Allen and Unwin, 1980; Boston: Houghton Mifflin, 1981.

The Old English Exodus: Text, Translation, and Commentary by J.R.R. Tolkien. Ed. Joan Turville-Petre. Oxford: Oxford University Press, 1981.

Finn and Hengest: The Fragment and the Episode. Ed. Alan Bliss. London: Allen and Unwin, 1982; Boston: Houghton Mifflin, 1983.

Mr. Bliss. London: Allen and Unwin, 1982; Boston: Houghton Mifflin, 1983.

The Monsters and the Critics and Other Essays. Ed. Christopher Tolkien. London: Allen and Unwin, 1983; Boston: Houghton Mifflin, 1984.

The History of Middle-Earth. Ed. Christopher Tolkien. 12 vols. London: Allen and Unwin, 1983–95; Boston: Houghton Mifflin, 1984–96.

The Annotated Hobbit. Annotated by Douglas A. Anderson. Boston: Houghton Mifflin, 1988.

"Mythopoeia." In *Tree and Leaf, Including the Poem "Mythopoeia."* Introduced by Christopher Tolkien. Rev. ed. London: Allen and Unwin, 1988; Boston: Houghton Mifflin, 1989. Pp. 97–101.

Reading of "The Homecoming of Beorhtnoth Beorhthelm's Son," with readings by Christopher Tolkien of "Beorhtnoth's Death" and Tolkien's "Ofermod." Commemorative Cassette Tape for "Tolkien: The Centenary, 1892–1992." London: Grafton, 1992.

Roverandom. London: Allen and Unwin, 1992; Boston: Houghton Mifflin, 1993.

Select Bibliography

OTHER PRIMARY AND SECONDARY WORKS

Abbott, Joe. "Tolkien's Monsters: Concept and Function in *The Lord of the Rings* (Part II)." *Mythlore* 60 (winter 1989): 40–47.

Allen, Jim, ed. *An Introduction to Elvish.* Frome, Somerset: Brian's Head, 1978.

Augustine, Saint. *On Christian Doctrine.* Trans. D.W. Robertson Jr. Indianapolis, Ind., and New York: Bobbs-Merrill, 1958.

Avery, Gillian. *Nineteenth-Century Children: Heroes and Heroines in English Children's Stories, 1780–1900.* London: Hodder and Stoughton, 1965.

Barkley, Christine, and Muriel B. Ingham. "There But Not Back Again: The Road from Innocence to Maturity." *Riverside Quarterly* 7 (1982): 101–4.

Barnfield, Marie. "'Túrin Turambar and the Tale of the Fosterling." *Mallorn* no. 31 (1994): 29–36.

Battarbee, K.J., ed. *Scholarship and Fantasy: Proceedings of the Tolkien Phenomenon, May 1992, Turku, Finland* (special issue). Anglicana Turkuensia, no. 12. Turku: University of Turku, 1993.

Blissett, William. "The Despots of the Rings." *South Atlantic Quarterly* 58 (1959): 448–56.

Bloom, Harold, ed. *Modern Critical Interpretations: J.R.R. Tolkien's "Lord of the Rings."* Philadelphia: Chelsea House Publishers, 2000.

Bloomfield, Morton W. *The Seven Deadly Sins: An Introduction to the History of a Religious Concept.* East Lansing: Michigan State College Press, 1952.

Boas, George. *Essays on Primitivism and Related Ideas in the Middle Ages.* Baltimore, Md.: Johns Hopkins University Press, 1948.

Boethius. *The Consolation of Philosophy.* Trans. Richard Green. Indianapolis, Ind., New York, New York, and Kansas City, Mo.: Bobbs-Merrill, 1962.

Brunsdale, Mitzi M. "Norse Mythological Elements in *The Hobbit.*" *Mythlore* 9 (1983): 49–50.

Bryce, Lynn. "The Influence of Scandinavian Mythology on the Works of J.R.R. Tolkien." *Edda* 7 (1983): 113–19.

Buchs, Peter, and Thomas Honegger, eds. *News from the Shire and Beyond: Studies on Tolkien*. Zurich and Berne: Walking Tree Publishers, 1997.

Callahan, Patrick J. "Tolkien's Dwarfs and the Eddas." *Tolkien Journal* 15 (1972): 20.

Callaway, David. "Gollum: A Misunderstood Hero." *Mythlore* 37 (1984): 14–17, 22.

Carpenter, Humphrey. *J.R.R. Tolkien: A Biography*. London, Boston, and Sydney: Allen and Unwin, 1977.

Carter, Lin. *Tolkien: A Look Behind "The Lord of the Rings."* New York: Ballantine, 1969.

Chance [Nitzsche], Jane. *The Genius Figure in Antiquity and the Middle Ages*. New York and London: Columbia University Press, 1975.

———. "King Under the Mountain: Tolkien's *Hobbit.*" *North Dakota Quarterly* 47 (1979): 5–18.

———. *"The Lord of the Rings": The Mythology of Power*. New York: Twayne/Macmillan, 1992. 2d ed. Lexington: University Press of Kentucky, 2001.

———. *Medieval Mythography*, vol. 1, *From Roman North Africa to the School of Chartres, 433–1177*. Gainesville and London: University Press of Florida, 1994.

———. "'A Mythology for England': Tolkien's *Silmarillion.*" *Houston Chronicle Zest*, Sunday, 11 September 1977, p. 13.

———. "Tolkien and His Sources." In *Approaches to Teaching Sir Gawain and the Green Knight*, ed. Miriam Youngerman Miller and Jane Chance, pp. 151–55. New York: Modern Language Association, 1986.

———, ed. *Medievalism: Inklings and Others* (special issue). *Studies in Medievalism* 3, no. 3, combined with no. 4, in one volume (1991): 231–392.

———, and David Day. "Medievalism in Tolkien: Two Decades of Criticism in Review." In *Medievalism: Inklings and Others* (special issue). *Studies in Medievalism* 3, no. 3, combined with no. 4, in one volume (1991): 375–88.

Chaucer, Geoffrey. *The Riverside Chaucer*. Ed. Larry D. Benson. 3d ed. Boston: Houghton Mifflin, 1987.

Christensen, Bonniejean. "*Beowulf* and *The Hobbit:* Elegy into

Fantasy in J.R.R. Tolkien's Creative Technique." Ph.D. diss., University of Southern California. *Dissertation Abstracts International* 30 (1970): 4401A–4402A.

————. "Tolkien's Creative Technique: *Beowulf* and *The Hobbit.*" *Orcrist* 7 (1972–73): 16–20.

Clark, George, and Daniel Timmons, eds. *J.R.R. Tolkien and His Literary Resonances: Views of Middle-earth.* Westport, Conn., and London: Greenwood Press, 2000.

Conley, John, ed. *The Middle English "Pearl": Critical Essays.* Notre Dame, Ind., and London: University of Notre Dame Press, 1970.

Cox, John. "Tolkien's Platonic Fantasy." *Seven* 5 (1984): 53–69.

Crabbe, Katharyn F. *J.R.R. Tolkien.* New York: Frederick Ungar, 1981.

Curry, Patrick. *Defending Middle-earth: Tolkien, Myth and Modernity.* Edinburgh: Floris Books, 1997.

Cursor Mundi. Ed. Richard Morris. Early English Text Society, o.s., nos. 57, 59, 62, 66, 68, 99, 101. London: Kegan Paul, Trench, Trübner, 1874–93.

Day, David. *Tolkien: The Illustrated Encyclopedia.* New York and London: Mitchell Beazley Publishers, 1991; London: Collier Books, 1992. Reprint, New York: Simon and Schuster, 1993.

Donahue, Thomas S. "A Linguist Looks at Tolkien's Elvish." *Mythlore* 37 (1984): 28–31.

Downing, Angela. "From Quenya to the Common Speech: Linguistic Diversification in J.R.R. Tolkien's *The Lord of the Rings.*" *Revista Canaria de Estudios Ingleses* 4 (1982): 23–31.

Dubs, Kathleen. "Providence, Fate and Chance: Boethian Philosophy in *The Lord of the Rings.*" *Twentieth-Century Literature* 27 (1981): 34–42.

Epstein, E. L. "The Novels of J.R.R. Tolkien and the Ethnology of Medieval Christendom." *Philological Quarterly* 48 (1969): 517–25.

Evans, Robley. *J.R.R. Tolkien.* New York: Warner Paperback Library, 1972.

Everett, Caroline Whitman. "The Imaginative Fiction of J.R.R.

Tolkien." Master's thesis, Florida State University, 1957.

The Exeter Book. The Anglo-Saxon Poetic Records. Vol. 3. Ed. George Phillip Krapp and Elliott Van Kirk Dobbie. Morningside Heights, N.Y.: Columbia University Press, 1936.

Flieger, Verlyn. "Medieval Epic and Romance Motifs in J.R.R. Tolkien's *The Lord of the Rings.*" Ph.D. diss., Catholic University of America. *Dissertation Abstracts International* 38 (1978): 4157A.

————. "Naming the Unnamable: The Neoplatonic 'One' in Tolkien's *Silmarillion.*" In *Diakonia: Studies in Honor of Robert T. Meyer,* ed. Thomas Halton and Joseph P. Williman, pp. 127–33. Washington, D.C.: Catholic University of America Press, 1986.

————. *Splintered Light: Logos and Language in Tolkien's World.* Grand Rapids, Mich.: William B. Eerdmans, 1983.

————, and Carl F. Hostetter. *Tolkien's Legendarium: Essays on "The History of Middle-earth."* Contributions to the Study of Science Fiction and Fantasy, no. 86. Westport, Conn., and London: Greenwood Press, 2000.

Foster, Robert. *A Complete Guide to Middle-earth from "The Hobbit" to "The Silmarillion."* Rev. ed. New York: Ballantine, 1978.

Fuller, Edmund. *Books with Men behind Them.* New York: Random House, 1959.

Giddings, Robert, ed. *J.R.R. Tolkien: This Far Land.* London: Vision Press; Totowa, N.J.: Barnes and Noble Books, 1983.

Gilson, Etienne. *Reason and Revelation in the Middle Ages.* 1938. Reprint, New York: Charles Scribner's Sons, 1966.

Green, Roger Lancelyn, and Walter Hooper. *C.S. Lewis: A Biography.* New York and London: Harcourt Brace Jovanovich, 1974.

Green, William Howard. *"The Hobbit": A Journey into Maturity.* New York: Twayne Publishers, 1994.

————. *"The Hobbit* and Other Fiction by J.R.R. Tolkien: Their Roots in Medieval Heroic Literature and Language." Ph.D. diss., Louisiana State University. *Dissertation Abstracts International* 30 (1970): 4944A.

————. "The Ring at the Center: *Eaca* in *The Lord of the Rings.*"

Mythlore 4 (1976): 17–19.

Grotta-Kurska, Daniel. *J.R.R. Tolkien: Architect of Middle-Earth.* Ed. Frank Wilson. Philadelphia: Running Press, 1976.

Hall, Robert A., Jr. "Tolkien's Hobbit Tetralogy as 'Anti-Nibelungen.'" *Western Humanities Review* 32 (1978): 351–59.

Hammond, Wayne G., with Douglas A. Anderson. *J.R.R. Tolkien: A Descriptive Bibliography.* Winchester, England: St. Paul's Bibliographies; New Castle, Del.: Oak Knoll Books, 1993.

Hammond, Wayne G., and Christina Scull. *J.R.R. Tolkien: Artist and Illustrator.* New York: Houghton Mifflin, 1995.

Helms, Randel. *Tolkien and the Silmarils.* Boston: Houghton Mifflin, 1981.

―――. *Tolkien's World.* Boston: Houghton Mifflin, 1974.

Hillegas, Mark R., ed. *Shadows of Imagination: The Fantasies of C.S. Lewis, J.R.R. Tolkien, and Charles Williams.* Rev. ed. Carbondale and Edwardsville: Southern Illinois University Press, 1979.

Hodge, James L. "Tolkien's Mythological Calendar in *The Hobbit.*" In *Aspects of Fantasy: Selected Essays from the Second International Conference on the Fantastic in Literature and Film,* ed. William Coyle, pp. 141-48. Westport, Conn.: Greenwood Press, 1986.

Holmberg, Annika. "J.R.R. Tolkien, Kalevala och det finska språket." *Horisont* 5 (1986): 73–74.

Hood, Gwyneth E. "Sauron as Gorgon and Basilisk." *Seven* 8 (1987): 59–71.

Hostetter, Carl F. "Over Middle-earth Sent Unto Men: On the Philological Origins of the Earendel Myth." *Mythlore* 65 (spring 1991): 5–8.

Huttar, Charles A. *Imagination and the Spirit: Essays in Literature and the Christian Faith presented to Clyde S. Kilby.* Grand Rapids, Mich.: William B. Eerdmans, 1971.

Irwin, W.R. "There and Back Again: The Romances of Williams, Lewis, and Tolkien." *Sewanee Review* 69 (1961): 566–78.

Isaacs, Neil D., and Rose A. Zimbardo, eds. *Tolkien and the Critics: Essays on J.R.R. Tolkien's "The Lord of the Rings."* Notre

Dame, Ind., and London: University of Notre Dame Press, 1968.

——. *Tolkien: New Critical Perspectives.* Lexington: University Press of Kentucky, 1981.

Jeffrey, David Lyle. "Tolkien as Philologist." *Seven* 1 (1980): 47–61. Revised and reprinted as "Recovery: Name in *The Lord of the Rings,*" in Neil D. Isaacs and Rose A. Zimbardo, *Tolkien: New Critical Perspectives,* ed. Neil D. Isaacs and Rose A. Zimbardo, pp. 106–16; and in Harold Bloom, pp. 125–32.

Johnson, J.A. "*Farmer Giles of Ham:* What Is It?" *Orcrist* 7 (1972–73): 21–24.

Jones, Alexander, ed. *The Jerusalem Bible.* Garden City, N.Y.: Doubleday, 1966.

Kalevala: The Land of Heroes. Compiled by Elias Lönnrot. 1849. Translated by W. F. Kirby. London: J.M. Dent and Sons, 1907.

Kilby, Clyde. *Tolkien and "The Silmarillion."* Wheaton, Ill.: Harold Shaw Publishers, 1976.

Klaeber, Friedrich, ed. *Beowulf and the Fight at Finnsburg.* 3d ed. Boston: D.C. Heath, 1950.

Knowles, David. *The Monastic Order in England: A History of Its Development from the Times of Saint Dunstan to the Fourth Lateran Council, 943–1216.* Cambridge: Cambridge University Press, 1949.

Kocher, Paul H. *Master of Middle-earth: The Fiction of J.R.R. Tolkien.* Boston: Houghton Mifflin, 1972.

——. *A Reader's Guide to "The Silmarillion."* Boston: Houghton Mifflin, 1980.

Krantz, Gisbert. "Der Heilende Aragorn." *Inklings-Jahrbuch* 2 (1984): 11–24.

Levitin, Alexis. "J.R.R. Tolkien's *The Lord of the Rings.*" Master's thesis, Columbia University, 1964.

Lewis, C.S. *Letters.* Ed. W.H. Lewis. 1966. Reprint, New York and London: Harcourt Brace Jovanovich, 1975.

——. *Out of the Silent Planet.* [The *Perelandra* trilogy, vol. 1.] London: John Lane/Bodley Head, 1938; New York: Macmillan, 1942.

——. *Perelandra.* [The *Perelandra* trilogy, vol. 2.] London: John

Lane/Bodley Head, 1943; New York: Macmillan, 1944.
———. *That Hideous Strength.* [The *Perelandra* trilogy, vol. 3.] London: John Lane/Bodley Head, 1945; New York: Macmillan, 1946.

Lewis, Lionel S. *Scaling the Ivory Tower: Merit and Its Limits in Academic Careers.* Baltimore, Md., and London: Johns Hopkins University Press, 1975.

Lobdell, Jared. *England and Always: Tolkien's World of the Rings.* Grand Rapids, Mich.: William B. Eerdmans, 1981.

———, ed. *A Tolkien Compass.* La Salle, Ill.: Open Court Press, 1975.

Macrobius. *Commentary on the Dream of Scipio.* Trans. William Harris Stahl. 1952. Reprint, New York and London: Columbia University Press, 1966.

Madsen, Catherine. "Light from an Invisible Lamp: Natural Religion in *The Lord of the Rings.*" *Mythlore* 53 (spring 1988): 43–47.

Miesel, Sandra L. "Some Motifs and Sources for *Lord of the Rings.*" *Riverside Quarterly* 3 (1968): 125–28.

———, "Some Religious Aspects of *Lord of the Rings.*" *Riverside Quarterly* 3 (1968): 209–13.

Miller, Miriam Youngerman. "'Of sum mayn meruayle, þat he myȝt trawe': *The Lord of the Rings* and *Sir Gawain and the Green Knight.*" In *Medievalism: Inklings and Others* (special issue), ed. Jane Chance. *Studies in Medievalism* 3, no. 3 (1991): 345–65.

Muscatine, Charles. *Chaucer and the French Tradition: A Study in Style and Meaning.* Berkeley and Los Angeles: University of California Press, 1957.

Nitzsche, Jane Chance. *See* Jane Chance.

Noel, Ruth S. *The Languages of Tolkien's Middle-earth.* Boston: Houghton Mifflin, 1980.

———. *The Mythology of Middle-earth: A Study of Tolkien's Mythology and Its Relationship to the Myths of the Ancient World.* London: Thames and Hudson, 1977.

Norman, Philip. "The Prevalence of Hobbits." *New York Times Magazine,* 15 January 1967, pp. 30–31, 97, 100, 102.

Parker, Douglass. "Hwæt We Holbytla. . . ." Review of *The Lord of the Rings*. *Hudson Review* 9 (1956–57): 598–609.

Pearce, Joseph. *Tolkien: Man and Myth*. London: HarperCollins Publishers, 1998.

Petty, Anne C. *One Ring to Bind Them All: Tolkien's Mythology*. University: University of Alabama Press, 1979.

Purtill, Richard. *Lord of the Elves and Eldils: Fantasy and Philosophy in C.S. Lewis and J.R.R. Tolkien*. Grand Rapids, Mich.: Zondervan, 1974.

Rateliff, John D. "J.R.R. Tolkien: 'Sir Topas' Revisited." *Notes and Queries*, n.s., 227 (1982): 348.

Rawls, Melanie. "The Feminine Principle in Tolkien." *Mythlore* 38 (spring 1984): 5–13.

———. "The Rings of Power." *Mythlore* 40 (1984): 29–32.

Ready, William. *Understanding Tolkien and "The Lord of the Rings."* New York: Warner Paperback Library, 1969.

Reckford, Kenneth J. "Some Trees in Virgil and Tolkien." In *Perspectives of Roman Poetry: A Classics Symposium*, ed. G. Karl Galinsky, pp. 57–92. Austin and London: University of Texas Press, 1974.

Reynolds, Patricia, and Glen H. Goodknight, ed. *Proceedings of the J.R.R. Tolkien Centenary Conference, Keble College, Oxford, 1992*. *Mythlore* 80 and *Mallorn* 30, in one volume. Milton Keynes, England: Tolkien Society; Altadena, Calif.: Mythopoeic Press, 1995.

Robertson, D.W., Jr. "Chaucerian Tragedy." *ELH* 19 (1952), 1–37. Reprinted in *Chaucer Criticism*, vol. 2, *"Troilus and Criseyde" and the Minor Poems*, ed. Richard J. Schoeck and Jerome Taylor, pp. 86–121. Notre Dame, Ind.: University of Notre Dame Press, 1961.

Russell, Mariann. "The 'Northern Literature' and the Ring Trilogy." *Mythlore* 5 (1978): 41–42.

Ryan, J.S. "Death by Self-Impalement: The Prudentius Example." *Minas Tirith Evening Star* 15 (1986): 6–9.

———. "Uncouth Innocence: Some Links Between Chrétien de Troyes, Wolfram von Eschenbach and J.R.R. Tolkien." *Inklings-Jahrbuch* 2 (1984): 25–41; and *Mythlore* 11 (1984): 8–13.

St. Clair, Gloria Ann Strange Slaughter. "*The Lord of the* Rings as Saga." *Mythlore* 6 (1979): 11–16.

———. "Studies in the Sources of J.R.R. Tolkien's *The Lord of the Rings.*" Ph.D. diss., University of Oklahoma. *Dissertation Abstracts International* 30 (1970): 5001A.

Sale, Roger. *Modern Heroism: Essays on D.H. Lawrence, William Empson, and J.R.R. Tolkien.* Berkeley, Los Angeles, and London: University of California Press, 1973.

Salu, Mary, and Robert T., eds. *J.R.R. Tolkien, Scholar and Story-Teller: Essays in Memoriam.* Ithaca and London: Cornell University Press, 1979.

Sarti, Ronald Christopher. "Man in a Mortal World: J.R.R. Tolkien and *The Lord of the Rings.*" Ph.D. diss., Indiana University. *Dissertation Abstracts International* 45 (1984): 1410A.

Schindler, Richard. "The Expectant Landscape: J.R.R. Tolkien's Illustrations for *The Hobbit.*" In *J.R.R. Tolkien: "The Hobbit" Drawings, Watercolors, and Manuscript,* pp. 14-27. Milwaukee, Wis.: Marquette University Press, 1987.

Scott, Nan C. "War and Pacifism in *The Lord of the Rings.*" *Tolkien Journal* 15 (summer 1972): 23–25, 27–30.

Shippey, Tom. *J.R.R. Tolkien: Author of the Century.* London: HarperCollins Publishers, 2000.

———. *The Road to Middle-earth.* 1982. Rev. ed. London: Allen and Unwin, 1992.

Simpson, Dale W. "Names and Moral Character in J.R.R. Tolkien's Middle-earth Books." *Publications of the Missouri Philological Association* 6 (1981): 1–5.

Slethaug, Gordon E. "Tolkien, Tom Bombadil, and the Creative Imagination." *English Studies in Canada* 4 (1978): 341–50.

Stimpson, Catharine R. *J.R.R. Tolkien.* Columbia Essays on Modern Writers, no. 41. New York and London: Columbia University Press, 1969.

Strachey, Barbara. *Journeys of Frodo: An Atlas of J.R.R. Tolkien's "The Lord of the Rings."* London: HarperCollins, 1998; Boston: Houghton Mifflin, 1999.

Thomson, George H. "*The Lord of the Rings:* The Novel as Traditional Romance." *Wisconsin Studies in Contemporary Literature* 8 (1967): 43–59.

The Tolkien Papers (special issue). *Mankato Studies in English* 2 (1967).

Tyler, J.E.A. *The Tolkien Companion.* Ed. S.A. Tyler. London: Pan Books Ltd.; New York: St. Martin's Press, 1976.

Ugolnik, Anthony J. "*Wordhord Onleac:* The Medieval Sources of J.R.R. Tolkien's Linguistic Aesthetic." *Mosaic* 10 (winter 1977): 15–31.

Unwin, Rayner. "Publishing Tolkien." *Mallorn* 29 (1992): 41–42.

West, Richard C. *Tolkien Criticism: An Annotated Checklist.* Rev. ed. Kent, Ohio: Kent State University Press, 1981.

Wilson, Colin. *Tree by Tolkien.* London: Covent Garden Press, 1973; Santa Barbara, Calif.: Capra Press, 1974.

Wilson, Edmund. "Oo, Those Awful Orcs!" *Nation* 182 (1956): 312–13. Reprinted in *The Bit between My Teeth: A Literary Chronicle of 1950–1965.* New York: Farrar, Straus and Giroux, 1965.

INDEX

on *The Lord of the Rings,* 20,
31, 118–19, 143, 147, 160,
170, 218–19(n2), 221(n7);
translations of, 27–28;
feasting in, 63; influence of,
on Tolkien's fairy-story
aesthetic, 76, 77; and the
fairy-stories, 79, 83, 84–85;
Tolkien's parody of, 112; as
elegy, 113; in "Ofermod,"
113, 135–36; and the medieval parodies, 113–14; and
"The Homecoming of
Beorhtnoth," 117–19, 135–
36; as epic, 142; general
importance of, in Tolkien's
works, 183; and *Exodus,* 196
"Beowulf: The Monsters and the
Critics": and *Farmer Giles of
Ham,* 5, 127–28; general
influence of on Tolkien, 5–6,
13, 183, 202–3(n1); influence
of on *The Hobbit,* 8, 50–53,
54, 55, 56–57, 63, 70, 127,
208(n11); and *The Lord of the
Rings,* 9–10, 142, 143–44, 146,
182; critic in as monster, 14,
16–17, 20–21, 24, 37–39, 127;
and "On Fairy Stories," 14,
21–23, 76, 77, 83; metaphors
in, 14–21; and "*Ancrene Wisse*
and *Hali Meiðhad,*" 29; hero
of as *Beowulf* poem, 33–34;
on allegory, 43–44; on
feasting, 63; and "Leaf by
Niggle," 76, 83, 85; on elegy,
77, 113; influence of on Old
English studies, 201(n9);
critical studies of its influence on Tolkien's fiction,
201–2(n10)
Beowulf poet, 7, 14, 16, 18, 20,
79, 112, 118
Beren, 197, 199
"Beren and Lúthien," 225(n1)

Bernard, Saint, 100
Bibire, Paul, 201(n10), 203(n3),
209–10(n20)
Bible, 10, 37, 80, 188, 192,
224(n27). *See also individual
books*
Bilbo: in *The Adventures of Tom
Bombadil,* 29; like Beowulf,
119; in *The Fellowship of the
Ring,* 147–48, 149, 150, 153,
154
—in *The Hobbit:* as heroic artist,
8, 52–73 *passim;* divided self
of, 46, 138; like Beowulf, 52,
147; maturation of, 52–73
passim, 86, 115, 145; the
monsters and, 52–73 *passim;*
as monster, 127, 147, 182; like
Tolkien reader, 183; as Master
Cook in "Smith of Wootton
Major," 211(n6)
bildungsroman, 145
Black Gate of Mordor, 178
Black Riders, 145, 151, 159, 160
blacksmith, 132–33
Blessed Realm, 193
Bloom, Harold, x, 201(n10)
Boethius, 81, 150, 222(n13)
Bombadil, Tom, 156, 157, 161,
166, 222(n19)
Bombur, 66, 67
"Book of Lost Tales, The." *See
The Silmarillion*
Book of Lost Tales, The, 228(n23)
Book of the Duchess, The, 122
Boromir, 9, 46, 145, 151, 154,
161, 168, 171, 172, 175
Brandybucks, 151, 152
Bratman, David, 226(n14)
Bratt, Edith, 228(n23)
Bree, 25
Brendan, Saint, 114–15, 116,
120, 139–40, 214(n7)
Bretherton, Christopher,
228(n23)

Index

Index

Workhouse, 86, 88, 93, 94, 96, 98, 99
World Soul, 88
World War I, 33
World War II, 32–33
Worm, 39, 181. *See also* Wormtongue

Wormtongue, 39, 164, 165, 166, 167, 176, 218(n2)

Yavanna, 191, 194
Younger Eddas, 2

Zimbardo, Rose A., 221–22(n13), 222(n15)